Staten Island

Wills & Letters of Administration

Richmond County, New York

1670 - 1800

Charlotte Megill Hix C.G.R.S.

HERITAGE BOOKS
2007

HERITAGE BOOKS

AN IMPRINT OF HERITAGE BOOKS, INC.

Books, CDs, and more—Worldwide

For our listing of thousands of titles see our website
at
www.HeritageBooks.com

Published 2007 by
HERITAGE BOOKS, INC.
Publishing Division
65 East Main Street
Westminster, Maryland 21157-5026

Other books by the author:
CD: Staten Island Wills and Letters of Administration in Richmond County, New York 1670-1800

International Standard Book Number: 978-155613-811-9

INTRODUCTION

This project was initially conceived after much time had been spent as a certified record searcher specializing in Staten Island, looking through the seventeen volumes of the <u>Collections of The New York Historical Society</u>, Publication Fund Series, for the abstracts of wills from Staten Island, New York. Volume I of the Abstracts of Wills was printed in 1892 and is the 25th volume of the series that were published under the provisions of the Publications Fund of the Society. One volume was added each year and ended with volume XVII in 1908.

The wills that the Society abstracted are on file at the Surrogate's Court, New York County, New York. Early wills from many counties are on file there, and William S. Pelletreau abstracted and included all of them. These books are a very useful tool for researching early testators in the New York City area.

In her work at the Staten Island Historical Society, Marjorie Decker Johnson of Staten Island uses these books frequently and we mutually agreed that it would be wonderful if all the Staten Island wills could be combined into one book. I proceeded to check every page of the seventeen volumes, all references to Staten Island were copied, and all items finally entered into a computer.

As with all secondary sources, primary sources should be checked, if possible. In 1975, while assisting in the research on early craftsman of Long Island, New York, for Dean Failey's book <u>Long Island is my Nation</u>, 1976, I did locate the original will of my ancestor Jean Crocheron of Staten Island [1696] in the storage room of Queens College, Queens County, New York. It was thrilling to have found it, even though it was dirty, worn and hard to read. We should be very grateful to the New York Historical Society for doing the task that resulted in the seventeen volumes of abstracts.

The Society stated in the volumes that exact wording of the wills, when used, was indicated by quotation marks. I have kept their quotation marks. The last two volumes, XVI and XVII, contain corrections to the earlier volumes. All of these corrections have been incorporated into this volume. They are indicated as follows: an item that was changed in the corrections has a line through it, i.e. ~~Killyer~~, followed by the correction, Hillyer. Additions from the corrections have been bracketed {}. Any information that has been added by me has been followed by my initials, C.M.H. The abstracts have been arranged in alphabetical order, rather than by date of probate. Original spellings have been preserved in the abstracts of the probate records. As in all early records, names were spelled as they sounded, and care should be taken to make sure all possible spellings are checked. Cruser, in some records is spelled with a K, Mersereau appears as Mercereau, Latourette as La Tourette and even Lea Tourette, Simonson as Symonse, Symonson and so on. To figure out these various spelling, think, sound the name out and then use your imagination!

Long before all the bridges connected Staten Island to New York and New Jersey, Staten Islanders traveled by boat to these surrounding areas. For this reason, I have included several items re. Staten Island found in the <u>Documents relating to the Colonial History of New Jersey</u>, ed. William Nelson, 1899. They can be found on pp. 211-216.

This book has been compiled for all those researchers who have an interest in the early settlers of Staten Island.

Charlotte Megill Hix C.G.R.S.

TABLE OF CONTENTS

In the name of God, Amen, August 29, 1760. I, **JOHN** ~~ANDROUET~~ **ANDROVET**, of Staten Island, boatman, being sick. I leave to my wife LEAH the use of all my estate during her life or widowhood. I leave to my youngest daughter, MARY, a negro girl and a bed and furniture. Also that part of my Plantation next the water side, with the house, orchard, barns, and other buildings. And the meadow near the water side, beginning at the water side and running along PETER ~~ANDROWVET'S~~ ANDROVET'S land to the road, thence along the road to JOSEPH SOPER's land, thence along his land to the river. I leave to my daughters, ELINOR and LEAH, all the rest of my Plantation, beginning at the road and running along PETER ~~ANDROWVET~~ ANDROVET and ISRAEL DISSOSWAY's land to Sandy Brook, and from Sandy Brook along the rear of the water side to the road, and along the road to PETER ~~ANDROWVET's~~ ANDROVET's land. I give to ELINOR WOGLOM and LEAH TOPPING two pieces of meadow, one piece lying in Fresh Kill, commonly called the Long Neck, being 7 acres, and the other at Woodbridge, called the Sunken Marsh, also 7 acres. All the rest of my movable estate I leave to my three daughters. I make my wife and my daughter MARY executors.

Witnesses, REBECCA ~~ANDROWVET~~ ANDROVET, CATHARINE ~~ANDROWVET~~ ANDROVET, LAUGHLEN FALLEN. Proved, December 8, 1760.
Liber 22:288   WNYHS VI:19

"In the name of God, Amen. I, **JOHN ANDREVET**, of Richmond County, being sick. I leave to my two sons, JOHN and LEWIS, all my lands and messuages and improvements in Richmond County. I leave to my son JOHN a negro boy, my wagon, two horses, one plow, and my Sloop called the Susannah, with all the appurtenances, and he is to pay to his brother LEWIS £50. But if he lose the Sloop by accident within five years he is not to pay. I leave to my son LEWIS a negro boy. To my daughter SUSANNAH £30 and a bed and a negro girl, and I have given to my four other daughters each a negro girl. The rest of my personal estate is to be sold and the money paid to my five daughters, ELIZABETH, ANN, REBECCA, TABITHA, and SUSANAH. I leave to my son JOHN the possession of my estate after my death to enable him to bring up and maintain his brother LEWIS and his sister SUSANAH till they are of age. When my son LEWIS is of age, the estate is to be divided between them. I make my son JOHN and my two sons-in-law, GILBERT JACKSON and JACOB COLE, executors."

Dated January 14, 1780. Witnesses, PAUL MICHEAU, ELIZABETH ANDREVET, HENRY BUTLER. Proved, April 18, 1780.
Liber 32:229   WNYHS IX:105

In the name of God, Amen. October 6, 1761, I, **PETER ANDREVET**, of Richmond County, "having at this time my usual sence". All debts to be paid. {mentions wife REBECCA}. I leave to my wife the use of my farm or Plantation that I now live on, lying and adjoining to the river on the west side of Staten Island, Containing two lots, and all the meadow adjoining; Also a negro wench and child, and a horse and chair, and two cows, a bed, and household goods sufficient to furnish a room. After her death, I leave all the said farm to my son PETER, also the movable estate. I leave to my son ANDREW all my land or farm at the South side where he now lives, with all the salt meadow adjoining to JOSEPH ~~STRAGGE~~ SPRAGG, "And 10 acres of salt meadow lying on Cannuns Point, adjoining the meadow of ANTHONY ~~STOTTENBORGH [STOUTENBURGH]~~ STOTTENBOROUGH; Also two negroes. I leave to my son PETER a lot of meadow and small island lying in the Fresh Kill adjoining to BARENT DE PUE. I leave to my daughters, REBECCA, wife of JOHN ~~STORREY~~ STOREY, ELIZABETH, wife of AARON ~~CORTILEW~~ CORTILEU, ANNE, wife of ZACHEUS VAN DIKE, SUSANAH, wife of DANIEL WINANTS, and RACHEL, wife of DANIEL WINANTS, Jr., each a negro slave. I leave to my two grandsons, PETER NOE and JOHN NOE, each a negro boy, and all the rest of my movables to my daughters

2

and grandsons. I make my sons, JOHN and PETER, and my son-in-law, AARON CORTILEW, executors.

Witnesses, LEUIS GRONDAIN, mariner, CORNELIUS VAN DIKE, SARAH ~~MONETT~~ MANNETT. Proved, October 9, 1769, before BENJAMIN SEAMAN.

Liber 27:158 WNYHS VII:289

-B-

In the name of God, Amen, January 26, 1750/1, I, **JACOB BAKER**, of Staten Island, yeoman, being sick. I leave to my wife REBECCA, the use of all my estate and lands, "she making no waste or destruction" until my son NICHOLAS is of age; and after that she is to have the use of the best room in the house, and firewood, and the improvement of 1/3 of my estate during her widowhood, and the best bed, and Great Looking Glass, and the large cupboard. I leave to my son NICHOLAS the whole of my homestead, containing about 60 acres, with my horses and wagons, "and a silver tankard and six silver spoons left in pledge by JOHN POST, of Hanover, for the sum of £12;" But if the owners redeem them, then he is to have the money. I also give him six silver spoons, marked J.B.R., and my furniture, and a bond of £20 against EPHRAIM BAKER; also cows and saddles and bridles. The rest of movables I give to my daughter CATHARINE, wife of JOHN LAWRENCE. I make my son executor.

Witnesses, MATHIAS DE HART, RICHARD SANDERS, ROBERT OGDEN. Proved, November 20, 1751.

Liber 18:38 WNYHS IV:368

In the name of God, Amen. I, **NICHOLAS BAKER**, of Staten Island, being very sick. I leave to my son, JACOB BAKER, all my farm or Plantation on Staten Island, where I now dwell, with the house and orchard, and all cattle and implements. All the rest of my personal property I leave to my four daughters, NEELKIE, ELIZABETH, ANN and CATHARINE, and my son JACOB is to pay to them £5 each. I leave to my wife CATHARINE my best bed and proper furniture thereto belonging, and she is to live in my house with my son JACOB, and be sufficiently maintained. I make my son JACOB, executor.

Dated July 15, 1726. Witnesses, LAURENCE DE RAMP, JOHN DOYLE, WALTER DONGAN. Proved, August 27, 1726.

Liber 10:310   WNYHS II:366

In the name of God, Amen. I, **WILLIAM BANCKER**, of Staten Island, being at present of sound mind. I leave to my wife ANNA, and to my three children, CATHARINE, ELIZABETH and HENDRICK, and to such children as I shall hereafter have, all my estate real and personal. If all my children should die, then I leave 1/3 to my wife and 2/3 to the children of my brothers ~~ERNEST~~ EVERT, ADRIAN, and RICHARD BANCKER. My children are to be educated till of age. I make my brothers, EVERT BANCKER, HENDRICK RUTGERS, Jr., and RICHARD BANCKER, and my wife, executors.

Dated November 12, 1770. Witnesses, JOHN MARLING, JAMES DUFFE, LAURENCE ROOME. Proved, in New York, April 9, 1772. In the probate, all the witnesses are said to be of Dutchess County.

Liber 28:278   WNYHS VIII:51

In the name of God, Amen. The twenty-ninth day of April, 1783. I, **CORNELIUS BARKELO**, of the County of Richmond, yeoman, being weak in body. All my honest debts and funeral charges to be paid. I leave to my beloved wife WINTIE, the best bed and its furniture, the choice of one milch cow and one horse; one third part of all the household furniture. Unto my eldest son, ABRAHAM, my silver hilted sword. Unto my son JOHN, my silver watch. Unto my son NICHOLAS, my gun. Unto the said three sons, all my real estate of lands and meadows, with all Rights and Interest equally to be divided between them.

4

My sons to pay to my two daughters, CATHARINE and SARAH, £50 to each when they become of age or years of maturity. My wife WINTIE shall hold and occupy all my real estate until my youngest child shall reach said age. Unto my wife £50, in lieu of dower to be paid at the above term by my three sons out of my real estate. The remainder of my estate to be sold by my Executors in publick vendue for cash. Any remaining cash to be used for the support of my family. Should any of my sons died under age and without heirs, then the shares of them so dying are to be equally divided among the survivors of my sons, or their heirs. The share of a daughter so dying to descend in like manner to the surviving daughter, or her heirs. I make my beloved friend, NICHOLAS STILLWELL, my uncle, and CORNELIUS CORSEN, executors.

(Signed)   CORNELIUS BARCKLOW.

Witnesses, PETER HOUSEMAN, and DANIEL SIMONSON and DANIEL SALTER (both tanners). Proved, June 9, 1783.
Liber 35:265

WNYHS XII:55

Page 118. **CORNELIUS BARKELO**, yeoman, of the County of Richmond, New York. To my wife WINTIE, the bed with all the furniture thereunto belonging, one milk cow, the choice of my cattle, one horse, one third part of all my house furniture; to my eldest son ABRAHAM, my silver hilted sword, to my son JOHN, my silver watch; to my son NICHOLAS, my gun; to my three sons before named, ABRAHAM, JOHN and NICHOLAS, to them and heirs forever, all my real estate of lands or meadows, to be equally divided among them, share and share alike; my aforesaid sons to pay unto my daughters, CATHARINE and SARAH, their heirs £50 to each of them when they become of age; my wife WINTIE to hold and occupy all my real estate of lands and meadows for and during to the end and time until my youngest child shall become of age; then I give my wife WINTIE £50, in lieu of her thirds or dower right, to be paid to her by my three sons, aforesaid out of my real estate. All the remaining part of my movable estate, as is not disposed of heretofore, shall be sold by my executors, in public sale, to highest bidder for cash, my just debts and funeral charges to be paid out of moneys so arising from said sale; if any cash shall remain it shall be used in support of my family. If any of my sons die before they become of age and without issue, then such share shall be equally divided among the survivors of my sons and the heirs of such as are dead if any there be, and if any of my daughters shall die before they be of age and without heirs, her share to the surviving sister or her heirs. I appoint NICHOLAS STILLWELL and my Uncle, CORNELIUS CORSEN, my executors.

Dated April 29, 1783. Witnesses, PETER HOUSEMAN, DANIEL SIMONSON and DANIEL SALTER, both farmers. Proved, June 9, 1783.
Liber 39:118   WNYHS XIII:377

WILLIAM BARKER........I, WILLIAM BARKER, of Southampton, in the County of Suffolk, Gentleman.....The rest of my estate, my farm on Staten Island, and my house in New York I leave to my cousin, MARY MENTOSS, daughter of my uncle, MATTHEW BARKER, Esq. Dated March 16, 1699/1700.
Liber 7:35   WNYHS I:345

"I **ROGER BARNES**, of New Dorp, in Richmond County. After all debts and funeral charges are paid, I leave to my daughter BETHIAH £200. To my daughter MARGARET £200, when 21. To my daughter ELIZABETH, wife of PAUL MERSEREAU £170. To my daughter MARY, wife of LEGGETT LAWRENCE, £170. If I die before my daughter MARY has had her outset, my executors shall make it equal to that of my daughter ELIZABETH. I leave to my wife all my silver spoons, and a bed and furniture. I leave to my two sons ROBERT BARNES and JOHN WESTON BARNES, all my lands and meadows and real estate. My children GEORGE and MARGARET shall have their schooling out of my estate, and be clothed until married. All the rest I leave to my two sons, and they are to support their mother. My daughter MARGARET is to be brought up out of my estate. My executors may sell estate if for the benefit of my sons. I make AARON CORTELYOU, and my brother GEORGE BARNES, and my son ROBERT, executors."

Dated January 5, 1777. Witnesses, BENJAMIN HUTCHESON, ISAAC CUBBERLY, THOMAS CUBBERLY. Proved before BENJAMIN SEAMAN, August 15, 1778.
Liber 32:23   WNYHS IX:46

Letters of administration of **TYSE BARNSE** of Staten Island, granted to PAULUS RICHARDS, February -. 1682. His widow SCYTIE having refused. [Note: See The Swaim-Tysen Family, Mullane, Joseph F., 1984:20; C.M.H.]
Liber 1-2:456   WNYHS I:123

Whereas **JOHN BARTELEAU**, of Richmond County, lately died intestate, Letters of Administration are granted to his wife MARGARET BARTELEAU. February 25, 1707/8.
1IBER 7:443   WNYHS I:454

In the name of God, Amen. I, **THOMAS BAYEUX**, at present residing on Staten Island. My estate is to be charged with all debts and funeral charges. Although THOMAS BAYEUX and HENRY BAYEUX, who bear my name, have been exceedingly undutiful to me, and have behaved themselves altogether unbecoming the relation that children stand to a parent, and therefore cannot seriously expect any testimony of my regard; yet, as I hope that they may come to a due sense of their misconduct, I have thought best, and do give to the said THOMAS BAYEUX £300. And my executors shall lay out the sum of £500 in the purchase of lands, at some place they shall judge best, but not in Westchester County, and shall cause the same to be settled upon the said HENRY BAYEUX during his life, and then to his eldest son. These two devises are upon this express condition, that whereas I sold my farm or

7

plantation in New Rochelle to BERNARD RYNLANDER, and gave him a bond against any claims of dower, the said THOMAS and HENRY shall procure a release of dower for him. I leave to my sister MARY, wife of Rev. RICHARD CARLTON, £700. To my niece, MARY MAGDALEN NICOLL, wife of BENJAMIN NICOLL, £200. To my niece Magdalen, wife of THOMAS DONGAN, £500. All the rest of my estate, real and personal, I leave to my sister, ANN GROESBECK. I make my nephew, BENJAMIN NICOLL, executor. Dated October 10, 1755.

Witnesses, JOHN HILLYER, BENJAMIN HILLYER, ANN SIMONSON. Proved September 27, 1760, before BENJAMIN SEAMAN, Surrogate. Confirmed by CADWALLADER COLDEN, Esq., October 16, 1760, and BENJAMIN NICOLL being dead, letters of Administration were granted to ANN GROESBECK, widow, the residuary legatee.

Liber 22:225

In the name of God, Amen. I, **JOHN BEATTY**, of the South Division of Richmond County, yeoman, make this will. I leave my beloved wife, ANN BEATTY, during her natural life, one bed with all the bed furniture belonging to it, six chairs and a table, one pot, one kettle, six tea-cups and saucers and tea spoons, one tea and sugar pot; at her decease whatever is left shall go to the children. Unto my wife and son JOHN the use and possession of the farm I now live upon; together with two horses, two cows, one waggon, one plough and harrow, and other farming utensils, for the term of three years after my decease; they paying yearly for the same, £10, if they choose to accept the conditions of this article. My three daughters, ELIZABETH, ANN and CHARITY, shall live with their mother and brother, and work for their mother, who shall provide them with every necessary during the three years as she now provides for them. At the expiration of said term the remaining part of my whole estate to be sold and turned into money. If

my wife and son JOHN shall agree to live on the place as above mentioned, then all the rest of my personal Estate that is not allotted for their use to be sold and turned into money; my just debts and funeral expenses to be forthwith paid. When said term expires and the residue of my estate is turned into money, the proceeds shall be divided into seven equal parts; of which my wife and five children, EDWARD, JOHN, ELIZABETH, ANN and CHARITY shall each have one part, and the remaining seventh part to be equally divided among the four children of my daughter, ISABEL VANDERBILT, deceased, viz.: JOHN, ARIS, CATHARINE, and ISABEL VANDERBILT. Should any of my children die under age his or her part shall be equally divided among the surviving grand- children. I make my loving wife ANN, and my two sons, EDWARD and JOHN BEATTY, and my trusty friend, DANIEL LEAKE, jr., now living at the mill on the Great Kills, executors. Dated August 27, 1778. Witnesses, PETER CORTELYOU, JOSEPH GUYON, and JOHN GUYON (yeoman). Proved, May 7, 1781.
Liber 34:188   WNYHS X:80

In the name of God, Amen. April 30, 1780. I, **JOHN BEDEL**, of Richmond County, Esq., being very sick but having my usual senses. All debts to be paid. I leave to my wife HANNAH £200, and my negro wench TENAH, and two beds with their furniture, and as much other household goods as shall be sufficient for her to keep house with, and my riding chair and horse, and two cows. I leave to my granddaughter HANNAH, wife of ABRAHAM COLE, £300. To my granddaughter, CHARITY BOGART, £250, when of age, and a negro girl, and a cupboard commonly called her mother's cupboard, and a bed. I leave to my son, ISRAEL, £1000, including £600 already advanced, and a negro boy. I leave to my son JOHN the Plantation he now lives on at Smoking Point, being all the lands and meadows I purchased of ANTHONY WATERS. I leave to my son CORNELIUS the Plantation I now

9

live on, with houses, buildings, and mills. Reserving to the use of his mother, during her widowhood, the room next to the kitchen and the back bedroom, with the use of the kitchen and cellar and firewood at the door, for her own use. And my son CORNELIUS shall provide hay and pasture, and the privilege of one hog to run with his own, and grain and fruit. And he shall furnish her yearly twenty bushels of wheat, ten of Rye, and ten of Corn. All the rest of my estate to be sold, and I leave all to my sons, JOHN, ISRAEL, and CORNELIUS, and my daughter HANNAH, wife of ABRAHAM COLE. I make my sons, JOHN and ISRAEL, executors.

Witnesses, JAMES WHITEMAN, Surgeon of 22d Regiment, CATHARINE BEDELL, BENJAMIN SEAMAN. Proved, January 26, 1781.
Liber 34:83   WNYHS X:28

In the name of God, Amen. October 13, 1760. I, **JOSEPH BEDELL**, of Richmond County, being weak and low. I leave to my wife HANNAH my best bed and furniture, and a negro girl and £60. All the rest to be sold by my executors. I leave to my daughter ANN, wife of ISRAEL DISOSWAY, £100; To my daughter MIRIAM, wife of MATTHEW DECKER, Jr., £100 and a negro girl. I leave to my grandchildren, RACHEL and ANN TELLIER, £50 each when 18; To my sons, SILAS and JOSEPH, each £50. All the remainder of my estate I leave to my three sons, JOHN, SILAS, and JOSEPH. I make my sons and my son-in-law, ISRAEL DISOSWAY, executors.

Witnesses, JAMES WOOD, JOSEPH WOOD, BENJAMIN SEAMAN. Proved, May 23, 1768.
Liber 25:337   WNYHS VII:186

In the name of God, Amen. I, **JOHN BEEK**, of Richmond County. All real and personal estate to be sold, and the money paid to my wife. When my son JOHN is of age, my wife is to have 1/3, and 1/3 to her son, JOHN SIMONSEN. I make my friends JOSEPH ROLPH and JOSHUA NESSEREAU, executors. December, 1760.

Witnesses, JACOB ~~CORSON~~ CORSEN, JOHN LAGRANGE, PETER VAN PELT. Proved, January ~~21~~

In the name of God, Amen, September 22, 1750, I, **JACOB BERGEN**, of Staten Island, Gent., being very sick. I leave to my son JACOB, a negro man and my Dutch Bible, my silver Beaker, and my best horse, 3 cows, and £12 in cash. To my daughter ELSIE, a negro girl, ½ of my silver spoons, and ½ of the apparell of my wife MARIA, deceased. To my daughter CORNELIA, 3 cows and £12, and my best feather bed and furniture for one room complete, and ½ of my late wife's apparell. As to my houses and lands in Richmond County, I positively order my executors to sell the same, and the money to be paid to my son JACOB, and my daughters, ELSIE, wife of JAHANES VAN WAGENEN, and CORNELIA. I leave all my wearing apparell to my son JACOB. I make my son JACOB and my daughter ELSIE and her husband, and my brother-in-law, CORNELIUS KROSSE, and DANIEL CORSON, executors.

Witnesses, JOHN VANDEVENTER, STEPHEN MARTINO, CORNELIUS VANDEVENTER. Proved, December 13, 1750.

BILYOU, includes BIYOU, BILLOU, BILJOU, BELEW

ISAAC BILJOU. In the name of God, Amen, the 7th of September, 1696. I, ISAAC BILJOU, of Richmond County, planter, being of sound health. I give to my eldest son JACOB, £20, in preference to all others, when he is of age. I leave to my wife IDA, one third of all lands and personal estate for life, and the use of all until the children are of age. After my wife's decease, all my estate is to go to my children, JACOB, JOHN, and PETER, and they are to pay legacies to my daughters FRANCINA and ARIANTIE. I make my wife IDA and my father, PETER BILJOU, and PETER LE COMTE, and CORNELIUS BARENS VAN DER WYCK and DAVID POLHEMUS, tutors to my children.

Witnesses, N. BOGARDUS N. BAYARD, PETER

LAKEMAN, SAMUEL BAYARD. Proved before Richard Ingoldsby, Esq., December 22, 1709.
Liber 7:562   WNYHS II:34

PETER ~~BIYON~~ BIYOU/BILLOU/BALYOU. "In the name of God, Amen. Be it known and manifest unto all to whom these presents may come, that I, PETER ~~BIYON~~ BIYOU, of the County of Richmond". I leave to my wife ~~PERIZE~~ PERRIYE GERRIAGE, £10, and also £15 per annum for life, as agreed by an ante nuptial contract. I also leave her the use of all household stuff. I leave to my eldest son, ISAAC BIYON, £25 for his birth right. I leave to the two children of son JACOB, deceased, £50 each, I having sufficiently done for their father in his life time. I leave to the four sons of my daughter CATHERINE, by her husband, RICHARD CURTIS, a certain tract of land adjoining to DANIEL LAKE, in County of Richmond, being 84 acres, to be equally divided. I having paid a certain mortgage of £125 to PAUL RICHARDS, which he had upon a certain piece of land belonging to NICHOLAS LARGILLIER, deceased, the husband of my daughter FRANCES, who is since intermarried with JOHN MORGAN, which piece of land lyeth in Richmond County, whereby the title is devolved upon me. And whereas NICHOLAS, the son and heir of said NICHOLAS LARGELLER, is heir to his estate, whom I had specially provided for on the marriage of my daughter FRANCES, my said daughter is to enjoy the benefit of the same till the said NICHOLAS shall come of age, and he shall pay £125 to the children of his mother, whether by his own father or of JOHN MORGAN. I leave the rest of my estate to my son, ISAAC ~~BIYON~~ BIYOU/BILLOU/ BALYOU, and to the children of my daughter MARIA, wife of ARENT PRALL, who is deceased, MARTHA, wife of THOMAS STILLWELL, CHRISTENSE, wife of ABRAHAM MARLET, CATHERINE, wife of RICHARD CURTIS, and FRANCES, wife of JOHN MORGAN. Makes ABRAHAM GOUVERNEUR, JACQUES POUILLON, and JASPER NISSEPAT, executors.
        Dated September 11, 1699. Witnesses,

12

NICHOLAS JAMAINE, JACOB ~~THIBON~~ THIBOU. Proved in New York, January 6, 1702.
Liber 7:79   WNYHS I:358

Inventory of the estate **PETER BELEW.** Taken February 2, 1702. Total £351.
Liber 5-6:362   WNYHS I:315

Whereas **JOSEPH BILLOP** of Staten Island died intestate, Letters of administration are granted to THOMAS ~~FORNER~~ FARNER, Esq., who hath intermarried with ANNE the daughter of CHRISTOPHER BILLOP, brother of said JOSEPH BILLOP, April 21, 1712.
Liber 8:105   WNYHS II:87

In the name of God, Amen. I, **THOMAS BILLOPP**, of Staten Island, Esq., being in health and of sound mind, my temporal estate I dispose of as followeth. "And although I will as the Law wills, in several cases, yet I think it best to declare my mind therein". My executors are to sell all personal property not herein disposed of at public vendue. I leave to my wife SARAH a negro woman, and her child, and my riding chair and the choice of my horses, and £500, in lieu of dower. I leave to my eldest daughter ANNE, whom I had by my first wife, £100, and my silver tea pot. I leave to my eldest son, CHRISTOPHER BILLOPP, all the certain part of my lands called the Manor of Bently, on Staten Island, Beginning at the south side of Staten Island on the bay, by the water fence which divides the lands now in possession of JAMES BUTLER and JAMES SEGUIN, my tenants, and then running up toward the woods northward, nearly as the said division fence runs between said Butler and Seguin, on a straight line, until it extends within 15 feet on a course northwest from the southwest corner of said Seguin's house, then northerly nearly along the road which leads from said Seguin's to JACOB RECKHOWS, to where it falls in with the main road, but upon a straight line, thence running as the said main road runs, easterly to the line between my

13

land and the land of MATTHIAS JOHNSON, thence as the line runneth, the several courses thereof to the Sound or River, that parts Staten Island from the main to low water mark, thence along said Sound at low water mark to Billopps Point, and thence continuing along low water mark to the place of beginning; And also all the mines and minerals in the other part of the manor of Bently. And he is to have the overplus of my personal estate after paying debts, when he is of age. If he dies under age, the said lands are to go to my son THOMAS, and if he dies, then to my son, JASPER FARMER BILLOPP. All the rest of my lands are to be sold by my executors, and after paying debts and legacies, the remainder is to be paid to all my children except CHRISTOPHER. If my wife shall bear me a child, it shall have an equal share. If I should purchase any lands after the date of this will, all such are to be sold and the proceeds to go to my children. I make my wife SARAH, and my friend, PAUL MICHAUX, and my son CHRISTOPHER (when of age) executors. *(The names of other children are not given.)*

Dated October 5, 1749. Witnesses, ELIZABETH SEAMAN, RACHEL LEONARD, BENJAMIN SEAMAN.

Codicil. "The testator did on this 10 of October 1749, call for his will," and ordered that all his silver plate (except the silver teapot) be given to his wife, and she shall have her choice of the feather beds, with pillows, etc., and all table linnen, and chest of drawers and dining table. He leaves to his eldest daughter ANNE, a large white bed quilt. He leaves to his son CHRISTOPHER all the family pictures, and looking glass, etc., "and my large square copper kettle".

Witnesses, RICHARD CHARLTON, JASPER FARMER {BENJAMIN SEAMAN. Proved August 6, 1750.}
Liber 17:218   WNYHS IV:297

In the name of God, Amen. I, **ANTHONY BIRD**, of Staten Island, Richmond County, being

14

weak in body. All my estate, real and personal, shall be disposed of by my Executors and the monies due and arising from such sale to be put out at interest for the benefit of my children, to wit: My son ANTHONY shall receive £20 when twenty-one years of age, and the remainder of my estate shall bè equally divided amongst my children, that is to say, my son ANTHONY, one seventh part, my daughters CATHERONE, ELIZABETH and JUDIAH, and my sons, ABRAHAM, JOSHUA and THOMAS, each one seventh respectively as they come of age. "My will is that my children be put out by my Executors till they shall respectively come of age and be maintained and edicated out of such moneys as shall be the parts or share of each". If any of my children die before twenty-one without issue, the share of such to be divided among the survivors. I make WILHALMUS VREELAND and THOMAS SEAMAN, my trusty and well-beloved friends, my Executors. No date.

Witnesses, PETER AMERMAN (Gent.) JOSHUA MERSEREAU, JOHN MERSEREAU (Esq., Clerk of Richmond County). Proved, Richmond County, January 6, 1786. At the Proof it was sworn that ANTHONY BIRD signed the above will on the 17th or 18th of May, 1785.

Liber 38:305   WNYHS XIII:263

BENJAMIN FLETCHER, Governor, etc. Whereas **JOHN BODEIN**, late of Richmond County, lately died intestate, Letters of administration are granted to PAUL RICHARDS as principal creditor, March 4, 1694/5.

Liber 5-6:75   WNYHS I:249

Inventory of estate of **JOHN BODEIN**: 14 cows and steers, £35; 3 horses and a colt, £13; 100 sheep, £50; 80 Scheppels of wheat at 3s, £12; 2 negro men and a negro woman, £100. Total, £242.

[Note. A Scheppels was about 3 pecks.]

Sworn to by RICHARD MICHELL, HANS ~~LOUVENS~~ LOURENS, ABRAHAM ~~LOCONERS~~ LAKEMAN. Richmond Co., February 11, 1695

Liber 5-6:87   WNYHS I:254

Account of Paul Richards, as administrator of estate of **JOHN BODEIN**, presented and approved, and Quietus granted by Governor FLETCHER, December 26, 1695
Liber 5-6:105   WNYHS I:260

"In the name of God, Amen, January 4, 1778. I, **JOHN BODINE**, of Richmond County, farmer, being weak in body. All debts to be paid. I leave to my wife DORCAS full possession of all lands and tenements until my youngest child is of age. And she is to keep my children together with her until they come of age, viz., JAMES, MARTHA, VINCE, and ANN. My wife DORCAS is to give to my son VINCE and my daughter ANN Learning as to read and write. And when my youngest child is 18, then to make a vendue to sell all my personal property, lands and tenements, and the whole to be divided among all my children, viz., RACHEL, JAMES, MARY EGBERTS, JOHN, MARTHA, VINCE and ANN. I leave to my eldest son, JOHN, he being heir at law, 8 shillings more than the rest. I make my wife DORCAS and my son JAMES, executors."
Witnesses, THOMAS KINGSTON, schoolmaster, WILLIAM SMITH, NATHANIEL LOKERMAN. Proved, March 27, 1778.
Liber 31:128   WNYHS IX:24

In the name of God, Amen. I, **SIMON BOGART**, of Richmond County, yeoman, being well in health, I leave to my eldest son SIMON, my big guns, sword, and a horse and saddle for his birth right as heir at law. I leave to my wife MARY the feather bed that I lie on, with all the furniture, and likewise the cupboard that she brought into my estate, and all her clothing, and all the goods in said cupboard. Also 2 iron pots, 2 pewter platters, 6 pewter plates, her side saddle, and little wheel I leave to my youngest son, ISAAC, a negro boy, and my silver tankard, and 2 silver spoons, and a sorrel horse. I leave to my daughter, ELIZABETH, all my Dutch books, and a feather bed, and a cupboard and a little wheel. To my daughter, SARAH, a cupboard and a bed. To my daughter-in-law (step daughter) CATHARINE WINANT, 1 bed and furniture, which her mother brought unto me. My executors are to sell all my lands and meadows upon Staten Island, lying between the land of WILLIAM JOHNSON and the land of NATHANIEL JOHNSON, And all my salt meadow lying on the north side of the Fresh Kills, as by deed from TUNIS BOGART; Also my horses and buildings on said lands. Out of the proceeds they are to build a convenient house for my wife. And all the rest of the money, and the money in the hands of my brother, TUNIS BOGART, on Long Island, shall be paid to my wife and children, SIMON, GILBERT, JANE, wife of WILLIAM PERINE, ELIZABETH, and SARAH. If my son GILBERT should not return, his part is to go to my son ISAAC. I make my friends, PAUL MISHSHO (MICHEAU) and ABRAHAM COLE, executors.

Dated, January 23, 1746/7. Witnesses, BARENT SLEGHT, ~~JAMES~~ ISAAC COLE, JOHN WOGLUM. Proved, April 8, 1747.
Liber 16:121   WNYHS IV:122

In the name of God, Amen. I, **RACHEL BRAISTED**, of the County of Richmond (spinster), being sick and weak. I leave to my son, JOHN BRAISTED, "a silver clasps and sleve buttens", and five dollars. Unto my daughter (CATHERINE) CATERINE, a gold ring and a silver spoon. Unto my son EGBERT, a pair of silver shoe buckles. All my real and personal to be sold by my friend, ANTHONY EGBERTS, whom I appoint executor. All my children, JOHN, CATHERINE, and EGBERT to share equally, after my just debts and funeral charges be paid. Should any child die under age and leave no issue, then the share of the one so dying is to be equally divided amongst the survivors, when they shall come of age.

(Signed)   RACHEL BRESTED.
Dated October 31, 1778. Witnesses, JOHN BODINE, WILLIAM SMITH, farmers; DARCUS BODINE. Proved January 7, 1783.
Liber 35:177   WNYHS XII:14

FRANCIS BRETON. In the name of God Amen, the seventh day of November 1703. I FRANCIS BRETON of Staten Island being very sick do make this my last will. I leave to my son FRANCIS BRETON, one shilling, for his portion of my estate. I leave to my daughter SUSANNAH RUSSKEA, one bed and one cow. To my daughter HESTER BEDINE £80 and I make her executor.

Witnesses WILLIAM TILLYER, DE BONREPOS, ANDRE CANON. Proved before Lord Cornbury May 12, 1704.

Liber 7:168   WNYHS I:387

In the name of God, Amen, November 10, 1724, I, **SUSANAH BRIDON**, of Staten Island, widow, being in good health, I leave to my well-beloved cousin JOHN BODIN, all that certain messuage, or Point of land on Staten Island on the north side of the Fresh Kill in Charles Neck, between the land of said JOHN BODIN and the land of TEUNIS GRIGGS, containing 10 acres, with all the salt meadow, house, barn, and other buildings, Also £175 which he oweth me. All this to him for life, and then it shall come into the hands of my well-beloved cousin ESTHER BODIN, wife of said JOHN BODIN, for life, and then to their children. I leave to my niece JUDITH, wife of JOHN CHADINE £50, and a feather bed and bedstead, and a rug and blanket. I give to JUDITH CHADINE, ELIZABETH TILLON and ANN TILLON all my linen, brass and pewter vessels, and other household goods. I leave all the rest to JOHN TILLON, PETER TILLON, ELIZABETH TILLON, and ANNE TILLON. I make my friend JOHN ~~CASSON~~ COSSON, executor.

Witnesses, DANIEL LOW, ENGELBART VAN ~~SANE~~ NAME, ABRAHAM COLE. Proved, December 5, 1724.

Liber 10:5   WNYHS II:304

{Whereas **ELIZABETH BRIDGES** late of Staten Island died intestate, Letters of Administration are granted unto THOMAS SUTTON son-in-law to ELIZABETH BRIDGES, May 20, 1704.}

Liber 7:172   WNYHS XVI:43

A true and perfect inventory of all the goods, etc., of **ELIZABETH BRIDGES**, late of Staten Island, widow. Taken July 31, 1704: 12 pewter plates, 18s.; 2 feather beds, with all furniture to them, £18. Total, £145. Taken by LAMBERT JOHNSON and JACOB JOHNSON. Liber 5-6:476   WNYHS I:330

William Burnet, Governor, etc. Whereas, **FRANCIS BRIDON**, of Staten Island, died intestate, Letters of administration are granted to wife SUSANAH, August 1, 1723. Liber 9:398   WNYHS II:272

BRITTAIN, includes BRITTON, BRITTEN

Whereas **NATHANIEL BRITTAIN**, of Richmond County, died intestate, Letters of admini-stration are granted to his wife, MARY ~~DUCKLAN~~ DUCHAN, April 10, 1708. Liber 7:485   WNYHS II:1

In the name of God, Amen. June 1, 1729. I, **NATHANIEL BRITTON**, of Richmond County, Esq., being at this time dangerously ill. Whereas it has pleased God to give unto me thirteen children, which are all now living, being six sons and seven daughters, namely, NATHANIEL, RICHARD, NICHOLAS, ABIGAIL, ELIZABETH, ALICE, REBECCA, JOHN, SAMUEL, MARY, SARAH, RACHEL, and WILLIAM. And whereas the first four have been portioned and provided for out of my estate, and the fifth and sixth have been partially provided for. I will that all funeral charges and debts be paid. I leave to my wife ELIZABETH, a negro woman, and one third of my personal estate. I leave to my son WILLIAM, a lot of land, 60 acres, and 6 acres of salt meadow, thereto belonging, situate at the head of Fresh kill, which was sold to me by JAMES DYE. And he is to pay to my grandson, NATHANIEL, son of my son ABRAHAM, deceased, £30, when he is of age. If my son WILLIAM dies without issue, then I leave the above to my sons, JOHN and SAMUEL. I leave to my sons, JOHN and SAMUEL, all my farm or

Plantation where I now live, in the South
Precinct of Richmond County; lying between the
Plantations of Col. NICHOLAS BRITTON and
VINCENT FOUNTAIN, Jr., with all appurtenances.
The northeast part, joining Col. NICHOLAS
BRITTON, is to be for my son JOHN; and the
southwest part to my son SAMUEL. The
Hommachs, in the Fresh meadow are to be in the
part of my son SAMUEL; and the rest of the
meadow equally between them. And they are to
pay £250 to six of my daughters, viz:
ELIZABETH, wife of JAMES POILLON, ALICE, wife
of JOHN COWELL COWARD, each £25. And to my
daughters, REBECCA, MARY, SARAH, and RACHEL,
each £50 when of age or married. I leave to
my grandson NATHANIEL, 2 cows and 2 mares. I
leave to my son WILLIAM, £100. To my son
NICHOLAS, 6 shillings. I leave to my sons,
JOHN and SAMUEL, two thirds of my personal
estate, and to my wife the use of the farm. I
make my wife and my son JOHN, executors.
Witnesses, LEWIS STILLWELL, JAMES CARMAN,
DANIEL SAYRE, Jr. Proved, November 11, 1729.
Unrecorded will   WNYHS IX:150

In the name of God, Amen, October 2,
1736, I, **NATHANIEL BRITTAIN**, of Staten Island,
being very sick. After payment of debts I
leave all estate to my wife MARTHA and my two
children MARY and FRANCIS. "As also I do
suppose my wife to be pregnant, now with
child, if soe, that to have as much as any of
the rest". I make my father, NICHOLAS
BRITTAIN and PAUL MUSHO, executors.
Witnesses, BARENT MARTLING, CHRISTOPHER RILEY,
EBENEZER SALTER. Proved, October 10 18, 1736.
Liber 13:29   WNYHS III:213

In the name of God, Amen. I, **NATHANIEL
BRITTON**, of Staten Island, being in perfect
health of body, "but now resolved, with God's
assistance, to adventure on the present
expedition against Kenede (Canada) now in the
possession of the French". I leave to my wife
FRANCES my house and lot in Richmond County,
for the support of my family; Also 2 lots of

20

land in Somerset County in the Jerseys, and my negro wench and all movable estate, and I make her executor.

{Dated July 2, 1746}. Witnesses, JAMES EGBERTSE, BENJAMIN BRITTON, JOHN ~~McCAWL~~ McCARROL. Proved, February 24, 1746/7.
Liber 16:78   WNYHS IV:110

In the name of God, Amen, January 5, 1740. I, **NICHOLAS BRITTAIN**, of Richmond County, Gent., being very sick. My wife FRANCKE is to have a good and sufficient maintenance, and to be furnished with good clothes, and a good horse and saddle when she wants to go abroad, also a negro man, with the proviso that she surrender and relinquish the 60 acres of land that she claims to be her own. I leave to my two daughters, MARTHA MOORE and RACHEL BRITTAIN, all my lands, messuages, and tenements, and other estate, and they are to pay to my son NATHANIEL'S 3 daughters, MARY, FRANCKE, and ~~NATALIE~~ MARTHA BRITTAIN, £50 each when of age. They are also to give to RANDAL SLIVE my apprentice, a good horse, saddle, and bridle. I make SAMUEL MOORE and SAMUEL HOLMES, and my two daughters, executors.

Witnesses, RICHARD STILLWELL, VINCENT FOUNTAIN, ~~SALEM~~ SOLOMON COMES. Proved before WALTER DONGAN, Esq., February 27, 1739.
Liber 13:345   WNYHS III:287

"In the name of God, Amen, October ~~22~~ 27, 1777. I, **SAMUEL BRITTEN**, of Richmond County being very sick. I direct all debts to be paid. To my wife MARY the use of all my estate, real and personal, while she remains my widow or until my youngest child is 21, she bringing them up and schooling them. If she marries, she is to have £100 and a negro wench, and as much household furniture as will furnish a room. I leave all the rest of my estate to all my children, reconing for one, the child my wife is now pregnant with. Only to my eldest son, JAMES, £20 before any division. *[Other children not named.]* I make

21

my wife and my uncle, JOHN POILLON, and my brother-in-law, JAMES GUYON, executors".

Witnesses, THOMAS FROST, JOSEPH LAKE. {Add as witness, SAMUEL WARD}. Proved, November 22, 1777.

Liber 31:71   WNYHS IX:14

Whereas **WILLIAM BRITTAIN**, of Richmond County, lately died intestate, Letters of Administration are granted to his wife, ANN WHITMAN, April 10, 1708.

Liber 7:486   WNYHS II:1

In the name of God, Amen. I, **SAMUEL BROOME**, of Staten Island. "I leave to my wife £400, and her choice of a feather bed, with compleat furniture, and a chest and cupboard, and all that may be therein, that she claims to be her own"; "Also her choice of one room in the house and my negro Sam, and our ould Ginney, to wait upon her in her old age"; Also two silver spoons and my watch. I leave to my stepdaughter, MARY LE CONTE, £400, and my negro girl "Betty", and two silver spoons. I leave to the children of my daughter ABIGAIL, viz., ABIGAIL, MARY, SAMUEL, JOHN, and DAVID, each £100, "when they are of age, or sooner if need require". I leave to my granddaughter ABIGAIL one silver spoon, and the same to my daughter MARY. I leave to my daughter ELIZABETH, wife of JOHN VANDERBILT, £400, and a negro girl, and two silver spoons. She is to have only the interest during the life of her husband, and if she survives him, she is to have the principal. I leave to my son SAMUEL the lot of land which was laid out formerly for FRANCIS LEE, and two silver spoons; Also £10, "over and above, for his Birth right". I leave to my son JOHN the lot of land which was formerly laid out for ABRAHAM LACKMAN; Also two silver spoons. I leave to my dear and loving friend, Mr. AARON RICHARDS, £20, "and if he dye before myself, then to his wife and children". "As for my poor Debtors who owe me some Debts, which because they are in a low condition, and not

22

well able to pay them, I hereby remit them to the value of £50, at the discretion of my executors, in favor of those who are the least able to pay their debts." My wife is to have a living out of my estate until she receives the greater part of her dower. All the rest I leave to my sons, SAMUEL and JOHN. "And now my dear wife and children. It is my hearty sincere advice to you all not to fall out or differ in any wise, but to endeavor to follow Peace with all men, and Holyness, without which no man can see the Lord. And I entreat one and all of my children to be mindfull and not forget to honor and obey your aged mother, and be kind to her". I make my wife and sons executors.

Dated April 5, 1771. Witnesses, ARTHUR ALINGTON, JOHN LA TOURETTE, HENRY LA TOURETTE. Proved, November 26, 1771.
Liber 28:122   WNYHS VII:457

In the name of God, Amen. ~~April 8~~ May 16, 1718. I, **SAMUEL BURNET**, of New York, cordwainer, being very sick. I leave to my wife ANN, all my personal estate and household goods. I leave to my child begotten on the body of my said wife, not as yet born, all my real estate, being 10½ acres, bounded by ENGLEBART LOTT, at the Fresh Kills at Staten Island. If the child dies under age, my wife is to have the use of the same, and I make her executor.

Witnesses, JOHN MYER, JOHN POLL, REM CLASON. Proved, May 16, 1718.
Unrecorded will   WNYHS XI:23

"In the name of God, Amen, January 14, 1779. I, **HENRY BUTLER**, of Richmond County, farmer, being very low in health. All debts to be paid. I leave to my eldest son, HENRY, my brown colt, saddle, and bridle. To my son JAMES my bay colt. To my wife ~~BELEYTA~~ BELITYA the use of all my estate so long as she remains my widow, she making no waste, and giving my younger children proper education. If she marries, I leave her a bed and

23

furniture, a horse and chair and £100. After her death or marriage, all to be sold by executors. I leave to my son HENRY £100. To my son JOHN £100. To my son NATHANIEL £100. The remainder I leave to all my children, HENRY, JAMES, NATHANIEL, FRANCES, and SARAH. I make my wife and my son HENRY and my friend, HENRY PERINE, executors."

Witnesses, JOSHUA MERSEREAU, ABRAHAM COLE, Jr., THOMAS BUTLER. Proved, May 4, 1780.

Liber 32:273   WNYHS IX:118

In the name of God, Amen, March 18, 1759. I, **JAMES BUTLER**, of Richmond County, being very low and weak. My estate is to be sold in some convenient time, and from the money and the rest of my estate to my sons JAMES and JOHN each 2/9. To my daughter ELIZABETH, wife of CHARLES LAFARGE, 1/9, reckoning the sum of £25 already paid to her. To my ~~wife~~ daughter MARY 1/9. To my daughter ~~NETTY~~ NELLY 1/9. The shares of my sons are to be kept by my executors to bring them up till they are fit to be put to trades. I make my friend and brother in law, LEWIS DUBOIS, and my son in law, CHARLES LAFARGE, executors.

Witnesses, BENJAMIN SEAMAN, JAMES SEQUIN, Jr., JOHN SEQUIN. Proved, June 5, 1759.

Liber 21:317   WNYHS V:312

JOHANES BYVANCK. In the name of God, Amen. I, JOHANES BYVANCK, of Staten Island, turner, being very sick. I leave to my eldest son EVERT BYVANCK all my wearing apparel and my tools; Also my great Bilested chest and £5. I leave to my wife ~~ALSKE~~ AELTIE the sole use and benefit of estate during the nonage of my children. After her decease all estate to my two children, EVERT and BELLIKIE, when of age. I make my wife executor.

Dated March 23, 1711/12. Witnesses, JAN WOGLUM, JOHN ~~CARSON~~ CORSON, OSWALD FOORD. Proved, May 13, 1712.

LIBER 8:110   WNYHS II:88

In the name of God, Amen, November 26, 1747. I, **ABRAHAM CANNON**, of Staten Island, being in good health. I leave to my dearly beloved wife JANAKE my bed which I lie on and the furniture thereto belonging, and a horse and saddle, and all the pewter that she hath bought since she has been my wife. I leave to son ISAAC, my sword as being my eldest son. I leave to my son DAVID all my lands and meadows and buildings on Staten Island and 4 horses, a plow, and my gun and cane, and £40. I leave to the children of my son ABRAHAM £40, "but £25 of the said £40 is to be paid to ANTHONY DOSHEN, son of ISRENE DOSHEN, deceased",. I leave to my son ANDREW £40. To my son JOHN £40 and 2 horses. These legacies are to be paid by my son DAVID. I leave to my wife £6 yearly. I make my son DAVID and HENRY CORSEN executors.

Witnesses, ALSE MERRELL, JOHN MERRELL, RICHARD MERRILL. Proved June 9, 1755. DAVID CANNON was then the surviving executor. Liber 19:276   WNYHS V:70

ANDREW CANNON. In the name of God, Amen, the 12 day of March, 1710. I, ANDREW CANNON, of Richmond County, being sick and weak, but praised be God of perfect remembrance. I leave to my eldest son, ABRAHAM CANNON, one cow, in full of his pretence as heir at law. I leave to my son ANDREW all that my Plantation on Staten Island at a place called the Long Neck adjoining to PHILIP CHASHEE, with all the improvements. When he is of age the Plantation is to be appraised, and he shall pay to his sister ANNA one third of its value. If he die under age then the Plantation is to go to my four children, ABRAHAM, JOHN, CATALINA and the heirs of my daughter HESTER, and they are to pay to my daughter ANNA one third. All the rest of my estate I leave to my wife ANNA, the better to enable her to pay my debts and for her comfortable living, and I make her executor.

Witnesses, AUGUSTUS GRASSETT, ELIAS NEAU, WILLIAM HUDDLESTON. "The above is in the handwriting of ANDREW CANNON". Proved, March 27, 1711.
Liber 8:10   WNYHS II:62

JOHN CASHIRE. In the name of God, Amen. I JOHN CASHIRE, of Staten Island, being sick. I leave to my wife SUSANNAH £40, and two beds and furniture, and the use of the best room in the new dwelling house during her life, if she remains my widow; and she is to have a barell of cider and a cow, and her firewood, and 50 ells of linnen, and her chest and £12 per annum. I leave to my son PHILIP, £1.16s before any division, he being my eldest son. I also leave him one half of all the estate of houses and lands. I leave to my younger son PETER the other half of the estate. I leave to my daughter SOPHIA £10, and to my daughter ELIZABETH £200, and her spinning wheel and a cow. I make my sons PHILIP and PETER, executors.

Dated December 26, 1709. {Witnesses JOHN CORCHON, CHARLES GARRESON and OSWALD FORD}. Proved, January 24, 1709/10.
Liber 7:565   WNYHS II:35

Richard Ingoldsby, Lieutenant-Governor, etc. Whereas **PETER CASHIE** of Staten Island, died intestate, Letters of administration are granted to his only brother PHILIP CASHIE, March 29, 1710.
Liber:574   WNYHS II:39

JOHN CHADYNE, Sr. In the name of God, Amen. The 27 March, 1708, I, JOHN CHADYNE, Sr., of the County of Richmond, ship carpenter. I leave to my wife MARY all of my estate, with full power to sell, during her widowhood. After her decease, to my children, JOHN, HENRY, MARTHA, and ELIZABETH, except that JOHN is to have £5 more than the rest. I leave to my daughter MARY, wife of JOSHUA MESEREAU, £20. Signed JEAN CHEADEAYNE.

Witnesses, JOHANES VAN ~~EYSELAM~~ ENGELEN,

26

BARENT SCHLECT, ABRAHAM COLE. Proved, October 27, 1708.
Liber 7:521   WNYHS II:17

"In the name of God,Amen.   I, **RICHARD CHARLTON**, Rector of St. Andrew's, in Richmond County.   I leave my Body to the Earth to be interred with the decency and frugality as shall seem meet to my executors.   I leave to the children of THOMAS BAYEUX, of New York, and HENRY BAYEUX, of Poughkeepsie, £300, £100 of which I leave to THOMAS BAYEUX, who served his time to my son JOHN CHARLTON. Of the rest of my estate I leave one-third to my son JOHN, one-third to my grandson, JOHN CHARLTON DONGAN, when he is of age, and one-third to the children of my daughter, CATHARINE BAYLEY, deceased.   I leave to my granddaughter, MARY BAYLEY, a negro girl, and to her two sisters a negro boy.   To my grandson, JOHN CHARLTON DONGAN, a negro man.   To my son JOHN three negroes; Also my gold watch, stock buckles and sleeve buttons, with my silver spurs.   I leave to ELIZABETH NICOLLS a negro girl and £30, upon this express condition that she live with me till my decease.   It is my positive and express will that no legacies be paid before my debts are discharged.   I make my son JOHN, executor."

Dated June 23, 1777. Witnesses, THOMAS FROST, JOSEPH GUYON, ISAAC DOTY.   Proved, October 10, 1777.
Liber 31:61   WNYHS IX:12

In the name of God, Amen.   I, **RICHARD CHARLTON**, Rector of St. Andrews, Richmond County.   I give my soul to the Omnipotent God that gave it in stedfast hope of pardon and forgiveness of my numerous sins thro' his mercy and the merits of Jesus Christ, my body to be interred with decency and frugality.   I leave to the respective children of THOMAS BAYEUX of New York and HENRY BAYEUX of Poughkeepsie, £300 ; £100 of which I bequeath to THOMAS BAYEUX, son of THOMAS BAYEUX, of New York, who served his time to my son, JOHN

CHARLTON; the other £200 to be divided between the other children. The remainder of my personal estate I bequeath as follows: one third to my son, JOHN CHARLTON; one third to my grandson, JOHN CHARLTON DONGAN when twenty-one, or if he dies sooner then half to my son JOHN and half to the children of my daughter, CATHERINE BAYLEY, deceased, share and share alike; the remaining third to the children of my daughter, CATHERINE BAYLEY, share and share alike, in case they all die before eighteen or married the said third to be divided between my son JOHN and my grandson, JOHN CHARLTON DONGAN, if he live to twenty-one, otherwise to my son the whole. I authorize my Executor to advance what sums out of the interest of said bequest as he shall deem to the advantage of the said children of my daughter. Notwithstanding the above bequests I leave to my granddaughter, MARY BAYLEY, my negro girl Bett, and to her two sisters [not named] my negro boy, formerly named Brennus. To my grandson, JOHN C. DONGAN, my Negro man, Adam; in case the above Legatees do not arrive of age then the said Negroes shall become my son JOHN's property, he directing the management and employment of said Negroes until the times above specified arrive. To my son JOHN, my Negro boy, Titus, my Negro wench, Phebe, and Negro man, Carlos, but if said Carlos be disposed of before my decease I hereby give him his choice of my remaining servants. To my son JOHN also my gold watch, stock button, and sleeve buttons, with my silver spurs. To ELIZABETH NICOLLS my Negro wench, Nan, and £30 to be paid twelve months after my decease upon this express Condition that she shall live with me till my decease, if not, the wench and £30 to be joined to the rest of my estate. It is my positive will that no legacies be paid before my debts are paid. My son JOHN my sole Executor.

Dated June 23, 1777. Witnesses, THOMAS FROST (Doctor), JOSEPH GUYON (farmer), ISAAC DOTY. Proved, Richmond County, October 10, 1777. Confirmed, New York, October 30, 1777.

Recorded, January 7, 1786.
Liber 38:278   WNYHS XIII:249

William Burnet, Esq., Captain-General and Governor. Whereas **CHRISTOFELL CHRISTOPHERS**, of Staten Island, died intestate, Letters of administration are granted to his wife ~~CHRISTANTIE~~ CHRISTENTRE, December 2, 1727.
Liber 10:124   WNYHS II:328

HANCE CHRISTOPHER. In the name of God, Amen, December 30, 1718. I, HANCE CHRISTOPHER, of Staten Island, being very sick. I leave to my wife SUSANNAH, all my estate, real and personal, during her widowhood. If she marries again, then she is to have my house, messuage, and tenements, and one half of my land adjoining to said tenements, for her and her heirs and assigns. The other half of my lands I leave to NICHOLAS and HANS, the sons of my brother BARENT CHRISTOPHER, and they shall pay to HANS PRALL £5. I leave to DANIEL GARRISON my gray horse, and to HANS SIMONSEN, son of AERT SIMONSEN, two young cattle. Also my brother BARENT CHRISTOPHER shall have my wagon. I leave the rest of my movables to my wife, and I make LAMBERT GARRISON, Sr., and BARENT CHRISTOPHER, executors.
Witnesses, JAN DU PUY, AERT SIMONSE, WILLIAM ~~TILLOW~~ TILLYOU. Proved, May 5, 1719.
Liber 9:39   WNYHS II:187

HENRY CLARK, of ~~Poynig~~ Poging Creek, Virginia, May 26, 1679. "I, HENRY CLARK, of New York, late come from Virginia, being sicke".....directs Mr. THOMAS CLARKE and ABRAHAM CORBETT shall see my negro Francis, delivered unto Captain JOHN PALMER, of Staten Island, and he is to pay £33, Boston money for him.... Proved July 19, 1679.
Liber 1-2:216   WNYHS I:54

Return of the jurors concerning the death of **ANN COFFIN**. We doe finde by the testimony Captain of RICHARD STILLWELL, of Staten

29

Island, that the body of ANN COFFIN, taken up this day, was one of the five persons that were drowned the 23 day of August, 1681.
Liber 19B:10   WNYHS II:428

In the name of God, Amen. I, **ABRAHAM COLE**, of Staten Island, being in good health. I leave to my eldest son RICHARD COLE, 60 acres of land now in my possession, which I bought of WILLIAM ELLSTONE, and is 3/4 of the lot which begins at the west side of the brook, and runs along the dividing line of the land of JOHN MARSHALL and my plantation, up to the rear, according to the divisions of the Patent, and bounded in front by the highway. With the due proportion of salt meadow. I leave to my younger sons, ABRAHAM and ISAAC, my lot of land which I now live on, between the land of CORNELIUS WYNANT and the lot I have left to my son RICHARD, and all the rest of my lands, which is ¼ or 20 acres which is next adjoining, with the salt meadow belonging to it. "As for my eldest son RICHARD COLE, he hath had of me that which is considerable, at his first beginning of his keeping house". I also give him, and each of my sons, a negro slave. To my daughter ANNE, now wife of WYNANT WYNANTS, £30. To my daughter REBECCA, wife of PETER ANDREWENT, £30. To my daughter MARY, wife of CORNELIUS WYNANTS, £30. I make my wife and three sons, executors.
Dated February 3, 1732/3. Witnesses, ANTHONY WRIGHT, ELIZABETH WRIGHT, HEZEKIAH WRIGHT. Proved, March 29, 1733.
Liber 11:481   WNYHS III:95

In the name of God, Amen, August 10, 1751. I, **ABRAHAM COLE**, of Richmond County. I leave to my son ABRAHAM £5, and my silver headed cane marked A.C. for his heir ship as heir at law. I leave to my wife SUSANNAH £50, and full possession of al lands during her widowhood. All the rest of my estate, real and personal, I leave to my children, ABRAHAM, SUSANAH, CORNELIUS, STEPHEN, JACOB, and DAVID, "and likewise the child that my wife is now bigg with". I make my wife and friends, BENJAMIN SIMMONS, and my son ABRAHAM, executors.

Witnesses, ABRAHAM PEARSE, ISAAC COLE, ABRAHAM COLE. Proved, October 13, 1752.
Liber 18:182   WNYHS IV:408

"In the name of God, Amen. I, **DAVID COLE**, of Richmond County. I leave to my brother STEPHEN COLE, all my wearing apparell. To my father-in-law, JOHN MARSHALL, my silver watch. An inventory to be made of all my estate. My son CORNELIUS is to be maintained and educated out of the money that is left to my wife REBECCA by her father, JOHN ANDROVET, deceased. If my son CORNELIUS should live to be 21, he is to have half the estate and my wife the other half. If he dies under age, then all to my wife. But the money left to me by my father ABRAHAM COLE, is to go to my sister, MARY LACKMAN, and DAVID, son of JACOB COLE, and DAVID, son of HENRY PERINE. I make CORNELIUS COLE and HENRY PERINE, executors."

Dated April 25, 1780. Witnesses, PHILIP BOWNE, OBADIAH BOWNE, JOHN MARSHALL. Proved, September 7, 1780.
Liber 32:323   WNYHS IX:133

In the name of God, Amen. I, **ISAAC COLES**, of Richmond County, January 27, 1762. I direct all debts and funeral charges to be paid. I leave to my wife MARY the use of all lands during the time she remains my widow, or until my youngest child is of age. Then all lands to be old by my executors and the money paid to my wife and 7 children, ABRAHAM, ISAAC, PETER, RICHARD, JOHN, BENJAMIN, and HESTER, wife of CHRISTIAN SMITH. I make my brother RICHARD COLES, and JACOB ~~REZEAN~~ REZEAU, executors.

Witnesses, WRIGHT ~~SHIMER~~ SKINNER, MATTHIAS ~~SULAM~~ SWEEM, JACOB ~~REZEAN~~ REZEAU, Jr. Proved, March 15, 1762, before BENJAMIN SEAMAN, Surrogate.
Liber 23:277   WNYHS VI:140

In the name of God, Amen. I, **JACOB COLE**, of Staten Island in the County of Richmond, being weak in body. My executors to take so much of my movable estate as shall discharge all my just debts and funeral expenses; also, to take the sum of £25, and keep and apply it for the best use of my son DAVID; it being a legacy given him by his uncle, DAVID COLE. All the residue of my estate, both real and personal, I leave to my beloved wife ANNE during her widowhood, upon condition she brings up my children. But if she marry, then my executors are to sell the whole of my estate, real and personal, at vendue or otherways and the proceeds to be equally divided, between my wife and five sons, JOHN, CORNELIUS, DAVID, WILLIAM, and JACOB COLE. If my wife marry, my executors to take that part of my estate which falls to the children, and out of the same to support them so long as the youngest is no longer chargeable to my estate. I make my brother, CORNELIUS COLE, and WILLIAM LAKERMAN, my brother-in-law, executors, and my loving wife ANNE, executrix.

Dated October 28, 1781. Witnesses, EPHRAIM JOHNSON, ABRAHAM COLE, ISAAC DOOTY. Proved, February 21, 1782.
Liber 34:432   WNYHS X:194

"In the name of God, Amen. I, **RICHARD COLE**, of Richmond County, yeoman, being in a middling state of Health. I leave to my wife ESTER my best bed and bedding, and my cupboard and all linnen and my cow. All my houses and lands and the rest of my personal property to be sold at public vendue, and after debts are paid I leave all the rest to my wife, and I make her and CORNELIUS COLE, executors.

Dated January 13, 1776. Signed "ISAAC COLE" *(probably this is an error)*. Witnesses, JAMES FORREST, DOWE JOHNSON, ~~DAVID~~ DANIEL HOOPER. Proved, December 24, 1777.
Liber 31:121   WNYHS IX:23

PETER COLON, chairmaker, of New York City, to my wife MARY,.....my four children

32

DANIEL, ABRAHAM, ELIZABETH and MARY MAGDALENE........... I appoint my brother, JAMES COLON, of Staten Island, Captain J. JACOBSEN, of Staten Island, executors.

Dated August 22, 1781. Witnesses, JONAS COLON, New York City, chairmaker; PHILIP SYKES, ABRAHAM WILLSON. Proved, July 10, 1786.

Liber 39:169   WNYHS XIV:20

CORSEN, includes COURSON

In the name of God, Amen. I, **CHRISTIAN CORSEN**, Esq., of Richmond County. I order all debts paid. I leave to my daughter NEETIEA(?), wife of FRANCE GERBRANTZ, all that my two lots of land situate at the north side of Richmond County, "over against Shooters Island", during her life, and after her decease to her two sons, CHRISTIAN and DANIEL GERBRANTZ. The former to have his choice, and they are to pay £50 each to their sisters. I leave to my two grandsons CORNELIUS and DANIEL, sons of my son CORNELIUS, deceased, 10 acres of salt meadow adjoining to the meadow of RICHARD ~~MERALL~~ MERRILL and MATHEW ~~DEAKER~~ DECKER. I leave to my grandson DANIEL, son of my son DANIEL CORSEN, Esq., deceased, all the rest of my lands and meadows and tenements, when he is of age. But MARY CORSEN, widow of my said son, DANIEL CORSEN, is to have the use of it to maintain and educate the three children of my son DANIEL. I leave to my grandsons, PETER, CHRISTAIN, CORNELIUS, and DANIEL, sons of my son, CORNELIUS CORSEN, deceased, all my lands in New Jersey. I leave to my three grandchildren, RICHARD, DANIEL, and ANN, children of my son DANIEL, deceased, ½ of all my movable estate. I leave to my grandchildren, PETER, CHRISTIAN, CORNELIUS, DANIEL, MARY, JANE, KATHERINE, and ANN, children of my son CORNELIUS, deceased, the other half. I make my daughter-in-law, MARY CORSEN, widow, and my grandson, CORNELIUS CORSEN, and ABRAHAM SPEER, and DANIEL LAKE, executors. My two grandsons, children of my

33

son DANIEL, deceased, shall have a liberal education. My grandson DANIEL shall pay to his sister ANN £50. Dated February 5, 1762.

Witnesses, HENRY ~~WILDMAN~~ VELDTMAN, WALTER ~~CLENDRE~~ CLENDNE, JOHN HILLYER.

Codicil. Confirms the will. I leave to my four grand-daughters, MARY, JANE, KATHARINE, and ANN, an equal share in my lands in New Jersey. The 5 acres of salt meadow left to my grandson CORNELIUS I give to my three grandchildren, ~~SARAH, CATHARINE~~ CORNELIUS CORSON, and PETER CORSEN, and MARY MACLEAN. Dated July 9, 1763.

Witnesses, JOHN HILLYER, PIERRE DE GROUT, THOMAS LISK.

Codicil. My daughter-in-law, MARY CORSEN, having died without leaving a will, and her eldest son RICHARD is her heir at law, which will give him a suitable provision. I hereby revoke my legacy to my said grandson, RICHARD CORSEN, and I leave the same to my granddaughter ANTEE, daughter of my son DANIEL, deceased. I also leave her a negro man and negro girl which were lately purchased for me at the vendue of the estate of JOHN BEEK. Dated December -, 1764.

Witnesses, RICHARD LAWRENCE, ABRAHAM ~~BARKELOW~~ BARCKLOW or BERKELAU, DEBORAH SMITH. Proved, January 7, 1766, before BENJAMIN SEAMAN, Surrogate.
Liber 25:201   WNYHS VI:432

CORNELIUS ~~CORSOEN~~ **CORSEN**, Staten Island. "In the name of God Amen. I, CORNELIUS ~~CORSOEN~~ CORSEN of Staten Island in County of Richmond, yeoman". Leaves all estate, real and personal to his wife, ~~MATTIE CORSOEN~~ MARITIE CORSEN, for life, and then to their children equally. If she remarry then the children are to take one half, each to have their share when of age (no names given). Makes his wife sole executor.

Dated December 9, 1692. Witnesses: CORNELIUS ~~NEPHEWS~~ NEVIUS, PETER ~~STAERS~~ STAES/STAATS, THOMAS CARHART.
Liber 5-6:12   WNYHS I:230

Page 13. BENJAMIN FLETCHER, Governor, &c. To all &c. Know ye that at the city of New York, on the 7th of December, 1692 before me, the last will of **CORNELIUS** ~~CORSOEN~~ **CORSEN**, of Staten Island was proved and the widow ~~MATTIE CORSOEN~~ MARITIE CORSEN is confirmed as executrix.
Liber 5-6:13   WNYHS I:230

      In the name of God, Amen, February 2, 1755. I, **CORNELIUS CORSEN**, of Staten Island, Esq., being very sick. "I will and particularly order all just debts and funeral charges to be paid". All my negroes, lands, and tenements, in the North Precinct of the County of Richmond, whereon I now dwell, are to be sold by my executors. I leave to my two sons, CORNELIUS and DANIEL, all my lands and tenements in the Manor of Castleton, in Richmond County, purchased by me from THOMAS DONGAN. I leave to my sons PETER and JACOBUS £640. To my daughter MARY, wife of CHARLES McLEAN, £120. To my daughters CATHARINE, ANN and JANNETTIE, £465. To my son DANIEL my negro boy. To my daughter MARY a negro girl. To my sons, PETER, CORNELIUS, JACOBUS, and DANIEL, 4 cows and all my horses. To each of my daughters 2 cows. To my son JACOBUS £15. To my son CHRISTIAN's child, named CORNELIUS, £30 when of age. All the rest of my goods and chattels to my children, viz., PETER, CORNELIUS, DANIEL, JACOBUS, MARY, CATHARINE, ANN, and JANNETTIE. I make my son in law, CHARLES McLEAN, and my brother, DANIEL CORSEN, executors.
      Witnesses, JOHN JENNER, GERARDUS BEEKMAN, merchant, JOHN JENNER, Jr. Proved, May 1, 1755.
Liber 19:240   WNYHS V:60

      Whereas **DANIEL COURSON**, of Staten Island, died intestate, Letters of administration are granted to JACOB COURSON, his eldest brother and heir at law, August 13, 1712.
Liber 8:130   WNYHS II:91

In the name of God, Amen, October 8, 1742. I, **JACOB** ~~CORSON~~ **CORSEN**, of Staten Island, Gent., being weak in body. All debts and burial charges to be paid. I leave to my wife ELIZABETH the use of all lands and tenements and goods during her life. After her death I give to my son JACOB all that my messuage, lands, and tenements, situate on the north side of Staten Island, where I now live, and lying near or adjoining to the lands of WALTER DONGAN, Esq., and NICHOLAS GARRISON. I leave to my daughter SUSTER, wife of JOHANES ~~SIMSEN~~ SIMONSON, £70. To my daughter MARY, wife of JOSHUA MERSEREAU, £70. To my son DOWE £70. To my son BENJAMIN £70; all these to be paid by my son JACOB. I leave to my sons, DOWE and BENJAMIN, all my messuages and lands in Hunterdon County, in West New Jersey, at or near the township of Reading, and purchased by me from JOHN BUDD. I leave to my daughter ~~SARAH~~ SUSTER, wife of ~~MYNDERT MYNDERSE~~ JOHANNES SIMONSON, my messuage or lands situate on the west side of Staten Island, adjoining the lands of WYNANT WYNANTS and JOHN ~~ANDREWOIT~~ ANDROVETTE, and purchased by me from JOSHUA MESEREAU, Sr. I leave to my daughter REBECCA, wife of JOHN BLOM, £70, to be paid by my son JOHN. I leave to my son JACOB, my silver hilted sword and silk sash. I make my sons {and JOSHUA MERCEREAU}, executors, and leave all the rest to my children.

Witnesses, CHRISTIAN CORSEN, JOHN QUIN, DANIEL CORSEN.

Codicil, February 3, ~~1742~~ 1746. Whereas I have given to my son BENJAMIN ½ of my lands in Hunterdon County, West New Jersey, which I purchased of JOHN BUDD, my executors are to pay to JACOB CORSEN, son of my son BENJAMIN, £30 out of said lands, and the rest of the said lands to be divided among JACOB, SARAH, and ELIZABETH, the children of my son, BENJAMIN CORSEN. But if my grand son JACOB wishes to keep all of said lands, he shall pay to his sisters 2/3 of the value.

Witnesses, CHRISTIAN CORSEN, ANTYE CORSEN, DANIEL CORSEN. Proved, August 2,

1756.
Liber 20:51   WNYHS V:120

In the name of God, Amen. January 4,
1737. I, **JOHN ~~CASSON~~ COSSON or CORSON**, of
Richmond County, being weak in body. I leave
to my wife ESTHER, for her dowry, £100. To my
niece CATHARINE RENAUD, wife of VINCENT
RENAUD, of the Island of Gurnesey, in Europe,
£50. To my other niece, MARY OZANS, wife of
HENRY OZANS, Jr., of said Island, £50. To my
nephew, PAUL MICHAUX, of Richmond County, I
leave all the rest of my estate of lands and
houses. And I make JOHN LE COUNTE and PAUL
MICHEAUX, executors.
Witnesses, JACQUES LEGIN, PETER ~~KAVART~~
RAVART, ~~LEWIS GANS,~~ ~~JACQUES JEQUIEN~~ LOUIS
JACQUES JEQUIEN. Proved, February 6, 1738.
Liber 13:150   WNYHS III:237

In the name of God, Amen. The twenty-
fourth day of April, 1781, I, **GARRIT COSINE**,
of the County of Richmond, yeoman, being weak
in body. All my just and honest debts and
funeral charges to be paid. I leave to my two
sons, JACOB and CORNELIUS COSINE, a certain
piece or parcel of land lying and being on
Long Island at New Lots in Kings County, now
in the possession of the said CORNELIUS
COSINE, to be equally divided between them.
Also, to my son JACOB, £3 in consideration of
his being my eldest son. To my son JAMES,
£90. To my son WILHELMES, £100. To my two
sons, JAMES and WILHELMES, all my Farmer
utensils of all kinds; also, all my cattle,
horses, sheep and hogs, to be equally divided
between them. To my son JAMES, my brass
"cittle", but order that he shall pay to my
daughter, ALTIE DOUGAN, 40 shillings in lieu
of the said cittle. To my daughter ALTIE, one
pewter platter and three pewter plates. All my
estate, real and personal, to be sold at
publick auction or vendue at the expiration of
one year after my decease. After all my
estate shall be turned into cash the residue,
after paying debts, shall be equally divided

between all my children, viz: JACOB, CORNELIUS, JAMES, WILHELMES COSINE; AFFIE, wife of JOHN BLAW; ALTIE, wife of CORNELIUS DOUGAN. My executors to deduct £33 out of the share of AFFIE, wife of JOHN BLAW, in lieu of money as I have paid for her. My executors to retain in their hands the portions of my two daughters, AFFIE and ALTIE, and not pay their husbands, but distribute to my daughters as they shall have need or occasion for the support of nature; if their husbands shall die, my daughters to receive their remainder in full immediately. I make my dearly beloved sons JACOB, CORNELIUS, JAMES and WILHELMES, executors. Signed, GARRET COSYNE.

Witnesses, PETER HOUSEMAN, WILLIAM KINGSTON, yeoman, JOHN HOUSEMAN.

Dated February 20, 1782.

Liber 34:436   WNYHS X:196

In the name of God, Amen. I, **CORNELIUS CORTELYOU**, of Staten Island, carpenter, being weak in body. The whole of my estate to be sold and converted into money. My just debts and funeral expenses to be paid. If the legatees shall agree to a suitable and equitable division of my estate among themselves, then the same need not be sold. Unto my wife SARAH, one bed and its furniture, and £50. Unto my son JACOB, a like sum; unto my son PETER, £40 extraordinary. All my wearing apparel to be equally divided between JACOB and PETER. The remainder of my estate to be equally divided between my wife SARAH, and my five children, namely; ELEANOR, MARTHA, JACOB, MARY, and PETER. Should any children die under age, his or her share to go to survivors equally. Whereas my daughter ELENOR has already had about £30 more than the rest, that sum is to be deducted from her part. I make my trusty and well-beloved wife SARAH, my son JACOB and my son-in-law, EDWARD BEATTY, executors.

Dated July 14, 1778. Witnesses, CORNELIUS VANDERVENTER, PETER PERINE, JAMES COLON, of Richmond County, farmer. Proved,

In the name of God, Amen. I, **ABRAHAM
CROCHERON**, of Staten Island, yeoman, being in
good health, May 8, 1754. I leave to my wife
ARIANTIE, all the movable estate she had when
I married her, "and my will is that all her
movable estate that has been lessened or made
worse by me since she has been my wife shall
be made up to her". My wife shall live in the
southeast room in my house where I now live,
and have the use of the leanto thereto
belonging. Also the privilege to pasture two
cows and a horse in the common pasture with my
children, and fodder sufficient to winter
them, and to get firewood, during her being my
widow, and no longer. I leave to my son
Daniel during his life all that messuage or
tenement, with the appurtenances situate on
Long Neck, whereon he now lives, with all the
salt meadows. And after his death to his
children equally, unless he divides it among
his children by will. "And my will and
meaning is, that ABRAHAM, the eldest son of
his wife ~~MARIA~~ MARY, shall be deemed and
esteemed one of his children, and to have an
equal share". I leave to my daughter
CATHARINE, during her life, 40 acres of land,
being a part of the farm on which I now live.
Beginning at the southeast corner at a gum
tree, and them North 16 degrees, East 52
chains to a beech tree, and then so far in
breadth at the rear of said land, northwest,
and thence such a course down to the road as
shall include the house, barn, orchard, and 40
acres of land. Also 4½ acres of salt meadow
which I bought of PETER ANDREVET; and after
her death to her children. The rest of my
land where I now live I leave to my son
DANIEL, with all my wearing apparell. I leave
all the rest of my estate to my son DANIEL and
daughter CATHARINE, and make them executors.
And the High Sheriff of the County to be a
Trustee.
Witnesses, SIMON HILLYER, BARSHEBA DEY,

JOHN HILLYER. Proved, July 4, 1765, before BENJAMIN SEAMAN, Surrogate. JOHN HILLYER was then High Sheriff.
Liber 25:112

WNYHS VI:402

"In the name of God, Amen, December 5, 1777. I, **ABRAHAM CROCHERON**, of Richmond County, being weak in body. I leave to my wife the best room in my house while she remains my widow, with furniture and firewood, and two cows and a horse whenever she wants to ride, and £8 a year, and to have full possession of all lands until my sons are of age. I leave to my eldest son, JACOB, £5 more than the rest. All the rest of my estate to my four sons, JACOB, NICHOLAS, JOHN, and ABRAHAM. I leave to my grandson, JACOB WYNANT, £150, and to my granddaughter, ELIZABETH WYNANT, 100 pounds. I make my wife ELIZABETH and my son JACOB, executors."
Witnesses, THOMAS KINGSTON, ISAAC SIMONSON, MOSES CLENDENING. Proved, May 5, 1778.
Liber 31:160

WNYHS IX:30

In the name of God, Amen, March 21, 1766. I, **DANIEL CROCHERON**, of Richmond County, being in good health. I leave to my wife MARY the use of all estate while she remains my widow. I leave to ABRAHAM, the eldest son of my beloved wife, £20, and an equal share with the rest of my children, viz., JOHN, DANIEL, NICHOLAS and CATHARINE, "esteeming my wife's eldest son ABRAHAM to be one of my children". I make my wife, and her son ABRAHAM, executors.
Witnesses, RICHARD CRIPS, JACOB VANDERBILT, JOHN HILLYER. Proved, March 19, 1767.
Liber 25:496

WNYHS VII:71

BENJAMIN FLETCHER, Governor, etc. Know ye, that at his Majesty's Fort in New York, on the 3d day of September, 1696, the last will of **JOHN CROCHERON**, of Staten Island, was proved and Letters of Administration are granted to his wife, MARY, as executrix.

JOHN ~~CROCHERAN~~ **CROCHERON**. "In the name of God Amen. The 13 day of December, 1695, I, JOHN ~~CROCHERAN~~ CROCHERON, of Staten Island, planter, being of great age, but of good and sound memory." I leave to my beloved wife, MARY, the use of all the estate for life, and after her death I leave to my eldest son, NICHOLAS ~~CROCHERAN~~ CROCHERON, all that my dwelling house, situate, lying and being on the north side of Staten Island, and two lotts of land belonging thereto, with the privilege of Commonage, and all the fresh and salt meadows belonging to the same being 20 acres. Which said lots are bounded, south by the highway, that parts them from the land now in the tenure ARENT PRALL. Also 2 horses and 4 cows and a weaver's loom. I leave to my son, ANTHONY, my two other lots of land, on Staten Island, bounded by Long Neck at the side of Mr. JOHN CASIERS, with the fresh and salt meadow belonging thereto, being 20 acres, with the privilege of Commonage, and my utensils of husbandry. Rest of estate to all the children (*other children not named*). Makes his wife and his sons NICHOLAS and ANTHONY executors.

Witnesses, WM. TILLIER, THOMAS MORGAN, JEAN CASSIER, JOHN DUFROW. Proved, before Governor FLETCHER, by oaths of the above witnesses, September 3, 1696, and executors confirmed.
Liber 5-6:126   WNYHS I:267

Inventory of estate of **JEAN CROCHERON**, of Staten Island. Taken by THOMAS MORGAN and WILLIAM FILLYER, December 17, 1696. Money in his chest £286, 8; A negro man, an Indian woman and her child, £80; 8 cows left as a legacy to NICHOLAS and ANTHONY Crocheran, £22; 6 heifers, 2 steers and a bull, £9. Total £531. Sworn to, March 8, 1696/7.
Liber 5-6:152   WNYHS I:274

Inventory of **JOHN** ~~CROCHERAN~~ **CROCHERON**, of

41

Staten Island, taken by NATHANIEL BRITTAIN, SR.,and NATHANIEL BRITTAIN, Jr., January 9, 1696/7, before ELIAS DUXBURY and THOMAS STILLWELL. Live stock, £131; 200 sheffles of wheat, £20; 110 sheffles of rye, £13.15s. A negro man, negro woman and negro boy, £120; money in the house, Arabian gold and other gold, £72.8s.; English money £45; 468 heavy pieces of 8, £140 14s. 11d.; 15 books, one a large Bible, £4. Total amount £625.
Liber 5-6:137   WNYHS I:271

In the name of God, Amen. August 6, 1725. I, **JOHN CROCHERON**, of Staten Island, yeoman, being in health. My clear land and pasture land that lies within fence, running to the path that goes to the Long Neck, shall be equally divided into two parts. And I leave to my wife MARY, that part joining to the Great Swamp, to the westward of said Swamp. And 20 acres of meadow, beginning at Carles Neck run, during her widowhood. And my wood land that joins to my pasture land shall likewise be divided equally into two parts, and my wife shall have that part joining to the said Great Swamp, during her widowhood. But is she comes to marry she shall give good security to my executors, that it may not be embesseled from my children, that I had by my said wife MARY. I leave to my wife a bed with its furniture, and a great cupboard, and ½ of my movable estate, and she is to pay all debts and funeral charges, out of her share. The other half of my movables I leave to my children by my first wife, viz.: JOHN, ABRAHAM, MARY, and ELIZABETH. The other part of my pasture and clear land I leave to my sons, JOHN and ABRAHAM. My son JOHN is to have that part joining to the west by the salt meadow, and my son ABRAHAM is to have that part joining to the east by the land left to my wife. And they are to have the other part of my woodland. My son JOHN is to have the part lying toward the Long Neck; and my son ABRAHAM is to have his part joining to my wife. I leave to my son JOHN, 10 acres of

42

salt meadow joining to said land, and my son ABRAHAM is to have 10 acres of salt meadow joining to the length of his brother JOHN's meadow. My son JOHN is to pay to his sister MARY, £100. And my son ABRAHAM is to pay to his sister ELIZABETH, £100. My son JOHN is to have £1 out of my movable estate before any division. And my two sons are not to be disturbed on the places where they now dwell, until the whole is divided, and no division is to be made in 6 years from this date. And my son ABRAHAM is to have the liberty to take his house where he now lives, and bring it where he pleases; and to take the division fence from where it now stands, and bring it where he pleases. I make my wife executor.

Witnesses, THOMAS LAKE, EDWARD ~~HILYER~~ TILLYER, WILLIAM ~~HILYER~~ TILLYER. Proved, June 7, 1727.

The widow, MARY CROCHERON, married BENJAMIN AYRES, of Staten Island, and they gave bonds according to the terms of the will. June 3, 1730.

Unrecorded will   WNYHS XI:51

In the name of God, Amen. I, **JOHN CROCHERON**, of Richmond County, being in good health. All debts and funeral charges to be paid by my executors. I leave to my son ABRAHAM all that farm or Plantation whereon I now live, with all the salt meadow thereto belonging. And one third of the meadow I bought of LEWIS GANO, with all the appurtenances. And he is pay as legacies, to my daughters, ABIGAIL, wife of BARENT SIMONSEN, and JOHANAH, widow of HENRY MARSH, or to their heirs and assigns, each £150, in six months. I leave to my grandson, HENRY CROCHERON, all that my farm or Plantation with all the salt meadows, and one half of the salt meadow I bought of LEWIS GANO, with all the appurtenances. And he is to pay to my daughter SARAH, wife of JOHN DUPUY, £150, in six months after he comes of age. And my will is that my son-in-law, JOHN DUPUY, shall live on the farm where he now lives, free of rent until my grandson, HENRY CROCHERON, is of age. But he shall not commit any waste. And my grandson shall not sell any lands or meadows until he is 30 years old. If he dies without issue, his estate is to be sold by my executors, and the money paid to my four children, viz.: ABRAHAM, SARAH, ABIGAIL, and JOHANNAH. All the rest of my estate I leave to my four children. I make my son ABRAHAM, and JOHN DUPUY, and BARENT SIMONSEN, executors.

Dated May 25, in the first year of King George the III, 1761. Witnesses, CORNELIUS BADGLEY, JOHN HILLYER, JACOB HATFIELD. Endorsed. "Lodged the 20 of June, 1771, by ABRAHAM CROCHERON, one of the executors". (No Probate.)

Unrecorded will   WNYHS XI:189

In the name of God, Amen. I, **JOHN CROCHERON**, of the County of Richmond, carpenter, being in perfect mind and memory this 10th day of February, 1783. I leave to my oldest son, ABRAHAM, £20. All my lands, tenements, and moveable estate to be sold by my executors after my decease at their discretion for the benefit of my children, ABRAHAM, MARY, ELIZABETH and JANNE, in equal shares after all my funeral charges and just debts are paid (except what is given to my oldest son, ABRAHAM); should any die under age or have no issue, their share to go equally to the survivors; my executors to pay their shares when the youngest comes to eighteen years, unless they think proper to do so before that time. I make my brother ABRAHAM, executor, and my loving friend, ANTHONY EGBERTS, overseer of this my last will.

Witnesses, CORNELIUS FOUNTAIN, ABRAHAM EGBERTS, both of said County, yeomen; MARY EGBERTS. Proved, May 21, 1784.

Liber 36:535   WNYHS XII:306

Inventory of estate of **NICHOLAS CROCHERON**, now in possession of his widow ANN

44

CROCHERON. Appraised September 23, 1701 by JOHN BILLOP and JACQUES ~~POILLAN~~ POILLON. Total £475.
Liber 5-6:481   WNYHS I:330

NICHOLAS CROCHERON. In the name of God, Amen.   I, NICHOLAS CROCHERON, of Richmond County, planter, being in good health.   I give to the poor of the French Congregation on Staten Island, £5, to be paid to the Elders. I leave to the children of JOHN BODINE by his first wife, my nephews and nieces, as objects worthy of my charity, one half of all my paternal estate, goods, and chattels, in case I leave no children.   I leave all the rest of my estate to my loving wife, ANNE CROCHERON, and to her heirs and assigns.   I leave to all my other heirs, each 6 shillings.
Dated February 10, 1702/3.   Witnesses, JOHN   BELLVILLE,   ~~MOSES   BERND~~   MOYSE BERNAD/BERNARD, WILLIAM TILYER.   Proved before THOMAS WENHAM, Esq., July 24, 1707.
Liber 7:410   WNYHS I:445

CRUSER, includes CRUSE, KRUSE, KRUSEN

In the name of God, Amen, March 7, 1771. I, **ABRAHAM KRUSE**, of Richmond County, being weak and sick.   "My body to be buried in a decent like and Christian manner".   I leave to my brother HENRY KRUSE, all that piece of land situated at the rear of the land now possessed by the widow KRUSE and said HENRY KRUSE, bounded by NATHANIEL BRITTAIN, CAPTAIN CORSEN, HENRY KRUSE, and RICHARD CORSEN.   My executors have power to sell the rest.   I leave to my wife LEANA £200; To my daughters, CHARITY, MARY, and ANN, each £100;   To my son JOHN £5. All the rest to my sons JOHN and GERRITT.   "I make my two fathers-in-law, ~~FRANCIS~~ "HANNIS" SIMONSON   and   ANTHONY   ~~STANTON~~   STOUTEN BURROUGHS, executors".
Witnesses, PETER ~~HAUSEMAN~~ HOUSEMAN, JOHN QUIN, JEMIMA MYER.   Proved, April 30, 1771.
Liber 28:10   WNYHS VII:426

In the name of God, Amen. I, **CORNELIUS KRUSEN**, of the County of Richmond, yeoman, being at present in a poor state of health of body. I leave to my son HENRY £210, to be paid him immediately after my decease. To my grand-children, the children of my said son HENRY, my place or plantation in Mapletown at Raritan in the Province of New Jersey, whereon he now lives, divided equally between them, male and female alike, and if any of them die before twenty-one years of age their share to go to the survivors, but my son HENRY to live on the said plantation for life. Also to the said children of said HENRY £400, to be raised out of the money due for the mills I sold at Rocky hill at Raritan, divided equally, and if any die before twenty-one their share to the survivors; But if my son HENRY die before his wife ELIZABETH, and she should claim or have a dower right in the mills which her said husband suffered the sheriff to sell then the dower shall be paid out of the said £400 , and the residue to my grandchildren. I give to my son ABRAHAM that lot of land on Staten Island whereon JOHN STILWELL now lives, being part of the patent granted to JOHN VINCENT containing 26 2/3 acres; Also all the residue of the money due or as shall become due from the sale of my mills at Rocky hill, after the said legacy of £400 is paid; Also to my said son ABRAHAM £200, raised out of my moveable estate. I give to my son CORNELIUS the remaining part of my real estate, land and salt meadow on Staten Island and elsewhere, that is the farm on which I now live, also the farm on which the said CORNELIUS now lives, and the woodland thereunto belonging; Also half of all the cattle and horses belonging to me and my son CORNELIUS being undevided. My executors are empowered to sell all my personal estate, the proceeds to pay my debts and funeral expenses; Also the £200 to my said son ABRAHAM; Also £210 to my son HENRY aforesaid, the remainder to be equally divided between my three sons, HENRY, ABRAHAM and CORNELIUS. I appoint my dearly beloved

46

children, ABRAHAM and CORNELIUS KRUSEN, and my trusty friend, WILHELMUS VREELAND, Executors.

Dated June 25, 1782. Witnesses, ADR^N BANCKER (Surrogate of Richmond County), ABRAHAM ROLPH (yeoman), ABR^M BANCKER (sheriff of Richmond County).

Codicil dated January 26, 1784 If my son CORNELIUS should happen to die before me then all the estate, real and personal, devised to him, shall be equally divided between my grandchildren JOHN and LANA, the children of my said son CORNELIUS.

Witnesses to Codicil same as to will. Proved, Richmond County before ADRIAN BANCKER, Surrogate, January 19, 1786.
Liber 38:332   WNYHS XIII:274

In the name of God, Amen. I, **HENDRICK CRUSE**, of Staten Island, being in perfect health, "but being far advanced in years". I leave to my son CORNELIUS the land which I bought of GEORGE HOGLANT. Also the 20 acres which I bought of WILLIAM GEORGE BOWMAN, and 20 acres of the 90 acre tract which I purchased of Mr. GEORGE BOWMAN, and 20 acres of the 90 acre tract which I had of Mr. DONGAN. The said 20 acres to be taken off the east side by a line from front to rear. I also leave him my Silver tankard. I leave to my son CORNELIUS and my daughter ~~VIELTIE~~ NIELTIE all my salt meadow. I leave to my daughter ~~VIELTIE~~ NIELTIE all the rest of my lands, and all the corn and grain growing on the same. But she is to be charged with the sum of £350, and she is to maintain my negro wench "Sada". I leave to my son CORNELIUS £200 to be paid by my executors. I leave to my grandson ABRAHAM, son of GARRETT CRUSE, £50 to be paid by my daughter ~~VIELTIE~~ NIELTIE. To my grandson HENDRICK, son of GARRET CRUSE, £50 when of age. To my daughter-in-law CLAUSIA, widow of my son GERRITT, and to his children, ABRAHAM, MARITSE, CLAUSIA, HENDRICK, and CHARITY, £200 when they are of age, and to be paid by my daughter VIELTIE. To my

47

granddaughter, CORNELIA BERGER, now wife of JOHN SWAN, £50, and to the children of my grandson, JACOB BERGER, £50. All the rest of my estate to my son CORNELIUS and my daughter VIELTIE and the children of my son GERRITT. I make CORNELIUS CRUSE, JACOB CORSEN, and JOSEPH ROLPH, executors. Dated August 11, 1760, (Signed HENDRICK KROESEN.)

Witnesses, HELMUS FREELAND, ROBERT DEGROOT, CORNELIUS CRUSEE, Jr. Proved April 29, 1761, before BENJAMIN SEAMAN, Surrogate.
Liber 23:76   WNYHS VI:96

ISAAC CUBBERLEY, of the County of Richmond, New York, to my wife ANNE, £300, of which £200 is to paid her by my son JAMES, the other £100 by my executors; Also my riding chair, the choice of one horse, one bed and furniture for one room, my negro wench, Zelph, and my negro boy, Samuel; Also three cows, and that she live in my house during her widowhood with my son JAMES; and my son JAMES shall allow her a maintenance out of his own expense during her widowhood, which is to be in lieu of dower or power of thirds on my estate; to my son JOSEPH, £5, having advanced him his full proportion of my estate; to my son THOMAS, his heirs, £400, also my negro girl, Sarah; to my daughter, MARY TAYLOR, her heirs, £300, also my negro girl, Betty, and all such furniture as I have heretofore bought for her which is known to be hers: to my son JAMES, his heirs, the southerly part of my farm or plantation I now live on with all the buildings thereon; Also the one equal half part of my woodland in the Manor of Castleton; Also the half of the woodland in the south quarter, except ten acres thereof; my black colt; to my son ISAAC, ten acres of woodland in the south quarter, beginning by the land of ABRAHAM EGBERT and running along his line to the land of LAWRENCE CRIPS as far as shall comprehend ten acres to the road; Also all my salt meadow, including a hummock of land lying at new creek, to him, his heirs forever; to my son ISAAC, his heirs, £400, also my negro boy,

Harry; to my son STEPHEN, his heirs, all that westerly part of my farm that I now live on, to begin at the corner of land now in the possession of PETER CORTELYOU, being his northeast corner, and to run southerly along the road as far as shall take in three rows of apple trees of the young orchard, and then to run from the lane a direct course to the ditch near a hummock in the rear of said farm; Also the equal one half of my woodland in the south quarter, except the ten acres given to my son ISAAC; to STEPHEN, his heirs, my negro boy, Peter; to my daughter ANNE, her heirs, £300, £200 to be paid her by my son STEPHEN when she attains the age of eighteen years; Also my negro girl, Dina; Also one bed and furniture, equal to that given my daughter MARY; my daughter ANNE to live with my son JAMES until she arrive to the age of eighteen years; if either of my sons or daughters die under age or without issue, then his or her share shall be equally divided among the survivors (except with my son JOSEPH), share and share alike; to my son JAMES, my negro boy, Sam, after my wife's decease. I appoint my three sons, ISAAC, THOMAS, JAMES executors.

Dated January 24, 1786. Witnesses, PAUL MICHEAU, BARZILL^A GROVER, NICHOLAS LOZIER, doctor. Proved, June 5, 1786.
Liber 39:240   WNYHS XIV:54

RICHARD CURTIS. "Richmond County August 15, 1702, the last will of RICHARD CURTIS, being sicke". I leave to my wife CATHARINE, my dwelling house and 40 acres of land next adjoining, for her life, and then to my two sons, JOHN and JOSHUA. The other 40 acres of my land, I give to my sons SAMUEL and ISAAC. I give 1/2 of the remainder of my estate to my wife to bring up my younger children and the other 1/2 to all my children. Made his wife executrix.

Witnesses JOHN STILLWELL, STOEFFEL VAN SANT. Proved April 12, 1703.
Liber 7:96   WNYHS I:365

I, **ROPER DAWSON**, of Richmond County, being in perfect health. I leave to my wife RACHEL all my household furniture, Plate, linnen, and clothes, until my children are of age. I leave to my son GEORGE all my real estate "whatsoever and wheresoever", and when he is of age, all my Plate and books and implements of husbandry. I leave to my daughters, HARRIET and CHARLOTTE, each £250, and all the linnen when she is 18, and they are to live with their mother, to be clothed and educated at her expense. And so long as they remain with her she shall have the use of all my real estate and money. I make my good friends, AUGUSTUS VAN CORTLANDT, of New York Mr. GEORGE BARNES, and my wife, executors. I leave to my wife and son and daughters my 4 negroes. My executors are to sell all the rest in 12 months, and the money to be paid to all the children.

Dated March 22, 1771. Witnesses, GILBERT FORBES, NATHANIEL BRITTON, TIMOTHY HUGHES. Proved, August 15, 1771.
Liber 28:141   WNYHS VII:436

In the name of God, Amen, June 16, 1733. I, **DAVID DE BONREPOS**, minister of the Holy Gospel, in the County of Richmond. I leave to my wife MARTHA, for her dower, £50, and £3 in addition and two negro women which are at JACOB ~~BILYEAS~~ BILYOU, and she shall have the interest on all my lands. And as for my other negro wench name "Judde" and her child "Elisah", I give the child to my wife, and the mother to my heir. Also my wife is to have all household goods except a Tankard and Silver Cup. I leave to Mr. JOHN ~~LAFORT~~ LAFONT, of New York, £40. To BLANCHE DE BONREPOS, wife of HENRY CHADEN, of New Rochelle, £30. To ANNA PAMER *(PALMER)* and HESTER LE COUNT, my nieces, £10 each. To the three youngest sons of ALEXANDER DE BONREPOS, £10 each *(names not given)*. I leave my silver tankard and silver cup and all the rest of my estate to DAVID DE BONREPOS son of ALEXANDER DE BONREPOS. My negro woman "Sans" is to be maintained out of my estate. I appoint BARENT MARTLINGS, PAUL MICHAUX and NICHOLAS STILLWELL, "Grandson to my wife", executors.

Witnesses, CHARLES TAYLOR, JACOB BILLAN, SOLOMON MACLEAN. Proved before WALTER DONGAN, Esq., May 6, 1734.

Liber 12:175   WNYHS III:148

Know all men whom it may any ways concerne, that I, **MARTHA DE BONREPOS**, of Staten Island, widow, being very sick. All my estate is to be sold by my executors, except two beds, two brass kettles, a negro girl and an old negro wench. I leave to my daughter RACHEL, my negro wench, and large brass kettle, and I leave to her daughter MARTHA, my negro girl, and to her daughter MARY my best bed and brass kettle. I leave to my son-in-law, JACOBUS BILLVE, all that he owes me, and a silver cup of £5 value. And a cup of same value, to my children MARTHA BRITTAIN, WILLIAM BRITTAIN, and to NICHOLAS BRITTAIN's daughter MARTHA, and to JACOBUS BILLVEE's daughter MARTHA, and to PETER LE COUNT's daughter MARTHA. All the rest of my estate to my children FRANCIS BRITTAIN, ANNIE BILLVE, RACHEL BRITTAIN, and to THOMAS STILLWELL's three children, NICHOLAS, JANE, MUSHO(?) {instead of JANE, MUSHO(?), it should be ANNE MICHAUD, daughter of Thomas Stillwell, and to MARY HOFFER's {HOPPER's} two eldest daughters, MARY JURNE and ELIZABETH JURNE. I make JOHN LE COUNT and RICHARD STILLWELL executors.

March 3, 1734/5. Witnesses, WILLIAM RICHMAN, ~~SARAH~~ SUSANNAH RAMAH, EBENEZER SALTER. Proved, October 23, 1736.

Liber 13:29   WNYHS III:213

In the name of God, Amen, April 6, 1754. I, **CHARLES DECKER**, of Staten Island, yeoman being in good health. I leave to my wife ELENOR all my real and personal estate during her widowhood. I leave to my eldest son CHARLES £5 for his birth right. All the rest

51

of my estate I leave to my children, CHARLES, MATTHIAS, ~~MALLOR~~ MATTHEW, ELENOR, EVA and HESTER {and daughter MERCY}. I make my sons CHARLES and MATTHIAS and my brother MATTHEW DECKER executors.

Wittnesses, RICHARD MORELL, JOSEPH ~~LAKE~~ LEAKE, SARAH LAKE. Proved February 19, 1755. Liber 19:198   WNYHS V:51

"In the name of God, Amen. I, **JOHANES DECKER**, of Richmond County, March ~~16~~ 10, 1779. I leave to JAMES SIMON DECKER, son of my son JOHN, deceased, 10 shillings. To the other children of my son JOHN, deceased, viz., REBECCA, JEMIMA, MOSES, and SILVANUS, £100 between them. I leave to MARY DECKER, daughter of my son MOSES, and to ISABEL WOOD, the money that JOHN DECKER, son of PETER DECKER, owes me. I leave to my son MOSES £50; also a lot of 15 acres, bounded by the road and BARENT ~~DUPUY~~ DEPUY. I leave to my daughter ELIZABETH, wife of EDMUND CHRISTOPHER, and EVE, wife of BENJAMIN COLE, 19 acres of land adjoining the above. All the rest of my lands to my sons, MATTHEW and MATTHIAS, and MATTHIAS to have the north part. The house of MATTHIAS is to be made equal to that of MATTHEW. My three sons, MATTHEW, MATTHIAS, and MOSES, I make executors."

Witnesses, PETER HAUSMAN, AARON DUPUY, BARENT DUPUY. Proved, December 27, 1779. Liber 32:175   WNYHS IX:87

In the name of God, Amen. April 11th, 1785. I, **MATTHEW DECKER**, of the County of Richmond, having my usual senses and memory. I leave to my wife ELICE, one third of my land and a cow for life; to oldest son MATTHEW, 40 shillings; to daughter MARY, £30 , brass kittle, spinning wheel and one pair of smoothing Irons. Rest of estate equally divided between sons, MATTHEW and BARNET.

Executors, wife ELICE, and THOMAS RIDGWAY.

Witnesses, CHAS. DECKER, yeoman; BENJAMIN PRICE, JOSEPH RIDGWAY. Proved, May 6, 1785,

Richmond County. Confirmed, May 17, 1785, New York.
Liber 38:24

In the name of God, Amen, November 12, 1765. I, **MATTHEW DECKER**, of Staten Island, being sick. I leave to my wife ELICE all that estate given her by her father, RICHARD MERRILL. All the rest of my estate to my son MATTHEW when he is of age, and I make him executor.

Witnesses, JOHN MERRILL, JOHN EGBERT, MAGDALEN MERRILL. Proved, February 25, 1766.
Liber 25:209

"In the name of God, Amen, May 30, 1777. I, **MATTHIAS DECKER**, of Richmond County, farmer, being very sick. I leave to my wife MARGARET the use of all houses, lands, and chattels during her widowhood, and I make her executor. I leave to my eldest son, MATTHIAS, 40 shillings more than my youngest son, RICHARD. I leave to my said two sons all my houses and lands. My son MATTHIAS is to pay to his sister JENNY £30, and my son RICHARD to pay the same. All the rest I leave to my two sons. My eldest son, MATTHIAS, is to take 20 acres adjoining to MATTHIAS DECKER, and my son RICHARD is to have my homestead lot."

Witnesses, THOMAS KINGSTON, BENJAMIN PRALL, DAVID CANNON. Proved, June 21, 1777.
Liber 31:74

In the name of God, Amen, July 21, 1739. I, **JACQUES DENYS**, of New Utrecht, in Kings County, being very sick. I leave to my son DENYS, my whole farm or plantation in New Utrecht, where I live; also £1000. I leave to my son ISAAC my whole farm or plantation in New Utrecht "so as I have bought of WILLIAM VERDON", with all privileges; Also 25 acres of woodland on Staten Island. I leave to my son ISAAC, £300. To my son JACQUES, £700, and to my daughters HELMA and ANNE, £50 each. I appoint my brother, TEUNIS DENYS, and my brother-in-law, SIMON SIMONSON, and my cousin,

HERMANUS BOCKELL, executors.
Witnesses, ADAM BALDERIDG, SAMUEL WARNER, S. GERITTSE. Proved before RICHARD STILLWELL, Esq., July 31, 1739.
Liber 13:283   WNYHS III:271

DEPUY, includes DUPUY

Whereas **CATALYNA DUPUY** of Staten Island, died lately intestate. Letters of Administration are granted to her eldest son, JOHN DUPUY. July 13, 1705.
Liber 7:259   WNYHS I:408

In the name of God, Amen, the ~~1st~~ 15th day of May, 1725. I, **JOHN DUPUY**, of Richmond County. I leave to my son JOHN £5, and the use of the northwest chamber in my now dwelling-house, during his life, and also his board, firewood, pasturing, and a horse, and such attendance as his bodily infirmities may require. I leave to my four sons, JOHN, NICHOLAS, BARENT and MOSES, all my lands and tenements. I leave to my daughters, MAGDALENA, SUSANAH, ELIZABETH, PETRONELLA and MARY, and to the children of my daughter CATHARINE, deceased, all my movable estate after payment of debts. I leave to my wife PETRONELLA, the benefit of all property during her life, and I make her executor.
Witnesses, LAMBERT ~~GARRITSEN~~ GERRITSEN, PETER ~~DEANED~~ DEDICKER, ELIZABETH GARRITSEN. Proved, June ~~11~~ 14, 1732.
Liber 11:321   WNYHS III:64

"In the name of God, Amen. I, **MOSES DUPUY**, of Richmond County, blacksmith, September 16, 1776. I leave to my wife LEAH the possession of all lands and estate during her life or widowhood, and then all to be sold and divided among my children, JOHN, NICHOLAS, MOSES, and LEAH. I make STEPHEN BEDELL and ANTHONY EGBERTS, executors."
Witnesses, BARENT SIMONSON, ABRAHAM ~~JAMES~~ JONES, JACOB DECKER. Proved, November 24, 1779.

In the name of God, Amen.   I, **NICHOLAS DEPUY**, of the County of Richmond, being in a weak state of health, but of sound mind.   My executors to take of monies arising out of my moveable estate sufficient to discharge all my debts and funeral expenses.   All my movable estate to be sold and the balance of the proceeds to be equally divided in four parts for my daughter CATHARINE, my other daughter ELIZABETH, the children of my son, JOHN DEPUY, deceased; the other part to the children of my son, MOSES DEPUY, deceased.   All my real estate of lands, meadows, and buildings to be equally divided between my two sons, AARON and PETER DEPUY.   I make my trusty friends, RICHARD CONNER, Esq., and BARNET SIMONSON, both of Richmond County, executors.

Dated June 26, 1781.   Witnesses, RICHARD CONNER, BARNET SIMONSON, and ISAAC DOTY. Proved, March 25, 1782.

In the name of God, Amen.   I, **CORNELIUS DUSSOSWAY**, of Staten Island, Richmond County, yeoman, being weak and sickly in body.   I leave to my dear and loving wife MARY all the farm in the township of Woodbridge, New Jersey, about 900 acres, bounded southerly by the Highway, Westerly by land belonging to MICHAEL LONG, RICHARD WRIGHT, Junr, and land formerly belonging to JOHN PIERSON, deceased, Northerly by land belonging to MOSES BLOOMFIELD, and Easterly by land formerly belonging to NATHANIEL FITZ RANDOLPH, Esqr, deceased, to the only proper use of my said wife for life, and after her decease to be divided between my two sons, CORNELIUS and ISRAEL, when they attain the age of twenty-one or marry; if both or either of my said sons at my wife's decease be minors then his part to be rented out for his benefit till he arrive at Manhood, if either die before he is twenty-one or married then his part to be equally divided between my surviving daughters.   To my wife a Negro Man named Jack, a Negro woman named Ambo, my riding chair and her choice of one of my horses, for life, and at her decease to be divided among my sons and daughters then living by my said wife MARY. To my wife £200, to be paid within two years after my decease. To ISRAEL DUSSOSWAY and MARK DUSSOSWAY, the sons of my brother MARK DUSSOSWAY, deceased, 450 acres on the west end of Staten Island, part of the plantion on which I at present reside, beginning at a spring inclosed with a gum Barrell below the bank near the old Mansion house which shall be ceded to them or the survivor of them at my decease, and if both shall die before my decease the land to be divided between my surviving sons. To said ISRAEL and MARK half of an Island of salt meadow called the Big Island, lying near Buckwheat Island in the sound that separates Staten Island from the Main Continent of New Jersey, the division line to begin at the river and to run toward the upland easterly, in case they should not live to inherit it the land to go to my sons CORNELIUS and ISRAEL.

To my sons, CORNELIUS and ISRAEL, when twenty-one years of age, all the residue of my land, salt meadows, etc., in Richmond County, viz.: that plantation or farm on which I reside on the west side of said Island, nearly opposite the City of Perth Amboy, except that bequeathed already, then being after the said deductions about 600 acres, which with the houses, barns, mills, outhouses, etc., I bequeath to them and their heirs forever; Also that piece of salt meadow called the sunken Marsh nearly opposite to the place occupied by ABRAHAM WOGLOM and contiguous to the Jersey shore, about 14 acres; Also two pieces of salt meadow at Freshkill, and another piece opposite Merrills Mills next the meadow of ABRAHAM PRALL; and one half of the Big Island, near Buckwheat Island, to be divided into two equal parts, if either die before possessing the above, the share of the defunct shall belong to the survivor. If both my sons die before twenty-one the lands they were to inherit to be equally divided between my daughters, ANNA, CHARITY, CATHARINE, MARY, VIOLETTA and SUSANNAH or the survivors. To my son CORNELIUS my gold watch with the chain and trinkets thereto to be by him preserved in remembrance of the love and affection I bear unto him. To my son ISRAEL, a pair of gold sleeve buttons, and a silver tankard as a token of my regard towards him; the rest of my silver plate to be divided amongst my daughters CATHARINE, MARY, VIOLETTA and SUSANNAH, in such manner as my wife shall please. To my daughter CATHARINE a Negro wench, Phebe; to MARY a Negro wench, Dinah; to VIOLETTA a Negro wench, Peg, and to SUSANNAH a Negro wench, Jenny, when they shall attain the age of eighteen years; Also to my above four daughters when eighteen £200 each. The remainder of my personal estate shall be equally divided between my sons, CORNELIUS and ISRAEL, and my daughters, ANNA, CHARITY, CATHARINE, MARY, VIOLETTA and SUSANNAH. My executors to dispose of my stock and Negroes or such parts as they think advantageous and the monies to be divided among my sons and daughters, but my household furniture shall not be sold but divided among my wife and daughters CATHARINE, MARY, VIOLETTA and SUSANNAH equally. Whereas the Education of my children will be of great importance to them in life I order that those deficient in that respect shall at the time of my decease be educated from my estate. My wife shall be permitted to reside in the Mansion house for five years and my youngest daughters till they marry or are eighteen. I make my sons-in-law, ISAAC PRALL and JOSEPH GUYON, and my trusty friend, ABRAHAM BANCKER, Executors, and my wife MARY, Executrix.

(Signed) CORNELIUS DISOSWAY. Dated October 13, 1785. Witnesses, GILBERT JACKSON (Esquire), SAMUEL SKINER (yeoman), CATY F. RANDOLPH. Proved, Richmond County, January 4, 1786.
Liber 38:292   WNYHS XIII:257

In the name of God, Amen, October 13, 1753. I, **ISRAEL DISSOSWAY**, of Richmond county, Gentleman, being now of perfect mind. I leave to my eldest son ISRAEL £10 as heir at law. "My good will and desire is that all my real estate be equally divided among my sons, ISRAEL, CORNELIUS, GABRIEL, and MARK, and not one to have more than the other". My lots are to be surveyed and divided into four parts, and if my four sons can not agree, they are to cast lots for each share. I leave to my wife a negro man and woman, and two negro children and £100 and her choice of rooms in my house during widowhood. I leave to my daughter ANNETTIE, wife of JOHN BEDEL, £400 to be paid by my four sons. "All the rest of my movable estate to my four sons. "All the lands and meadows are on Staten Island, except a piece of land in Middlesex, in East New Jersey, and 5 acres of salt meadow at a place called Sunken Marsh in the Jerseys". I make my wife KERTRY, and my three sons, ISRAEL, CORNELIUS, and GABRIEL, executors.

Witnesses, WILLIAM ~~JACKSON~~ JOHNSON, ELIZABETH PARMER, MATHIAS VAN BROCKEL. Proved, October 4, 1754.
Liber 19:118   WNYHS V:33

MARK DUSOCHANY. In the name of God, Amen, December 23, 1713. I, MARK DUSOCHANY, of Richmond County, being very sick. I leave to my eldest son JOB, £15 in full of his pretence as heir-at-law. I leave to my wife JANE the use of one-third of my estate during her life. I leave to my eldest son JOB the farm on which my dwelling house stands, containing 85 acres of upland and 10 acres of salt meadow. I leave to my son ISRAEL the north lot fronting to the water side, containing 85 acres of upland, and 10 acres of meadow. I leave to my son GABRIEL the south lot fronting to the water side next unto the land of JOHN RUE, containing 85 acres of upland, and 10 acres of meadow. I leave to my daughter ELIZABETH a certain tract of land lying and fronting to a certain brook at the rear of the land of HENRY

JOHNSON, containing 85 acres of upland and 10
acres of salt meadow. I leave to my daughter,
SUSANNAH HENDRICKS, the north lot joining to
the land last above mentioned, containing 80
acres of upland and 10 acres of salt meadow.
I leave to my daughter DINAH a tract of land
joining to the northward of the above tract,
containing 80 acres of upland and 8 acres of
salt meadow. I leave to my daughter SARAH, a
certain tract of land joining northward of the
above tract, containing 80 acres of upland and
8 acres of salt meadow. The above tracts are
to be laid out and measured, and if there is
any land remaining it is to go to my sons.
None of the above tracts are to be sold, but
they are to leave them to their issue. I
order my negroes Jack and Betty to be sold.
They are valued at £70. My sons are to have
their lots when of age. My wife is to live
with any of my children she chooses, but if
she cannot agree with them a convenient house
is to be built for her at their charge. {The
will mentions daughter MARY}.

Witnesses, DAVID de BONREPOS, SAMUEL
BERINS, LEWIS GITTON. Proved, January 27,
1713.
Liber 8:294   WNYHS II:126

Whereas **JOHN DONGAN**, of the County of
Richmond, Gentleman, died intestate, Letters
of administration are granted to his brother
and heir at law, WALTER DONGAN, July 2, 1715.

[Note. JOHN and WALTER DONGAN, were two
of the nephews of Governor THOMAS DONGAN, Earl
of Limerick, who left to them and their
brothers a large estate. WALTER DONGAN was
the only one who left descendants, and their
representatives are now living in New York,
Staten Island and Brooklyn. W.S.P.]
Liber 8:399   WNYHS II:152

In the name of God, Amen. "I, **THOMAS
DONGAN**, of Richmond County, Esquire, do ordain
and publish this as my last will and
Testament." I make my wife MAGDALENA
executor, with full power to dispose of any

part of the estate, and I leave to her the use of all my estate during the minority of my son, JOHN CHARLTON DONGAN, directing that a decent and suitable Education and maintenance shall be allowed to him. I leave to my son, JOHN CHARLTON DONGAN, when he is 21, one-half of all my real and personal estate, and I leave the other half to my wife during her life. If my son dies, then I leave all to my wife.

Dated March 8, 1765. Witnesses, JOSEPH RALPH, MARGARET BUFFLERY, wife of JACOB BUFFLERY, WILLIAM HICKS. Proved, June 6, 1768.

Liber 26:340   WNYHS VII:187

In the name of God, Amen. I, **ISAAC DOTY**, of Richmond County, innholder, being very weak in body. I leave to my wife MARGARET the use of all my estate so long as she remains my widow; but if she marries I leave all my estate to all my children *(not named)*. I make my wife and my son SAMUEL and my friend, BENJAMIN SEAMAN, executors.

Dated January 1, 1774. Witnesses, SAMUEL ~~BARROW~~ BORROW, "Doctor", WOODHULL TURNER. Proved, March 29, 1774.

Liber 29:193   WNYHS VIII:208

Robert Hunter, Captain-General and Governor. Whereas **PETER DRAGOE**, late of Richmond County, died intestate, Letters of administration are granted to wife, ELIZABETH, April 3, 1712.

Liber 8:270   WNYHS II:120

In the name of God, Amen, ~~May 8, 1741~~ July 8, 1711. I, **LEWIS DUBOIS**, blacksmith, being in good health. I make RUTGER VAN BRUNT, of New Utrecht, and JOHN ~~GRANDEN~~ GRONDEN, of Staten Island, executors. I leave to my eldest son, LEWIS DUBOIS, for his heirship, the smith tools he now works with, and no more, for what he has already had. I leave to my wife CATHARINE, 1/3 of the rest of my estate, during her widowhood and no longer.

60

I leave to my sons AUGUSTUS and JOHN the Plantation which I now dwell on, both land and meadow, the eastern part for AUGUSTUS and the west part for JOHN. I leave to my son SAMUEL, that plantation which I bought of DANIEL STILLWELL at the south side. My son AUGUSTUS shall pay to his sister MARTHA, £20, or to her heirs, that she has or will have, by PETER ~~PORELIE~~ PARELIE; To be paid by him when of age. He is also to pay to my daughter MARY, £40. My son JOHN shall pay to my daughter ESTHER, £30. My son SAMUEL shall pay to my daughter ESTHER, £45; and to my daughter MARGARET, £45. I order that my land and meadow which I have bought of GEORGE PERSONET and JACOB WRIGHT, with all the buildings, to be sold at vendue. And I leave all the rest of my estate to my last named 7 children.

Witnesses, JAMES EGBERTSE, DANIEL ~~MOREAU~~ MERSEREAU, HENRY LA TOURETTE. Proved before WALTER DONGAN, Esq., October 1, 1745.
Liber 16:48   WNYHS IV:102

ANTHONY DUCHENE. In the name of God, Amen, the 3d of April 1711. I, ANTHONY DUCHENE, of Staten Island. I leave to my son MICHAEL DUCHENE, my whole estate, of a lot and a half of land, and "Mink" the negro boy. And all my movables, and he is to give my dear wife ANNA her whole and separate maintenance as long as she lives. I leave to my son JEROME, the lot of land he now liveth on. I leave to my son VALENTINE, £10. To my daughters, ANNA GOLDERS, JANETTE MANGLES, MAGDALENA CLAASON, and ~~FRANETTIE~~ FRANSENTIE EGBERTS, each £5.

Witnesses, JOHN ~~BAYHAM~~ BYBAN, BARENT SIMONS, BENJAMIN COOPER. Proved, May 12, 1712, and MICHAEL DUSEN appointed administrator, the widow and JEROME, the eldest son, having refused.
Liber 8:273   WNYHS II:121

ELLIS DUXBURY. In the name of God, Amen. I, ELLIS DUXBURY, of Staten Island, being in good health, I leave and bequeath all that my

61

Plantation or tract of land on which I now
live in the County of Richmond, to the
Corporation of the Minister, Church Wardens
and Vestrymen of St. Andrew's in Richmond
County, and to their successors forever. For
the only use and maintenance of the present
minister, the Rev. Master ENEAS MACKENZIE,
during his life, and at his decease to his
successors being orthodox ministers of the
Church of England. And I make and appoint His
Excellency, Governor ROBERT HUNTER, to see
that the said Plantation granted to me by
Patent under the seal of the Province be not
put to any other use. And I also leave £100
toward building a vestry room for St. Andrew's
Church, and a handsome porch for the church
door, and to pale in the church yard, and to
buy a pall to cover the bier. I also leave
£10 for such poor of the county as my
executors shall think fit, I leave all the
rest of my personal estate to Master ENEAS
MACKENZIE, the present minister, namely, my
negroes, money and bonds, and I make him sole
executor.
     Dated May 5, 1718. Witnesses, WALTER
DONGAN, WILLIAM TILLYOU, MARGARET TILLYOU.
Proved before Governor HUNTER, October 22,
1718.
Liber 9:4   WNYHS II:180

-E-

     In the name of God, Amen. October 26,
1765. I, **JAMES EGBERT**, of Staten Island,
being in perfect health. I leave to my wife
CATHARINE my best bed. And all the rest of my
estate, real and personal, is to be sold by my
executors. My wife is to remain on the place
and have her living till it is sold. From the
proceeds, my executors are to pay 1/3 for the
support of my wife, and the rest of my
children, CATY, TUNIS, CATHARINE, ANN, MARY,
JOHN, LAWRENCE, NICHOLAS, PETER, SUSANAH,
ABRAHAM, ELIZABETH, and BENJAMIN. I leave to
my son BENJAMIN £50. I leave to my
grandchildren, JAMES, MARY, and CATHARINE, the

62

children of my son JAMES EGBERT, £25. I make
my sons TUNIS and ABRAHAM, and HENRY LA
TOURETTE, executors.

Witnesses, JOHN POILLON, TUNIS EGBERT,
Jr., JEREMIAH CONNOR, schoolmaster. Proved,
April 16, 1768, before BENJAMIN SEAMAN.
Liber 26:272   WNYHS VII:165

In the name of God, Amen, July 6, 1721.
I, **TEUNIS EGBERTSE**, of the county of Richmond,
yeoman, being sick. I leave to my eldest son
EGBERT, 5 shillings as in full of all pretence
of being heir-at-law. I leave all my lands
and tenements to my seven sons, EGBERT, JOHN,
ABRAHAM, JACQUES, ISAAC, LAURENCE and TEUNIS.
My wife JANETTIE "is to reap all the benefit
of my estate during her life or widowhood." I
leave to my daughters, HARMITIE, MARY and
~~SARAH~~ SUSANNAH, each £20. I make my wife and
son JACQUES, executors.

Witnesses, WILLIAM BRAISTED, ENGELBERT
LOTT {and ELIAS GASTRAW?}. Proved, August 25,
1721.
Liber 9:258   WNYHS II:239

In the name of God, Amen, March 25, 1760.
I **BASTIAN ELLIS**, of Staten Island, being now
very sick. I direct all debts to be paid. I
leave to my wife all my whole estate, real and
personal, to support her so long as she
remains my widow. "But if she shall marry
again or come to die", then I leave the same
to all my children, in the following manner:
All my household goods and movables, to all my
children, viz., CORNELIUS, BASTIAN, CATHARINE,
EAGGE, ANATTIE, HENDRICA, and MARY. I leave
to my son CORNELIUS ½ of all my lands and
meadows. His share is to be the west side,
and from his share he is to raise £150 and pay
½ of the debts, and the rest to my three
daughters, CATHARINE, SARAH, and EAGGE. I
leave to my son BASTIAN the other half of my
lands on the east side, and he is to raise
£150 and pay ½ the debts, and the rest to my 3
daughters, ~~ANATTIE~~ ARIANTE, HENDRICA, and
MARY. I make my sons executors.

Witnesses, RICHARD LAWRENCE, THOMAS STEPHENSON, AARON VAN NAME. Proved, November ~~29~~ 26, 1763, before BENJAMIN SEAMAN, Surrogate.
Liber 24:227   WNYHS VI:279

In the name of God, Amen. I, **CORNELIUS ELLIS**, of Richmond County, weaver. I leave to my wife MAGDALEN, after all debts are paid, all the remainder of my estate for her maintenance and that of the children so long as she remains my widow. If she marries I leave all my estate to my executors for the support and maintainance of my children. I bequeath the reversion and fee simple of the real estate I possess, left to me by my father, BASTIAN ELLIS, after my mother's death, to my son, GERRITT ELLIS, and he is to pay to my daughter SARAH £80 when he is 21. I also leave him all my wearing apparell. I make my wife and my brother BASTIAN and my friend LAWRENCE ROOME executors. Dated August 1, 1763.
Witnesses, RICHARD LAWRENCE, ship carpenter; ABRAHAM SWAIM, HENRY HOLLAND. Proved, November 26, 1763.
Liber 24:230   WNYHS VI:280

-F-

Will of **RICHARD FLOYD**, of Town of Brookhaven, Suffolk County, NY, 27 February 1738. His daughter RUTH married WALTER DONGAN of Staten Island.
Liber 13:225   WNYHS III:260

In the name of God, Amen, January 4, 1731/2. I **VINCENT FOUNTAIN**, Sr., of the County of Richmond, Gent., being in good health. I leave to my son VINCENT, 150 acres of land and meadow in Middlesex County, New Jersey. It being ½ of a tract of land of 300 acres. The other ½ I have given by deed to my daughter ANNE and her husband HENRY PERINE. I leave to my youngest son, ANTHONY, all my farm or plantation where I now live, in the south quarter of the County of Richmond, with all the appurtenances. And he is to pay to my grandson ANTHONY, the son of my son VINCENT, £80. If he dies, then to the other children of my son VINCENT. And my sons are to pay to my daughter, ANNE PERINE, £10. "It is my will that my much honored mother SARAH DYE, shall be decently maintained, and sufficiently provided for, out of my estate, and to be tended attendance as her feeble and old age shall require". I leave to my wife ANNE certain slaves, and the use of property during widowhood. I make my wife and my sons, and "my beloved friend and nephew, STEPHEN MARTENEAU", Executors.

Witnesses, ~~WILLIAM VOORHIS~~ JAN VAN VOORHIS, REM VANDERBEEK, JOHN DUPUY. Proved, June 14, 1732.
Liber 11:323   WNYHS III:65

In the name of God Amen, this 28 September, 1740. I, **VINCENT FOUNTAIN**, of Richmond County. "Whereas it hath pleased God to give unto me six children, whereof all are at present alive, viz., ANTHONY, JOHN, ELIZABETH, VINCENT, SARAH, and MARTHA." I leave to my son ANTHONY, a horse and a new saddle. I leave to my wife MARTHA, the use of all estate during her widowhood. After her decease my executors are to sell all the estate and divide the proceeds among my children. I appoint my wife and STEPHEN MARTENS and RICHARD STILLWELL, executors.

Witnesses, REM VANDERBEEK, NICHOLAS ~~BRITTAIN~~ BRITTON, AVIS ~~BYERSE~~ RYERSE. Proved before WALTER DONGAN, Esq., November ~~12~~ 20, 1740.
Liber 14:1   WNYHS III:317

-G-

In the name of God, Amen. I, **JOHN GARREAU**, of Richmond County, merchant, being in good health. My will is that my dear beloved wife, MARY GARREAU, shall keep in full possession, and reap the benefit of all my estate, real and personal, as long as she remains my widow and no longer. I leave to my son JOHN, after my wife's decease, all my estate, houses and lands, shop and goods, and I make him executor. Signed JEAN GARREAU.

Dated, May 17, 1725. Witnesses, JOHN ~~TILLON~~ TILLOU, PETER ~~TILLON~~ TILLOU, ABRAHAM COLE. Proved, December 1, 1726.
Liber 10:239   WNYHS II:355

GARRISON, includes GARRETSON

Robert Hunter, Captain-General and Governor. Whereas **CORNELIUS GARRETSON**, of Richmond County, died intestate, leaving two children, JOHN and ELIZABETH, both infants of tender age. And his sisters AELTIE, wife of PETER PRALL, and ELIZABETH, wife of NATHANIEL GARRETSON, having petitioned that Letters of administration be granted to NATHANIEL BRITTAIN, they are granted, April 15, 1714.
Liber 8:313   WNYHS II:130

In the name of God, Amen, April 13, 1764. I, **JOHANIS GARRISON**, of Richmond County, being at this time in good health. I direct all debts to be paid. "I leave to my dearly beloved wife MARGARET the use of the best room in my house, which she shall chuse, and as much house furniture as she shall think necessary for her comfort, and a negro man and woman," Also 4 good cows and a good horse, and the privilege of all sorts of fruit on my plantation. My two sons, JOHANIS and AROMANUS, shall pay her, each £10 a year, and provide her beef, pork, and bread corn and firewood, and pasture and hay, during her widowhood. I leave to my daughter HANNAH my best bed and furniture, and my large brass kettle, and my negro woman "Sarah". I leave to my son JOHANIS a negro boy, and to each of my sons a negro slave. I leave to my son AROMANUS one half of the stock on the place, between him and me in partnership. I leave to my sons, JOHANIS and AROMANUS, all my carpenter tools. All the rest of my movables I leave to my four sons, CORNELIUS, JACOB, HENDRICK, and ABRAHAM, and my daughter HANNAH. I leave to my two sons, JOHANIS and AROMANUS, the Plantation that I dwell on, with all the improvements, and all my lands in Richmond County. My son AROMANUS is to have the house where I now live, and JOHANIS to have the house where he lives, and the land to be divided equally, and they are to pay to their brothers and sister £40 per annum, "until they make up £140". I make my sons, JOHANIS, CORNELIUS, and JACOB, executors.

Witnesses, AARON VAN NAME, SIMON VAN NAME, BENJAMIN HUBBARD. Proved, August 18, 1766, before BENJAMIN SEAMAN, Surrogate.
Liber 25:282   WNYHS VII:16

I, **JOHN GARRISON**, of Richmond County, being in a low state of health". All debts to be paid. I leave to my wife HANNAH £30, "to dispose of the same as she thinks best, among my children and grandchildren", Also two beds and furniture, and a cow, 2 pots, a large copper kettle, ½ dozen silver table spoons, and my riding chair. I leave to my son JOHN £10. I having already advanced him a full proportion of my estate. I leave to my grandson, JOHN KITCHEN, £50, after his grandmother's death. I leave to my grandson, ~~JOHANES~~ JOHN GARRISON, son of my son GEORGE, £25. {Also mentions his grandson JOSEPH KITCHEN}. All the rest of my estate, real and personal, in Richmond County, is to be sold by my executors, and the money put at interest, and the interest paid to my wife during her widowhood, and then to my three daughters, HANNAH, REBECCA, and HESTER, and my two grandsons, JOHN and WILLIAM, sons of my son WILLIAM. "If my daughter, who was unhappily married to RICHARD LOWRIE, of New ~~York~~ Jersey, and for just reasons is now separated from him, shall return and live with him again, she shall be debarred from any part". I make my wife HANNAH, and HENRY PERINE, executors {and BENJAMIN SEAMAN as Trustee}.

Dated November 18, 1774. Witnesses, DAVID LA TOURETTE, JAMES LA TOURETTE, ISAAC DOTY. Proved, December 19, 1774.
Liber 29:278   WNYHS VIII:233

In the name of God, Amen. October 7, 1723. I, **LAMBERT GARRISON**, of Staten Island, being very sick. I leave to my wife, MARY, a bed and furniture for the same, a woman's saddle, and one-half of all household goods, and £20. I leave to my eldest son, LAMBERT, 5 shillings. Considering what I have done for my daughter SUSANAH, I give her £5. I leave all the rest of my estate, houses, and lands, to my children, LAMBERT, CHARLES, NICHOLAS, ISAAC, JACOB, CATHARINE, and ELIZABETH; and to my grandsons DANIEL and NATHANIEL, sons of my son DANIEL, deceased. From these lands are excepted "that land which belongeth to the two eldest sons of BARENT CHRISTOPHERS, which is in the bounds of my Patent, and belongeth not to me". "I will that the burying place on my land shall continue for a burying place for my posterity forever". I make my brother SEGAR GARRISON, and my sons CHARLES and NICHOLAS, executors.
Witnesses, ELIAS ~~BARGER~~ BURGER, SUSANNAH ~~BARGER~~ BURGER, SEGAR GARRISON {and NICHOLAS GARRISON}. Proved, May 22, 1725.
Liber 9:471   WNYHS II:292

Power of Attorney given by **EDMOND GIBBON**, of New York, merchant, to "his trusty friend SAMUEL WINDER, of Staten Island", "to appear in an action that may be occasioned by the taking and carrying away several Casks of Rum, by the Porters of said city", and to prosecute all such ways and manners as the Law allows.
March 30, 1681. Witnesses WILLIAM COX, MATTHEW TAYLOR.
Liber 19B:10   WNYHS II:424

"In the name of God, Amen. I, **JOHN GIFFORD**, of Staten Island, ~~weaver~~ mariner, being very sick. My executors are to sell all real and personal estate at discretion. I leave to my daughter, MARY DUBOIS, during her life with her husband, JOHN DUBOIS, in peace, and no longer, one feather bed, bedstead, and pillows, a pair of sheets and blankets, a small mahogany bureau, one black walnut bureau, a round table and a square table, a pint silver cup, six spoons, silver tea tray. After her death, to her children. I leave to my grandson, EDWARD DUBOIS, all my right to the lands granted by his Excellency, BENNING WENTWORTH, Esq., Governor of New Hampshire, in 1763, and since granted by the Governor of New York, it being in this Province to the eastward of Wood creek; Likewise an Island called Gifford's Island in Mahone Bay, granted by Governor LAWRENCE. All the rest of my estate I leave to my wife, and after her death to my daughter MARY if she is a widow. Furthermore, if after my death my executors see any hopes of JOHN DUBOIS using his wife MARY with tenderness and kind usage, without any abuse, then the said JOHN DUBOIS is to give bonds to keep good my estate, and he is to have the use of her share, but my executors are to be very cautious about making over my estate to him. It is my desire that my daughter is not to suffer, but should be glad if she could live a peaceable, quiet, sober, Godly life with her husband, but if she cannot, then to live with her mother. I make my wife executrix, with Captain JOHN JOURNEY and JOSEPH BEDELL, Sr., executors."

Dated this - day of -, 1776. Witnesses, JACOB ~~REYAU~~ REZEAU, STEPHEN MERCEREAU, CATHARINE ~~BURROWE~~ BARROW, wife of Dr. BURROWE. Proved, March 28, 1780.
Liber 32:224   WNYHS IX:102

Inventory of the estate of **JAMES GLASSON**. Cash £541.13s 4 ½. Taken by THOMAS DAVENPORT, administrator. A true and perfect inventory of all and singular the goods, etc., of THOMAS STILLWELL, Jr., of Staten Island. Taken by NATHAN WHITMAN and LAMBERT JOHNSON. February 3, 1703/4. 6 cows, 2 heifers, £15; 17 head other cattle, £22. Seems to have been the owner of a small farm. Exhibited by MARY STILLWELL, administrator. October 3, 1708. Liber 5-6:479 WNYHS I:330

In the name of God, Amen. I, **JOHN GOULD**, of the west quarter of Richmond County, being in a reasonable state of health. After my debts and funeral expenses are paid I leave to my son PETER, a young sorrel horse. All the rest of my estate to my dearly beloved wife CATHERINE, so long as she lives or remains my widow, on condition she makes no unnecessary waste thereof; when she dies or marries I give my estate to my three sons, namely, JOHN, PETER and ABRAHAM GOLD, or the survivors, share and share alike. And whereas there appears by the will of Mr. ABRAHAM MANCE, deceased, my father-in-law, that a legacy is given to my wife, my will is for her to enjoy it so long as she lives or is my widow, and at her death or marriage for it to descend to my three sons as above. I appoint my three sons, JOHN, PETER and ABRAHAM GOULD, executors.
Dated March 10, 1783. Witnesses, STEPHEN BEDELL, JOHN WOOD, JOHN BEDELL. Proved, New York, September 10, 1784.
Liber 36:180 WNYHS XII:400

Robert Hunter, Esq., Captain-General and Governor. Whereas **AUGUSTUS GRASSETT**, of New York, died intestate, Letters of Administration are granted to LOUIS ~~DE BONIS~~ DUBOIS, who married his daughter HESTER, JOSEPH OLDFIELD, of Jamaica, Long Island, who married his daughter MARTHA, and HENRY MONEY of Richmond County, who married his daughter MARY. April ~~19~~ 16, 1712.
Liber 8:100 WNYHS II:86

In the name of God, Amen, February 2, 1749/50. I, **JOHN GRONDAIN**, of Richmond County, boatman. I direct all debts to be paid. I leave to my wife MARGARET £30 in liew of dower, and the use of all my estate except my boat, so long as she remains my widow.

70

"She bringing up my children and giving them schooling suitable for them". If my wife should marry she shall quit the estate. I leave to my son and heir, LEWIS GRONDAIN, my black mare and saddle and bridle and £25. To my son PETER £25. To my son SAMUEL £25. All the rest to my 6 children, LEWIS, PETER, SAMUEL, MARY, ESTHER, and MARGARET. My sons are to have my boat immediately after my decease, with all her rigging. I make my wife MARGARET and my son LEWIS and my brother-in-law, ISAAC ~~PRAWL~~ PRAUL, executors.

Witnesses, BENJAMIN BRITTAIN, STEPHEN MESSEREAU, BENJAMIN SEAMAN. Proved, December 17, 1764, before BENJAMIN SEAMAN, Surrogate. Confirmed by Governor Colden, December 22, 1764.
Liber 24:535   WNYHS VI:362

JACQUES GUYEN (Dutch). Appeared before the notary, WILLIAM BOGARDUS, May 3, 1680. JACQUES GUYON, planter, of Staten Island, and SARAH COZIER, his wife. Their will is that the survivor shall have all the estate. Proved December 1, 1694 and Letters of Administration granted to his widow SARAH.
Liber 5-6:62   WNYHS I:464

JACQUES GUYON (Dutch). The will of JACQUES GUYON was proved before Governor FLETCHER, December 5, 1694.
Liber 5-6:63   WNYHS I:246

George Clarke, Lieutenant-Governor. Whereas, JAMES GUYON, of Staten Island, died intestate, Letters of administration are granted to his wife MARY, and his son JAMES, October 30, 1742.
Liber 14:335   WNYHS III:377

In the name of God, Amen, September 27, 1759. I, JAMES GUYON, of Richmond County, farmer, being sick. I leave to my wife ADRANSHA, £300, and 1 silver tankard, and the use of one room and furniture while she remains my widow, and ½ the income of the

Plantation, clear, for bringing up the
children, and the rest to my sons and
daughters. I leave to my son JAMES all that
Plantation where I now dwell, except the lot I
bought of RICHARD CONNOR; and a piece of
meadow in fence, below that. And he is to pay
£800 to my sons PHILIP and JOHN, when of age.
And my son JAMES is to have my Sword, Pistols,
and holsters. I leave to my son JOSEPH £300.
I leave to my son PETER that lot of land and
meadow within fence, as above. I leave to my
daughter MARY £200. To my daughter ANDRASHA,
£200. I make SAMUEL HOLMES, JOHN POILLON, and
CORNELIUS GARRISON executors.
    Witnesses, PHILIP GUYON, JOSEPH HOLMES,
JOHN DANIEL. Proved, March 3, 1761.
Liber 22:402   WNYHS VI:42

    In the name of God, Amen. I, **JOSEPH
GUYON**, being weak, this 7 of December, 1757.
I leave to my cousin *[nephew]*, JOSEPH GUYON,
all my land and meadows and tenements, also
£100. I leave to my sister ANNE, wife of JOHN
GARRISON, £100. I leave to my brother,
STEPHEN GUYON, £40.   To my brother, JOHN
GUYON, £40.   To my sisters, SARAH and
ELIZABETH, £30 each. To my ~~mother~~ sister,
MARY GUYON, £30. To JOSEPH GARRISON, son of
JOHN GARRISON, £40.   To my uncle, PHILIP
GUYON, £15. "I leave to my brother's two
daughters, MARY and ARIANTIE, each £15." All
the rest I leave to my brother JAMES. I make
by brother JAMES and my uncle, SAMUEL HOLMES,
executors.
    Witnesses, DANIEL LAKE, WILLIAM BARNET,
JOSEPH HOLMES, Jr. Proved, June 15, 1758.
Liber 21:40   WNYHS V:243

-H-

    In the name of God, Amen. I, **RICHARD
HARRIS**, of Richmond County, Gentleman, "being
in my usual Health of Body". Executors are to
pay all debts and funeral expenses. I leave
to my wife MARGARET £50 yearly "during so long
as she remains my widow," and the use of a

72

negro wench. If my daughter, MARTHA HARRIS, is not married during my lifetime I leave her £60 in lieu of an outset, and she is to be maintained till she is of age or married, in such manner as my executors shall think fit and best. My executors are to provide for and educate my grandson, RICHARD HARRIS CRAVEN, until he is of age, and they and my wife are to have the sole guardianship of him. My executors may lease my lands at their discretion and to sell if necessary, and they are to sell all my plate at vendue, but among my children and devisees only. After the death or marriage of my wife, I leave to my son JAMES £5 "as an acknowledgement that he is my eldest son and heir at law, and in full bar to his claim". If my wife should marry I leave her 1/6 of my estate. All the rest of my estate I leave to my three sons, JAMES, ABRAHAM, and RICHARD, and to my daughter MARTHA, and to my grandson, RICHARD HARRIS CRAVEN. I make my brother-in-law, JOHN ALSTYN, of New York, and my son, executors.

Dated May 31, 1771. Witnesses, BENJAMIN LARZELERE, PAUL MERSEREAU, DANIEL VAN CLEFE. Proved, February 24, 1772, before BENJAMIN SEAMAN, Surrogate.

Liber 28:189   WNYHS VIII:19

In the name of God, Amen. I, **WILLIAM HARRISON**, of Richmond County, on Staten Island, Clerk, being in a state of perfect health. Being sensible of the necessity of doing Justice to all men. I think fit to leave this Instrument, in order thereto, and this is my last will. And I do by this cut off all other wills. Particularly, One made, On [account of] the Rev. Commisorys Vesey's being my chief creditor, by a bond now in the hands of JOSEPH PEARCE, of Trenton, in New Jersey; which will is in keeping of WILLIAM RICKETTS, of New York, Esq. But it is not now of any use, the said Vesey being paid in full. I commit my Body to the Earth from which it was taken, to be decently layed in the Grave until the General Ressurection. I leave to my loving friend and brother, the Rev. EDWARD VAUGHAN, of Elizabethtown, in New Jersey, all my wearing clothes, Books, Sermons, and Manuscripts. And the two half length Pictures, and four Oval pictures, now in possession of CAPTAIN RICKETTS. My executors are to sell in the best manner, all my stock of cattle, sheep, negroes, and household goods, for the paying of debts and legacies. I leave to the Poor of Staten Island, £20, if so much be left when debts are paid. I leave my Funerall, to be at the discretion of my executors, but to be plain and without show or ostentation, Decent and Humble such as becomes a Pilgrim who died Poor, in a strange land. I appoint Mr. ADR. ~~SHILER~~ SKILER (ADONIJAH SCHUYLER), Gent., of New York, and JOSEPH PEARCE, of Trenton, executors, they being my chief creditors. To this I set my hand and Seal this 16 day of September, 1735.

Witnesses, MARY CATHARINE BOUDINOT, MARY EMOTT, MARY VAUGHAN.

Endorsed, "Probate not issued."

Annexed to the will is the following: "MARY VAUGHAN, July 12, 1739, *jurat*, that she saw the other witnesses sign." "Mr. ADONIJAH SCHUYLER, one of the executors, sworn and Power given to JOSEPH PEARCE".

Unrecorded will   WNYHS XI:123

{Whereas Rev. **WILLIAM HARRISON** of Richmond County died intestate, Letters of Administration are granted to BARENT MARTIN principal creditor. October 6, 1739.}

Liber 13:283   WNYHS XVI:135

In the name of God, Amen. June 1, 1706. I, **JACOB ~~HASTA~~ HASTE**, of Staten Island, being in good health. I leave to my wife CATHARINE, all my estate during her life, but if she comes to marry she shall have two thirds. I leave to my 5 children by my said wife, viz.: CHARLES, SOPHIA, CORNELIA, JOHANES, and BENJAMIN, £10 each. My oldest son, BARTHOLOMEW, is to have the choice of my horses, or £8, in money, before the rest of my

74

children. The rest to all my children.

Witnesses, MATHIAS DE DECKER, WILLIAM ~~HILYER~~ TILLYER, SAMUEL OSBORN. Proved, December 12, 1717. Letters of Administration granted to wife CATHARINE.

Unrecorded will   WNYHS XI:31

HAUGHWOUT, includes HAGEWOUT, HOUGHWOUT

In the name of God, Amen, January 28, 1773. I, **EGBERT HAUGHWOUT**, of Richmond County, being weak in body. I direct all debts to be paid. I leave to my eldest son, PETER, £10. All my whole estate is to remain in the hands of my wife NELLY during the time of her being my widow. If she marries, my executors are to sell all, and my wife is to have £100. I leave all the rest to my 5 children "now born, and the child as my dear wife is like to have" *(names not given)*. I make JOSEPH CHRISTOPHER, DANIEL GERBRANTZ, and my wife, executors.

Witnesses, PETER HOUSMAN, MARCUS ~~MINER~~ MIER. Proved, March 11, 1773.

Liber 28:406   WNYHS VIII:96

In the name of God, Amen. I, **NELLY ~~HAZEWOUT~~ HOUGHWOUT**, of Staten Island, being sick. I leave to my son EGBERT, the Plantation and house where I now dwell, with the salt meadow belonging unto it, with all the buildings. And 2 horses, 3 cows, and "½ my Periawger", a good wagon and plough. This is in lieu of £100 left to him by his father, I leave to my son PETER 2 cows. To my son NICHOLAS £5. I leave to my grandson, JOHN ~~BRESTED~~ BREASTED, son of my daughter CATRINA, a loom and tackling. I leave to my two grandsons, PETER and EGBERT BRESTED, sons of my daughter CATRINA and JOHN BRESTED £5 each. I leave to my 4 daughters, CATRINA, widow of JOHN BRESTED, DIRCKJE, NELLY, wife of ANTHONY BRAT, and MARITIE, the house and land I bought of THOMAS DONGAN, lying in the Manor, and all the remainder of my movables. I make my son EGBERT and JOHN MERRALL executors. March 22,

1761.
Witnesses, MATTHEW ~~DEDER~~ DECKER, ELIZABETH EGBERTS, JEREMIAH CLARK. Codicil. "I having made my last will, and disposed of all my estate except £53, 9s and 6d which I had forgot to mention", All debts and funeral expenses are to be paid out of the same, and the remainder to my 4 daughters. March 24, 1761.
Witnesses, JOHN BURBANK, JOHN MERRILL. Proved April 15, 1761.
[Note: See will of PETER ~~HAZEWOUT~~ HAGEWOUT, Liber 15:569. W.S.P.], [p.76 C.M.H.]
Liber 22:494   WNYHS VI:67

In the name of God, Amen. I, **PETER HAGAWOUT**, of Richmond County, yeoman, being sick and weak. My executors are to dispose of all my estate at public vendue. All debts to be paid, and the remainder to my children, ALTIE, PETER, JOHN, GERITIE, HARMETTIE, ISAAC, JACOB, ~~LIPETTIE~~ LEFFERT, and LEAH, and to RACHEL and DIRITIE, the daughters of my son EGBERT, equally. I make my very good friends, HENDRICK CREUSE and JOHN MACHILERSE, executors.
Dated February 13, 1715/16. Witnesses, MARY BUTLER, NICHOLAS MANNING, AUGUSTINE GRAHAM. Proved, October 29, 1716.
Unrecorded will   WNYHS XI:21

In the name of God, Amen, November 27, 1745. I, **PETER** ~~HAZEWOUT~~ **HAGEWOUT**, of Staten Island, being very sick, I leave to my wife NEELTIE, all lands and tenements during her widowhood, and after her death to my two sons PETER and NICHOLAS; all my lands in Richmond County next adjoining to the land now in possession of DOWE VAN WOGELUM, with all meadows and messuages. I leave to each of my two younger sons, EGBERT and ~~JOHN~~ JACOB, £100. To my daughter DIRCKJE, £10. All the rest of my estate, real and personal, to my 5 children, CATHARINE, wife of JOHANS BRESTEDE, DIRCKJE, NEELTJE, GERTRUYD, and MARGARET. My daughter CATHARINE'S part is not to be paid till after the death of her husband, "and her husband is not in intermeddle or have anything to do with the same," nor shall it be liable to pay any of his debts. I make my wife and DANIEL CORSEN, executors.

Witnesses, GERRIT ~~KRASSE~~ KROESE, JOHN ROLL, Jr., ~~KLAAS~~ KLAES ~~KRASSE~~ KROESE. Proved, April 8, 1746.

Liber 15:569   WNYHS IV:77

George Clarke, Esq., Lieutenant-Governor. Whereas, **JOHN HEASTON**, of Richmond County, died intestate, Letters of administration are granted to JOHN BUTLER, of Richmond County, farmer, as principal creditor, May 12, 1740.

Liber 13:372   WNYHS III:293

In the name of God, Amen. I, **JOHN HILLYER**, Jr., of Richmond County, being sick. All debts to be paid. I leave to my son JOHN "that small lot of land whereon he now lives, with all the appurtenances, except the hides and leather, in the tan vats". I leave to my daughter FRANCES £30. To my wife HESTER the choice of my beds, and the use of all my estate, except that part bought of ABRAHAM LOCKERMAN, during her widowhood and no longer. My executors may sell my estate and put the money at interest for my wife and children. All the rest I leave to all my children, except what has been advanced to my son JOHN. If the amount should be more that £50 to each, the surplus to all my children. "Whereas I purchased certain real estate from ABRAHAM LOCKERMAN, late of Richmond County, deceased, for £1000, in order to discharge his debts, and extricate him from his difficulties, and save the overplus for his family. And having sold a part for £1238, I leave to his widow ELIZABETH, a piece of land unsold. Beginning at the line of the land he bought of his brother, WILLIAM LOCKERMAN, by the land of JOHN POILLON, and then running South 49 Degrees West, 3 chains, 60 links, to the corner of the land of JOHN and JAMES POILLON. Then running N. 24 ½, West 8 chains to a stake

14 links west of a spring, now used for a watering place. Then N. 18 W. 16 chains to a tree. Then south by the land he bought of his brother WILLIAM, to beginning, being 4 8/10 acres. {Also mentions land of ABRAHAM LOCKERMAN}. The rest to be sold by my executors, and the money used to pay his debts, so as that small place he bought of his brother WILLIAM shall go to the son of said ABRAHAM free of all incumbrance". The remainder of the money is to go to ELIZABETH LOCKERMAN to bring up the other children. The part of my estate that would have come to my daughter CATHARINE is to be paid to her by my executors at their discretion. I make my wife HESTER and my friends, JOHN JOURNEY and JOSEPH BEDELL, executors.

Dated July 29, 1775. I give to the said ELIZABETH LOCKERMAN 1 2/10 acres of the land ordered to be sold, beginning at a tree near a spring, at the northwest corner of the land bought of his brother WILLIAM, and then running north to the new road. Then South 12 degrees, west 9 chains, and then along the land bought of his brother, to the beginning. Witnesses, JOSEPH McDANIEL, miller, BENJAMIN DRAKE, BENJAMIN SEAMAN. Proved, September 8, 1775.
Liber 29:538   WNYHS VIII:298

In the name of God, Amen. I, **JOHN HILLYER**, Esq., of Richmond County. I leave to my wife MARY £25, in lieu of dower, "according to an agreement made before we were married." And she is to have all the household goods that did belong to her when married, and her side saddle. I leave to the children of my son JOHN, deceased, £10, besides an equal share of my estate, "equally between them, except CATHARINE." I leave to my son LAURENCE £20, and an equal share of my estate. I leave to my grandson JOHN, son of my son JAMES, £5. To my granddaughter RACHEL, eldest daughter of my daughter ELIZABETH, "the value of a good cow, and a new linnen spinning wheel, to be paid out of that part of the legacy that will fall to her mother's share." I leave all the rest to my children and to the children of my son JOHN. "I leave to my son BENJAMIN, the gun that my friend, JAMES MALDREN, gave to me, besides his equal share of my estate." I make my sons, WILLIAM and LAURENCE, executors. What my son LAURENCE owes to me is to be considered part of my estate.

Dated October 9, 1775. Witnesses, RICHARD CHARLTON, HECTOR GAMBOLD, minister of the Moravian Church, ~~AUS~~ ARIS RYERS. Proved, November 6, 1775.

Liber 30:28   WNYHS VIII:312

JOSEPH HOLMES. In the name of God Amen. This 31 day of December 1702. I, JOSEPH HOLMES, of Staten Island, being very sick. I appoint my wife ANNE sole executrix and manager of all my estate real and personal till my eldest son SAMUEL is of age, and then he is to possess the same and then is to pay my sons OBADIAH and JOSEPH £200. I leave to my daughters MARY and ANNE, each £50. I make my beloved cousin JONATHAN STILLWELL and my cousin NATHANIEL BRITING, to be trustees of this my will.

Witnesses WILLIAM TILLYER, HENRY ~~BARRY~~ BERRY, JOHN DAYLEY. Proved before Lord Cornbury May 12, 1704.

Liber 7:169   WNYHS I:388

In the name of God, Amen, August 3, 1756. I, **JOSEPH HOLMES**, Senior, of Staten Island, "being not well but of perfect memory". I leave to my wife SARAH all lands and tenements during her widowhood, and then to my son JOSEPH, and he shall pay to his mother £150 and to my daughter ANNE £150. I leave to my daughter ANNE a negro girl ~~"Patty"~~ "Polly". I leave to my wife a negro girl and a bed and furniture, and all the rest of my movables to my wife and daughter. I make my wife and SAMUEL HOLMES, executors.

Witnesses, FRANKEY RULYEA, HENRY RULYEA, ELIZABETH INYARD. Proved April 5, 1760.

Liber 22:80   WNYHS V:393

"In the name of God, Amen. I, **SAMUEL HOLMES**, of the South Quarter, of Richmond County, yeoman, being aged and infirm. I leave to my grandson, SAMUEL HOLMES, all the lands, meadows, and buildings belonging to the place which I live on, during his life, and then to his next heir, and so from heir to heir forever. I leave to my grandson, THOMAS HOLMES, all that farm with the meadow where he and his mother now live; She having the right to live on the farm with him for 10 years. After his death, to his next heir, and so from heir to heir forever. I leave to my grandchildren, JOSEPH and SARAH BARTON, all the land below the road now in their possession, and 20 acres of meadow fronting on the lower side of the land, so as to take in the first Hommock; also 1/2 of my woodland above the road. The other half I leave to THOMAS HOLMES, to extend northwesterly no farther than ISAAC LEWISES or Nelly's brook. To them for life, and then to their next heirs. I leave to my grandson, ISAAC ~~LACKMAN~~ LACKERMAN, and MARTHA his wife, all the land above and below the road, with the meadow. I leave to my grandchildren, ABRAHAM BURBANK and ANN his wife, the west half of my Plantation in the Manor (of Castleton), and a lot of salt meadow on the Great Kills, lying east of that above mentioned, and now in possession of Mr. JOHN BEATTY; Also a great Hummock, which ABRAHAM BURBANK has in his possession. All the meadow adjoining I leave to ABRAHAM BURBANK and ANTHONY McNEIL. I leave to ANTHONY McNEIL and MARY his wife a small piece of land northwest of Nelly's Brook. {The will mentions land of A. CORTELYOU, GEORGE COLON and JAMES BUTLER.} I leave to my daughter MARY £150. To my grand-daughters, LUCY and MARY HOLMES, each £100. To my granddaughter, ANN LEE, £200. I make my friends, LEWIS DU BOIS, Sr., and LEWIS DU BOIS, Jr., and HENDRICK PERINE, executors.

Dated July 9, 1778. Witnesses, HECTOR ~~GAMBOILD~~ GAMBOLD MARY McNEIL, PETER DURAND.

ADRIAN HOOGLAND. In the name of God, Amen. Be it known and manifest that I, ADRIAN HOOGLAND, of New York, merchant, being in good health. I leave to my eldest son DIRCK £5 when of age; I leave all the rest of my estate to my wife ANNE, during her life, with full power to sell during her widowhood. After her decease all estate is to go to my children, DIRCK, BEELTIE, ELIZABETH, and HELENA. Mentions "my brothers, JOHANES and JORAS HOOGLANDT", and sisters AELTIE, wife of JOHANES BYVANCK, MARITIE and SARAH. I appoint my friends and relatives, JOHANES HOOGLANDT, DANIEL RAPALYE, DAVID PREVOOST, Jr., and JACOBUS GOELET, guardians of my children, and my wife ANNE executor.

Dated September ~~9~~ 4, 1702. Witnesses, PETRUS BAYARD, EVERARDUS BOGARDUS, ABRAHAM ~~GANSEVORT~~ GOUVERNEUR. Proved, May 13, 1712, before Henry Wileman, Esq.
Liber 8:112
WNYHS II:88

DIRCK HOOGHLAND. In the name of God Amen, I, DIRCK HOOGHLAND of Staten Island being in good health. I leave to my wife ELIZABETH, all my estate, both real and personal, for life, and then to be divided among my children, namely JOHANES, GEORGE, ARIENT, ~~ALLETIE~~ ALTIE, MARY AND SARAH. Only my son JOHANES shall have £7 and my daughter SARAH shall have £3 over and above their proportion. And my will is that whichsoever of my three sons, JOHANES, GEORGE, and ARIENT, shall give the most for my lands and tenements, they shall have the same for the more benefit of the rest. I make my wife ELIZABETH sole executrix.

Dated April 21 1701. Witnesses ELLIS DUSENBURY, JAN WOGLUM, JOHN WOGLUM, JR. Proved before Lord Cornbury March 15, 1704/5.
Liber 7:231
WNYHS I:402

Robert Hunter, Esq., Captain-General and

Governor. Whereas **DIRCK HOOGLANDT**, of Staten
Island, died, leaving a will, and made his
wife ELIZABETH executor, and she having proved
the will has since died, intestate, Letters of
administration are granted to her eldest son
JOHANES HOOGLANDT, May 19, 1712.
Liber 8:120   WNYHS II:90

~~JORAS HOGLANDT~~ **JORIS HOOGLAND**.   In the
name of God, Amen.   I, ~~JORAS HOGLANDT~~ JORIS
HOOGLAND, of Staten Island, being sick and
weak.   Considering the shortness of the life
of man upon this earth, I leave to my eldest
son, DIRCK HOGLANDT, £5, and also my gun when
he is of age.   I also leave him all my lands
and meadows when of age, and he is to pay to
the rest of his brothers and sisters £500.   If
he die under age the lands are to go to my son
DANIEL.   I leave to my wife KATHARINE the sole
use and benefit of estate during the minority
of my sons, and after they are of age she
shall have the use of one third the estate.
If both my sons die then all the property is
to go to my children, KATHARINE, ELIZABETH,
MARITIE, DIRCK, ~~ALSKE~~ AELTIE, DANIEL, AMITIE,
and SARAH.   I appoint my wife executor.
{Dated May 19, 1711}.   Witnesses, JOHN
WOGLUM, Jr., ANDREIS BOWMAN, OSWALD FOORD.
Proved, May 13, 1712.
Liber 8:108   WNYHS II:87

In the name of God, Amen.   This 16th day
of December, 1783.   I, **PETER HOUSMAN**, of
Richmond County, New York, yeoman, being weak
in body.   I leave to my eldest son, JOHN, the
choice of my silver watches and the sum of £5
in lieu of his Birthright.   To my son
BENJAMIN, one silver watch; to my son PETER,
my silver hilted sword; to my three sons,
JOHN, BENJAMIN and PETER, all my wearing
apparel equally divided; to my daughter
MARTHA, two gold rings and one pair silver
buckles; to my daughter JOHANAH, one gold ring
and one pair of silver buckles; to my two
daughters, MARTHA and JOHANAH, all my wife's
wearing apparel, equally divided; to my

82

daughter MARY, one piece of "Pompidore Chince"; to NANCY KRUSE, daughter of my last wife, one "Cubbord" being in the widdow STOUGHTENBUROUG's care. I order my executors to sell the remainder of my estate, real and personal. To my brothers and sisters, AURT, JOHN, RICHARD, ABRAHAM, MAREGRET, MARY, ELISABETH, CATHRIN, JEMIMA and SARAH, £22 a peace in lieu of what I give them of their father's estate, "as I fell heir to", to be paid them one year after my decease. I reserve £50 for the purposes hereafter mentioned. I give to all my children here named, JOHN, BENJAMIN, PETER, ABRAHAM, ISAC, JACOB, ANTHONY, JAMES, MARY, MARTHA and JOHANAH, all the rest of my estate, equally divided, excepting my daughter MARY, wife of JOHN TYSON, I deduct out of her share the sum of £50 aforesaid in lieu of her outset. If any of my children die under age without issue, their shares to be divided among all my sons and daughters. Whereas I stand charged with the maintenance of a child the daughter of ELONER CHLINDINNY, now the wife of THOMAS DICKSON, the before reserved sum of £50, on condition the said child or some person shall give to my executors sufficient discharge that she shall never claim any more of my executors, and if she shall fail on the performance of her part the £50 to be divided among my children. To my daughter, MARY TYSON, one side saddle now in her care. I appoint my brothers, AURT and RICHARD HOUSEMAN and JOHN TYSON, my son-in-law, my trustees, to be executors, and guardians of my children.

Witnesses, GAMES COZINE, JAMES BODINE, WILHELMAS COZINE. Proved, Richmond County, October 18, 1784.
Liber 37:268   XIII:40

-I-

YELLIS INGART {or INIARD}. In the name of God, Amen. I, YELLIS INGART, of Staten Island, being very well in health, but

83

considering the brevity and shortness of my life. I leave to my son JOHN, £5 more than the rest of my children. I leave all the rest of my estate, real and personal, to my other children {which may come to me}. {The will mentions children JOHN, ANTEA CHRISTINE, ANNANETIA, CHARLES, TICE.} If my house and lot come to be sold, my son JOHN is to have the refusal if he shall see cause to buy. I leave to my wife TRIENTIE, the use of 1/3 of my estate for life, and the use of my dwelling house, unless my son JOHN, or whoever of my children shall buy the same, shall build another comfortable house upon the same land for her to live in. I make my two brothers in law, JOHN ~~WOGLAN~~ WOGLUN and URY ~~WOGLAN~~ WOGLUN, executors.

Dated January 2, 1706/7. Witnesses, PETER HOOGEWATER, JAN MAKLYS, OSWALD FORD. Proved, March 11, 1707/8.
Liber 7:462   WNYHS I:456

-J-

I, **CHRISTIAN JACOBSON**, on Staten Island, the County of Richmond, being in good health and of sound mind, this fourth day of January, 1782, ordain this will and testament. I leave to my loving wife, ANN JACOBSON, my house I now live in, with all the land now in my possession, and also my negroes, live stock, farming utensils, household furniture (except such articles as are given to each of my children); as long as she remains my widow. After her death to go to my son, JOHN B. JACOBSON. Unto my daughter CATHARINE, £1050; to my daughter ELIZABETH, £1000; to be paid to them when they come to age of twenty-one years; or till then, so much of the interest as is necessary for their bringing up. To my son JOHN the sum of £400; to be paid when he is of age; till then to have his maintenance on the place. To my loving wife ANN, the sum of £600, in lieu of dower in case she should marry again. I give to the Brethren's Church

84

on Staten Island, £20 and to the Reverend Mr. GAMBOLD, £10, also to him £20 for the use of the Missionaries amongst the Indians. The rest of my money after the foregoing legacies are paid shall be divided in equal shares between my wife and children. To my son JOHN, all my wearing apparel, my horse, clock, and watch; to my daughter CATHARINE, my silver tea pot and six silver table spoons; to my daughter ELIZABETH, my silver tankard and my little negro wench Suck, and also one good feather bed with furniture. I make my wife ANN, my brother-in-law, CORNELIUS VANDEVENTER, and my good friends, CORNELIUS CORTELYOU and LEWIS RYERSZ, executors.

Witnesses, CATHARINE RYERSZ, RICHARD SEAMAN, SAMUEL WOODWARD. Proved, February 20, 1782.

Liber 34:433   WNYHS X:194

"In the name of God, Amen. I, **CHARLES JANDINE**, of Staten Island, being of sound mind. I leave all my estate, real and personal, to my five daughters, SUSANAH JANDINE, CATHARINE LAMB, MARY LAMB, HANNAH LAWRENCE, and MARTHA ALLICOCKE. I bequeath to my two granddaughters, CATHARINE DAVIS and SALLY DAVIS, their full mother's share. I make JOSEPH ALLICOCKE and WILLIAM SMITH, one of his Majesty's Council, executors."

Dated September 22, 1779. Witnesses, DANIEL CROCHERON, MOSES CLENDENNING, blacksmith, BENJAMIN COLE. Proved, March 21, 1780.

His Excellency, JAMES ROBERTSON, Esq., Captain General and Governor of the Province of New York. To all whom these Presents shall come, Greeting. Know ye that at New York on the 21 day of March 1780, the last will of CHARLES JANDINE was proved before CARY LUDLOW, Esq., and the executors confirmed. In Testimony whereof I have set my hand and Seal in Fort James, March 30, 1780. A marginal note states, That on July 9, 1789, before THOMAS TREDWELL, Esq., Judge of Probate, it was shown that JOSEPH ALLICOCKE, one of the

executors, had departed from the state, and that WILLIAM SMITH was also absent from the state, and JAMES LAMB, who married MARY JANDINE, was appointed Administrator.
Liber 32:221   WNYHS IX:101

In the name of God, Amen. I, **CHARLES JANDINE**, of Staten Island, Richmond County. I leave to my five daughters all my whole estate, real and personal, such as lands, houses, household goods, wearing apparel, plate, jewels, etc., to my five daughters, to wit: SUSANAH JANDINE, CATHRINE LAMB, MARY LAMB, HANAH LAWRENCE and MARTHA ALLICOCKE, equally divided, and to my two granddaughters, CATHERINE DAVIS and SALLY DAVIS, I bequeath them their full mother's share. I nominate JOSEPH ALLICOCKE and WILLIAM SMITH, one of his Majesty's Council of New York, my executors.
Dated September 22, 1779. Witnesses, DANIEL CROCHERON, MOSES CLENDENNEY, BENJAMIN COLE. Proved, March 21, 1780. Administration granted to JAMES LAMB, of the City of New York, mariner, who intermarried with MARY a daughter and one of the residuary legatees of CHARLES JANDINE, late of Richmond County, gentleman, deceased, whereas administration was granted to JOSEPH ALLICOCKE, one of the executors whereas he has since departed this State, the estate not being fully administered, and whereas WILLIAM SMITH, the other executor, is likewise absent from this State, administration is hereby granted to the above. New York, July 9, 1784.
Liber 37:68   WNYHS XII:349

Whereas **JOHN JARMYN** of Staten Island, black-smith, died intestate. Upon application his wife ANNE is made administrator. November 20, 1679.
Inventory: Bellows and anvil £4,5s, 1/2 of House and plantation, £6.
Liber 1-2:246   WNYHS I:62

In the name of God, Amen, January 30, 1765. I, **ABRAHAM JOHNSON**, of Staten Island,

Gent. I leave to my wife RACHEL 1/3 of all my estate, and the rest to my daughter MARY, "and I leave her to be brought up with my father and mother". If she dies, her part is to go to my brother JAMES' children [not named]. I make JAMES JOHNSON and ABRAHAM WINANT executors, who are to sell all effects.

Witnesses, EDWARD YEATS DOWEL, [?] JOHNSON, ANNE JOHNSON. Proved, November 10, 1766, before BENJAMIN SEAMAN.
Liber 25:346   WNYHS VII:33

In the name of God, Amen, the 23 day of December, 1731. I, **ALBERT JOHNSON**, of the County of Richmond, Gent., being in perfect health. My will is that my wife MARTHA be honorably maintained out of my estate, during her widowhood. I leave to my son ROBERT the choice of my riding horses, and a good saddle and bridle, as his portion, as heir at law; Also a certain tract of land in Richmond County, in the rear of the land of Mrs. MARGARETTA LE COUNT, and the land of JOHN PERLEY, and between the land of JAMES SEGANY, and the land which I bought of PAUL DROILET and FRANCIS VINCENT, being 120 acres; Also a parcel of land adjoining the same, being the front part of the land which I bought of PAUL DROILET and FRANCIS VINCENT, and running along the rear of the land of HERMAN VAN PELT and STEPHEN WOOD, and the land of ISAAC LAKERMAN, to the line of the land formerly belonging to JOHN VAN NOY, and from thence along the line to a chestnut tree, which is in the corner, and thence on a straight line until it comes to the line of the said 120 acres, and along the same to the corner tree of the old Plantation, or said 120 acres; Also 13 acres of meadow adjoining the meadow of Mrs. LE COUNT, near the Fresh Kills. {I leave to my son ALBERT a lot of land on the south side of the Fresh Kills}, between the land of JOSEPH ~~CAMMAN~~ CANNON and the land of ISAAC LAKERMAN, being 80 acres; Also the salt meadow belonging to said lot; Also a parcel of land adjoining to the rear of said land, being the northwest part of the land I bought of PAUL DROILET and FRANCIS VINCENT, and adjoining the land of JOHN GUERING, ADAM MOTT, and JOSEPH ~~CAMMAN~~ CANNON; Also 3 acres of salt meadow "lying by a place commonly called the Burnt House," being part of a lot of meadow of 16 acres, of which I have given to my son ROBERT; Also an island of meadow lying in the mouth of the Fresh Kills, belonging to the land now in possession of my son-in-law, NATHANIEL ~~VAN BROCKETT~~ VAN BROCKELL. I leave to my daughter, RACHEL ~~VAN BROCKETT~~ VAN BROCKELL, £10, and to my granddaughters MARTHA, RACHEL, and MARY ~~VAN BROCKETT~~ VAN BROCKELL, £30, when of age. To ELIZABETH JOHNSON, my brother's daughter, £10, when of age. I leave to my grand daughter, MARY GOULD, 80 acres of land at Smoking Point, adjoining the land of ADRIAN VAN WOGLAM, with the meadow thereto belonging, and £10, when of age. To ELIZABETH MOTT, Jr., a gold diamond ring. I make ADAM MOTT, and my sons, ROBERT and ALBERT, executors.

Witnesses, STEPHEN WOOD, JOHN ~~PARKER~~ PARLIER, WILLIAM HOLLY. Proved, before WALTER DONGAN, Esq., July ~~2~~ 22, 1732.
Liber 11:351   WNYHS III:69-71

In the name of God, Amen, January 23, 1734/5. I, **ALBERT JOHNSON**, of Richmond county, yeoman, being weak in body. I leave to my wife CATHARINE, £100. To my sister RACHEL, wife of MATTHEW VAN BRAKELL, £100, to be put at interest by my executors, "and paid to her if she comes to want it". I leave to MARY JOHNSON, the daughter of my brother ROBERT JOHNSON, one side saddle, value £9, when she is of age. All the rest of my movable estate to my daughter MARTHA. Mentions "MATTHEW VAN BRAKELL, son of my sister RACHEL VAN BRAKELL". {Mentions his sister's three daughters, MARTHA, RACHEL and MARY VAN BRAKELL}. I appoint my wife CATHARINE, and Mr. JOHN LE COUNT, and Mr. PAUL MUSHAW *(MICHEAU)*, executors.

Witnesses, NICHOLAS ~~LAZBERE~~ LARZLERE, STEPHEN WOOD, ADAM MOTT. Proved, November 26,

In the name of God, Amen. September 29, 1729.   I, **CORNELIUS** ~~JACKSON~~ **JOHNSON**, of Richmond County, glazier. My wife MARY shall have as the Law directs, after my debts are paid. My executors may sell all lands, goods, and negroes, a year and a day after my decease, and divide among my five children, MARGARET, SUSANAH, ELIZABETH, SARAH, and MARY, when they are of age. I make ABRAHAM COLE and JOHN LE COUNT, executors.

Witnesses, ~~WYGANT~~ MARGUERITE LE COUNT, RICHARD COLE, ALBERT JOHNSON. Proved, October 10, 1729.

Unrecorded will   WNYHS XI:152

Will of ~~HARME~~ **HARMON JOHNSON**, of H e m p s t e a d ,   Q u e e n s   C o u n t y , yeoman......"Children of PETER HOOGWERT, of Staten Island, deceased"......... {Not mentioned by name.} Proved October 4, 1746.

Liber 16:23   WNYHS IV:95

In the name of God, Amen. April 6, 1726. I, **HENRY JOHNSON**, of Richmond County, husbandman, being sick, and knowing that it is appointed for all men, once to die. After all debts are paid, I leave to my son WILLIAM my riding horse, saddle, and bridle, for his birthright. I leave to my eldest daughter, ANNE JOHNSON, my brass warming pan, and side saddle. I leave to my three sons, WILLIAM, NATHANIEL, and MATTHIAS, all my lands, buildings, and meadows, on Staten Island. I leave to my six children, WILLIAM, NATHANIEL, MATTHIAS, ANNE, MARY, and SARAH, all my movable estate. I leave to my eldest daughter, ANNE, £30, which my son WILLIAM shall pay. To my daughter MARY, £30, which my son NATHANIEL shall pay, and to my daughter SARAH, £30, which my son MATTHIAS shall pay. I make JOHANES ~~DEPECE~~ DEPUE and my son WILLIAM, executors.

Witnesses,   THOMAS   ~~SHECKFIELDING~~

SHEEKFIELD, WILLIAM ~~BRITTERS~~ BRITTIN, ABRAHAM COLE. Proved, March 25, 1730.
Unrecorded will   WNYHS XI:106

"In the name of God, Amen, April 21, 1780. I, **LIDIA JOHNSON**, widow of WILLIAM JOHNSON, being in my common health. My executors are to sell all my estate and divide the proceeds among my children, HENRY, NATHANIEL, EPHRAIM, WILLIAM, JAMES, ABRAHAM, PHEBE, ABIGAIL, and ANN. Reckoning to my son HENRY £30 already advanced to him. I make my son EPHRAIM and my friend, PAUL MICHEAU, executors."

Witnesses, BENJAMIN SEAMAN, JOHN ~~MANCE~~ MANEE, weaver, ISAAC DOTY. Proved, August 7, 1780.
Liber 32:305   WNYHS IX:126

In the name of God, Amen. I, **MATTHEW JOHNSON**, of Richmond County, yeoman, being very sick {February 22, 1733}. I leave to my wife CHARITY 1/3 of all movable estate, "as the Law directs", and £50 as a legacy, and the use of all my Plantation during her widowhood for the bringing up of my children. I leave to my eldest son MATTHEW £5 and a riding horse as his part as heir at law. I leave to all the children I had by my first wife and the child I have by my present wife CHARITY, viz., ANNE, ELIZABETH, ~~BELICKY~~ BELICHY, RACHEL, MATTHEW, and WINANTS, all the rest of my movable estate. {A daughter MARY is also named}. If my wife marries, then all the real estate is to be sold and divided among my children. I make my friend, HENRY VAN GELDER, and my kinsman, WILLIAM JOHNSON, executors.

Witnesses, ~~SYMON SMITH~~ SIMON SIMONSON, NATHANIEL JOHNSON, ABRAHAM MOTT. Proved, May 15, 1756. Confirmed by Sir CHARLES HARDY, Governor, May 15, 1756. WILLIAM JOHNSON was then the surviving executor.
Liber 20:9   WNYHS V:106

William Cosby, Esq., Captain-General and Governor. Whereas, **ROBERT JOHNSON**, late of the west Precinct of Richmond County, died intestate, Letters of administration are granted to his wife SARAH, February 6, 1732/3. Liber 11:462   WNYHS III:92

In the name of God, Amen, February 24, 1760. I, **WILLIAM JOHNSON**, of Richmond County. I will that all debts be paid. I leave to my eldest son and heir, HENRY JOHNSON, the shop he now works in and the bellows thereto belonging. I leave to my wife LYDIA all the rest of my estate, real and personal, so long as she remains my widow, But if she marries, she shall have £100, "and she shall quit my estate". I leave all the rest of my estate to my children, WINANTS, NATHANIEL, EPHRAIM, WILLIAM, JAMES, ABRAHAM, PHEBE, ABIGAIL, and ANNE. I leave to my son NATHANIEL my gun and sword. I make my wife, and my son WINANTS, and my friend, BENJAMIN SEAMAN, executors. Witnesses, JOHN SLAGHT, ANNA SLAGHT, PAUL ~~MICHAW~~ MICHEAU. Proved before BENJAMIN SEAMAN, Surrogate, May 28, 1760. Liber 22:99   WNYHS V:397

Whereas **MALLIARD** ~~JOURD~~ **JOURNEE**, late of Staten Island, in his will, gave all of estate to his wife ELIZABETH ~~DAMAN~~ DU MON, for the maintenance of herself and children, and nominating DAVID DEMAREST and JOUST VAN OBLINUS, as executors in Trust. "And it soe happened that the said ELIZABETH hath since joyned herself in marriage to another person on Staten Island". And the said executors have neglected their duty in regard to said estate of which complaint was made to Court of Sessions at Gravesend in June last, who appointed Mr. PAULUS RICHARDS, merchant and OBADIAH HOLMES, of Staten Island to be executors. They are confirmed July 8, 1678. Liber 1-2:198   WNYHS I:49

-K-

"In the name of God, Amen. I, **JOHN KETTLETAS**, of Staten Island, September 4,

91

1779. I leave to my son JOHN, as heir at law, my House Clock. To my son STEPHEN my watch. To my sons, JOHN and STEPHEN, each £80 when of age. I leave to my wife ELIZABETH my house and farm where I live, with all household goods, and cattle, and my two negroes, for life. The other negroes are to be sold in six months. My wife is to have the use of my estate to bring up my children till of age. When they are of age, the estate is to be sold and the money paid to my sons, JOHN and STEPHEN, and my daughter, CATHARINE GUYON. The movable estate which I give to my wife is to be at her disposal. I make my wife and friends, CORNELIUS MARTINEAU and Dr. THOMAS FROST, executors."

Witnesses, CORNELIUS VANDEVENTER, NICHOLAS STILLWELL, BENJAMIN MARTIN. Proved, March 25, 1780.
Liber 32:231   WNYHS IX:105

George Clarke, Esq., Lieutenant-Governor. Whereas, **JAMES KIERSTEAD**, of Richmond County, died intestate, Letters of administration are granted to SAMUEL ~~HALMAN~~ HOLMES, principal creditor, June 3, 1740.
Liber 13:387   WNYHS III:296

William Cosby, Esq., Captain-General and Governor. Whereas, **SAMUEL KIERSTED**, shoemaker, late of Richmond County, died intestate, Letters of administration are granted to JAMES HAYWOOD, of the West Precinct of said county, as principal creditor, June 5, 1733.
Liber 12:49   WNYHS III:116

In the name of God, Amen, October 16, 1764. I **BENJAMIN KILSEY**, of Richmond County. I direct all debts to be paid. I leave to my dearly beloved wife HANNAH my best bed and furniture, also a horse and saddle and a negro wench. I leave to JOHANAH, wife of PETER HOUSMAN, £40. My executors have full power to sell lands. Of all the rest of my estate, I leave to my wife HANNAH ½, and the other half to the heirs of my brother, DANIEL KILSEY, and my sister, LIDDY (LYDIA) WINENCE, my sister to have ½. I make my friends, PETER HOUSMAN and RICHARD SANDERS, executors.

Witnesses, PETER HOUSMAN, RICHARD HOUSMAN, ABRAHAM HOUSMAN, JOHN HOUSMAN. Proved, August 21, 1765, before BENJAMIN SEAMAN, Surrogate.

Liber 25:137   WNYHS VI:411

KROESEN, KROESON, KROOSE, KRUSE, See Cruser.

-L-

"In the name of God, Amen. I, **ADRIAN LAFORGE**, of Richmond County, farmer, being very sick. All debts to be paid. I do order that my daughter MARY shall have a maintainance out of my estate. I leave to my two sons, ADRIAN and JOHN, all my real estate, lands, meadows, and houses; Also two horses and wagons and tackling, and four cows. I leave to my son ADRIAN my negro boy Warrick. To my son JOHN negro man BEN. I leave all the rest to my son DAVID and the children of my son CHARLES, deceased [not named]. A bond is to be given for the support of my daughter MARY. I make my friends, BENJAMIN SEAMAN and his son RICHARD and JAMES LATOURETTE, executors."

Dated November 1, 1777. Witnesses, RICHARD MERSEREAU, shoemaker, JOHN SILVESTER, taylor, OWEN LIMNERS. Proved, December 31, 1777.

Liber 31:125   WNYHS IX:23

"In the name of God, Amen, January 23, 1778. I, **ADRIAN LAFORGE**, weaver, of Staten Island. All debts to be paid. I leave to my brother, JOHN LAFORGE, all my estate, real and personal. And he is to pay to my sister MARY £50 in three months. I make my brother JOHN and HENRY LA TOURETTE, executors."

Witnesses, JOHN LA TOURETTE, OWEN LIMNER, REBECCA LIMNER. Proved, February 2, 1778.

Liber 31:123   WNYHS IX:23

In the name of God, Amen.   August 3,
1783.   I, **JOHN LA FORGE**, of Staten Island,
Richmond County, farmer, being weak in body.
All my just debts to be paid.   My whole
estate, both real and personal, to be sold and
turned into money.   I leave to my daughter
CATARAN, £500, payable as soon as she comes of
age.   Unto my wife's daughter MARY £100,
payable when she comes of age.   Unto my wife
SARAH, all the rest of my estate.   Should
either of the children die under age, or
without issue, then that part shall return to
my wife. I make CORNELIUS COLE and JOHN LISK
and SARAH, my wife, executors.
    Witnesses, RICHARD MERCEREA, CHRISTIAN
MERCEREAU, ANNE MERCERAU.   Proved, May 18,
1784.
Liber 36:536   WNYHS XII:306

In the name of God, Amen, January 19,
1767.   I, **NICHOLAS** ~~LAFARGE~~ **LAFORGE**,   of
Richmond County, being sick.   I leave to my
sister MARY £10; To my brother DAVID's son,
PHILIP, "one blue coat and Jacote Cote".   My
executors are to sell all estate, and after
paying debts and funeral charges, the rest to
go to my cousins [nephews] PHILIP and
NICHOLAS, sons of DAVID LAFARGE, and CHARLES
and NICHOLAS, sons of CHARLES LAFARGE.   I make
my brothers, DAVID and CHARLES, executors.
    Witnesses, JOHN LAFARGE,   JOHN ~~SEQUIN~~
SEGUIN.   Proved,   March 3, 1767,   before
BENJAMIN SEAMAN.
Liber 25:494   WNYHS VII:70

In the name of God, Amen.   August 2,
1727.   I, **DANIEL LAKE**, of Staten Island,
Gentleman, being not well, but of perfect
mind.   I leave to my wife SARAH, all my lands
and goods, both movable and immovable, during
her widowhood, to keep my children by her.   If
she marries, my estate is to be divided as
follows: I leave to my sons, DANIEL and
JOSEPH, all my lands and tenements where I now
dwell.   If either die under age, his share is

to go to my son WILLIAM. But if they both live, they shall pay to my son WILLIAM, £100 each. I leave to my wife SARAH, and my son WILLIAM, and my daughter ALICE, all my movable estate and household goods, except my riding horse, bridle, and saddle, and my gun, which I give to my son DANIEL. I leave to my grandson, DANIEL STILLWELL, all the land I bought of NELCHE SEVERIN, and JOHANES SEVERIN, and NATHANIEL BRITTEN, Esq. I make my wife and WILLIAM ~~HILLYER~~ TILLYER, RICHARD STILLWELL, and MATTHEW REEV, executors.

Witnesses, JOHN MITCHELL, SAMUEL HOLMES, JAMES KIERSTEDE. Proved, October 9, 1727.
Unrecorded will   WNYHS XI:54

In the name of God, Amen. I, **DANIEL LAKE**, of Staten Island. All my estate, real and personal, to be sold in four or five months. From the proceeds, I leave one half to my wife MARGRETHA and my daughter ALLEDAY, and one half to my son WILLIAM. I make my father-in-law, HARMANIS GERRITSON, and my brother, WILLIAM LAKE, executors.

Dated December 1, 1780. Witnesses, CHRISTIAN JACOBSON, CHRISTIAN SMITH, THOMAS DAGITY. Proved, January 23, 1781.
Liber 34:85   WNYHS X:29

In the name of God, Amen. I, **WILLIAM LAKE**, of the City of New York, being very weak in body. All my just debts and funeral expenses to be first paid. I leave to my dearly beloved wife ELIZABETH, all the household furniture and effects that I have which was given to her by her father; Also, £200 in lieu of dower. The remainder of my personal estate to be sold. The remainder of my estate unto my three children, namely: ELIZABETH, DAVID, and JOHN, in equal shares. The proceeds of sale of my estate, and all other monies, to be put at interest, which shall go to maintain and educate my children. My executors to pay to my said daughter ELIZABETH, her portion when she is sixteen years old; to my sons, when they are twenty-

one, or marry. I make my two brothers, DANIEL
and JOSEPH LAKE, of the County of Richmond,
executors.

Dated February 26, 1783. Witnesses, PAUL
MICHEAU, Esq., JOHN MICHEAU, Esq., JOSEPH
GUYON, yeoman; all of County of Richmond.
Proved, May 17, 1783.
Liber 35:255   WNYHS XII:50

In the name of God, Amen, March 25, 1734.
I, **ABRAHAM LAKERMANS**, of the County of
Richmond, Gent., being very sick. After the
payment of debts and funeral charges, I give
and devise my farm or plantation whereon I now
live at Old Town, in said County, to my three
daughters, HESTER, wife of NICHOLAS LAZELIER,
CATHARINE, wife of JOHN MORGAN, and ELIZABETH,
wife of JOHN VANDEVENTER, all of Richmond
County. I also leave to each of them £100.
My executors are to sell, "at a publick
vendue," my two dwelling houses in New York,
one fronting Wall Street, and now in tenure of
JAMES SEARLE; and the other on Dock Street,
now in tenure of SHARMIN GOLDSMITH, with the
lots; And also my grist mill and lot on the
Great Kill, in the County of Richmond; and
also my woodland in said County between the
Fresh Kill lots, and the land formerly of
WILLIAM BARKER. My personal estate is also to
be sold at a public vendue. If any of my
slaves prove stubborn, or obstinate, or
disobedient, they are to be sold by my
executors. And whereas I am bound that my
wife ANJE shall have £100, and a negro girl
"Beth", the said girl is to be delivered to
her. Out of the remainder of my estate, my
son JACOB, and my daughter MARY, wife or widow
of NICHOLAS MATISEN, shall be provided for
with reasonable dwelling, meat, drink,
washing, lodging, and apparell, during their
lives. After their decease, all my estate is
to be divided among my children in such
proportions as my executors may think proper.
I appoint my trusty and well-beloved friends,
GOSEN ADRIANS, of Richmond County, and REM
VANDERBEEK, of New York, Gent., and JAQUES

CORTELYOU, Sr., of New Utrecht, in Kings County, and my 3 sons-in-law, NICHOLAS LAZELIER, JOHN MORGAN and JOHN VANDEVENTER, Gent., of Richmond County, my executors. *(The names of part of the children are not given.)* Witnesses, JACOB BERGEN, NICHOLAS STILLWELL, SAMUEL THURSTON. Proved, April 23, 1734.
Liber 12:162   WNYHS III:144

In the name of God, Amen. I, **NICHOLAS LARZELERE**, of Richmond County, "being in my usual understanding". I leave to my granddaughter MARY PRAAL, daughter of my daughter ELIZABETH, deceased, who was wife of PETER PRAAL, my negro girl called "Sarah". I leave to my granddaughter, MARY SPRAGG, £20, "instead of a negro girl intended for her, but has been sold". My executors are to sell all the rest of movable estate and pay all debts, and I leave the rest of the money to my two sons, JACOB and BENJAMIN. I leave to my son BENJAMIN all my real estate in Richmond County, with houses, lands, mills, mill ponds, etc., and he is to pay legacies as follows, viz.: To my daughter CATHARINE, wife of THOMAS HADING, £50. To HESTER, wife of JOHN HILLYER, Jr., £50. To FRANCES WINANT, £50. To my grandson, JACOB SPRAGG, £10. To my granddaughter, DOROTHY SPRAGG, £10. To my niece, MARY WEBB, £50 out of my movable estate. To my granddaughter, HESTER SPRAGG, £10. "The £50 left to MARY WEBB is her part of a certain sum of money left in my hands by the executors of ABRAHAM ~~EAKERMAN~~ LAKERMAN." My negro man "Jack" is to be maintained by my son BENJAMIN, and my negro slaves are to be allowed to choose their masters. I make my sons, ~~JOHN~~ JACOB and BENJAMIN, and my son-in-law JOHN HILLYER, Jr., and my friend, JOHN MICHEAU, executors.
Dated September 1, 1774. Witnesses, PAUL MICHEAU, DAVID LAFARGE, CORNELIUS CHRISTOPHER. Proved, April 1, 1766.
Liber 30:137   WNYHS VIII:335

"Know all men by these Presents that I, **SOLOMON LATIMER**, of Richmond County, mariner, do make my trusty and loving friend, DAVID LYNN, my true and lawful attorney". And considering the uncertainty of life I declare this to be my last will and Testament, and I leave DAVID LYNN my chest and clothes, now in possession of SOLOMON ~~DOOTENIER~~ DOCTENIER, of Fresh Kills. I also leave to him all the rest and make him executor.

November {17}, 1731. {Witnesses JOHN THOMPSON, ANDREW KING, PETER ZENGER}. Proved, July 21, 1732.

Liber 11:349   WNYHS III:69

In the name of God, Amen, February 23, 1764. I, **DAVID ~~LA TOURETTE~~ LA TOURRETTE**, of Richmond County. My executors are to sell personal property to pay debts and funeral charges. I leave to my son JAMES my gun and sword. I leave to my sons JAMES and DAVID all my lands, tenements, and messuages in the following manner: JAMES is to have ½ of the clear land, the west part. DAVID is to have the east part, and the wood land to be divided equally. And they are to pay to their sisters MARY and CATHARINE £300 each. I leave to my wife CATHARINE the use of all my estate, real and personal, so long as she remains my widow. After her death or marriage all the estate to my two sons, but I first leave £100 to my daughter CATHARINE. I make my wife and sons and my son-in-law, JONATHAN LEWIS, and my brother HENRY LA TOURETTE, executors.

Witnesses, HENRY PERINE, EDWARD PERRINE, JOHN STILWELL. Proved, March 23, 1764.

Liber 24:384   WNYHS VI:315

In the name of God, Amen. September 1, 1780. I, **EASTER LATOURETTE**, of Staten Island, being sick. All my movable estate to be sold in three months, and the proceeds and money in hand to be put at interest, and I leave one half of the interest to my executors for their service and trouble, and the interest on the other half to be added to the stock. I leave to my grandson, JOHN PARKER, when of age, £25, and one fourth of the remainder. To my grandson, BENJAMIN PARKER, one third. To my grandson EPHRAIM one half of the sum that then shall be, and the other half to my granddaughter, EASTER PARKER, when of age. I make DAVID LATOURETTE and JONATHAN LEWIS, Sr., executors.

Witnesses, HENRY LATOURETTE, JOHN VANDERBILT. Proved, January 19, 1781. Liber 34:81   WNYHS X:28

In the name of God, Amen, January 24, 1737. We, **JAMES LA TOURETTE** and **HENRY LA TOURETTE**, both of Staten Island, being in perfect health, do make this, our will. "For the good affection and brotherly kindness we bear each other, we do give to each other all our estate, real and personal, wholly to the longest liver, and we make each other executor of him whom it shall please God to call first out of the mortal state." Each of them binds himself in the sum of £100, not to revoke or make void the said will.

January 24, 1737. Witnesses, SAMUEL BROOME, MARTIN ARMSTRONG, CORNELIUS DORLANDT. Proved before WALTER DONGAN, Esq., November 13, 1738. JAMES LA TOURETTE having died first.
Liber 13:183   WNYHS III:246

In the name of God, Amen. I, **JAMES LATOURETTE**, of Staten Island, Richmond County, being sick and weak in Body. I bequeath to my son JAMES that land that his house and Buildings stand on and that belongs to me, lying between my rear fence along the New Road and the fence of DONA JOHNSON; Also five acres of my woodland to begin at the said road at the northwest corner of DAVID LATOURETTE and to extend along his line so far as a straight line runs from thence to JOSEPH McDONALD's land shall contain the said quantity of five acres, reserving the privelidge of a road through the said five acres from my other land to said new road. To my said son JAMES, £250.

To my son DAVID £350 and my Bay Roan horse Colt. To my daughter PHEBE, wife of ANTHONY STOUTENBURGH, £80 and my negro girl Jane, and two of my best cows. To my two sons, JONATHAN and HENRY, all my lands equally divided between them when my son JONATHAN comes to the age of twenty-one, but if die under age and without issue then his part equally divided among my three sons above named. To my son JONATHAN, my sorrel horse, saddle and bridle. When my real estate shall be divided my executors shall rent out for my son HENRY, part or half thereof till he be twenty-one, and the monies arising from said rent to be applyed for his support and education, and the surplus paid him when of age. The remaining part of my personal estate (if any there be) after paying my debts and funeral expenses shall be equally divided among my four sons, JAMES, DAVID, JONATHAN and HENRY. I appoint my sons, JAMES, DAVID and JONATHAN, executors.

Dated January 27, 1785. Witnesses, PAUL MICHEAU, DAVID LA TOURETTE, house carpenter; JAMES LEWIS, Taylor. Proved, Richmond County, March 15, 1785. Confirmed, New York, March 23, 1785.

Liber 37:447   WNYHS XIII:123

In the name of God, Amen. I, **JOHN LAWRENCE**, of Staten Island, being weak in body, this January 24, 1767. I leave to my executors all my estate, real and personal, and all debts due to me, "to sell, as soon as they conveniently may, as much as shall seem meet to them," and they are to pay all debts and charges. The rest is to remain in the hands of my wife CATHARINE for the education and support of my children. After her death or marriage, the remainder is to be sold and divided among my children, ANN, CATHARINE, NICHOLAS, and EDSTEL. I make my wife and my brother, RICHARD LAWRENCE, executors.

Witnesses, WILLIAM LAURENCE, SAMUEL DE HART, Jr., JOSHUA MESEREAU, Jr. Proved, December 14, 1767, before BENJAMIN SEAMAN.

Liber 26:134   WNYHS VII:127

In the name of God, Amen. I, **JONATHAN LAURENCE**, of New York, mariner....I make my brother, RICHARD LAURENCE, of Staten Island, shipwright, executor.

Dated January 17, 1767. Witnesses, MARY MORSE, JACOB HALLETT, CHARLES MORSE. Proved, April 1, 1767.

Liber 25:448   WNYHS VII:56

Benjamin Fletcher, Governor &c. Know ye that at New York October 12, 1697, the will of **JOHN LACOUNT** was proved and PETER LACOUNT and ABRAHAM ~~LOCKERMAN~~ LAKEMAN are confirmed as executors.

Liber 5-6:198   WNYHS I:282

JOHN LECOUNTE. In the name of God, Amen. I JOHN LECOUNTE of the County of Richmond being in good health. I leave to my daughter, SUSANNAH, all my estate, real and personal, after the death of my wife, HESTER LECOUNTE, or when she shall marry again. If my wife HESTER should remarry before my daughter comes of age, then she is to have £120. But if she do not remarry, then she shall enjoy the use of all the estate, till my six daughters come of age. If the daughter SUSANNAH should died, then the estate is to go to PETER and WILLIAM LECOUNTE. Makes his brother PETER LECOUNT and his friend ABRAHAM ~~LOCKERMAN~~ LAKEMAN, executors. "I desire that my body may be buried in the garden by my own house, by my sister-in-law, the wife of my brother PETER LECOUNTE".

Dated October 2, 1697. (Witnesses not named).

Liber 5-6:199   WNYHS I:282

Richmond County, the 6 day of April Anno Dom 1698. A true and just inventory of the goods and money of the deceased Mr. **JOHN LECOUNTE** taken before EPHRAIM TAYLOR, JOHN ~~BELLVEALSEA~~ BELVEALLE, CHARLES MARSHALL and PETER ~~MAYDBONE~~ MANGLESONE ?, Constable. 9 cows, £27; 6 calves, £4; 6 shoats, £3; 2 young oxen, £6.15; 100 schepples rye, £12.10s; one old negro man, £20; 5 young steers, £12.10. Total £385. "To one silver cup, 5 silver spoons, 2 silver forks, and one silver dram cup to be left for the child YONESE, the daughter of Mr. JOHN LECOUNTE, till she comes of age". This is a true inventory taken before me, EPHRAIM TAYLOR and appraised by us, ~~ISAAC~~ JACOB CORBETT, JOHN ~~BELLVEALLSEA~~ BELLVEALLE, CHARLES MARSHALL, JOHN LECOUNTE, ABRAHAM ~~LOKERMAN~~ LAKEMAN.

Liber 5-6:229   WNYHS I:289

In the name of God, Amen, December 28, 1747. I, **JOHN LE CONTE**, of Richmond County, being in good health. I leave to my wife MARY £150, within six months after my decease, in full for her right of dower. I leave to my son JOHN all my lands and tracts of meadow, and my silver tankard, gun, and sword. I leave to my daughter FRANCES my great cup board, best bed, and all my rings and jewels. All the rest of my movable estate I leave to my two children when my son JOHN is of age. My executors are to rent my farm to some good and careful person who shall not commit any waste, but keep the farm in good repair, till my son JOHN is of age. I make NICHOLAS ~~LARRABIE~~ LARZELERE, JOHN MORGAN, ABRAHAM COLE, and my son JOHN executors.

Witnesses, ISAAC COLE, NICHOLAS ~~LARRABIE~~ LARZELERE, Jr., ESTHER LA TOURETTE.

Liber 20:17   WNYHS V:109

In the name of God, Amen, September 19, 1734. I, **MARGARET LE COUNTE**, widow of PETER LE COUNTE, of Richmond County. I leave to my son JOHN for his birth right, a certain half lot of land in Richmond County, lying between the land of JOHN CASON, and the land of JOHN MORGEN; Also my old negro man "Pine", and my negro woman "Margaret". I direct that my son shall pay £3 yearly to the poor. I leave to my son JOHN's daughter FRANCES, my little negro girl "Mary". I leave to my grand-daughter, MARGARET LE COUNTE, a negro boy, and she is to pay to her sisters, MARY and MARTHA,

102

£10 each when of age. I leave to my grand-daughters, MARY, wife of SAMUEL STILLWELL, and CATHARINE, wife of DAVID LATOURETTE, and ESTHER, wife of ISAAC COLE, each £10. I leave to my niece, CATHARINE JOHNDINS *(JANDINS)*, widow, the use of £30, so long as she lives with my son JOHN, and in case she goes to live elsewhere, she is to have the £30 paid to her. I leave to my daughter-in-law, now wife of PAUL MICHAUD, a negro girl. I leave the rest of my movable estate to my son JOHN, and my grand-daughters MARGARET, MARY and MARTHA LE COUNTE. I appoint my son JOHN and ADAM MOTT and ~~MICHELIS LARRERE~~ NICHOLAS LARZALERE, executors.

Witnesses, JOHN MARSHALL, ~~CLINTON GRIFFITHS~~ CHRISTIAN GRIFFITH, M. MILLER. Proved before WALTER DONGAN, Esq., May 13, 1736.

Liber 12:492   WNYHS III:201

PETER LE COUNTE. In the name of God Amen. "I, PETER LE COUNTE of Staten Island, in the County of Richmond, being weak of body". I leave to my well beloved wife MARGARET LE COUNTE, the use and benefit of all my real and personal estate during widowhood. Only she is to pay £50 to my son and heir, JOHN LE COUNTE when he is 21 years of age. I leave to son JOHN my two lots of land and meadow, to be appraised by three indifferent men of the neighborhood and he is to pay to his two brothers, PETER and JAMES 2/3 of the value. I leave all the rest of my estate to my three sons. I appoint my loving friends ~~JAMES GIRNEST~~ JACOB GARRIOT, ABRAHAM LOCKMAN, {JAMES BALLION} and JOHN COZEER, executors.

Dated October 11, 1702. Witnesses ~~JAMES~~ JEAN LATOURETTE, ABRAHAM COLE, JOHANNES FOUPET. Proved before Lord Cornbury by oath of the above witnesses April 10, 1704.

Liber 7:159   WNYHS I:385

In the name of God, Amen. February 6, 1728/9. I, **PETER LECOUNT**, of Richmond County, being very sick. My wife ANNE is to keep and

103

remain in full possession of my whole estate, lands, and movables, and to reap the benefit of the same, so long as she doth remain my widow. "But if she do marri again to an other man, she shall take her thirds according to Law". I leave to my daughters, MARGARET and MARY, all my lands and tenements when of age, and 2/3 of the movable estate. Whereas it is likely now, that my dearly beloved wife is with child, if it be a son, it is to have an equal share of my lands and £50 more. But if a daughter, she is to have an equal share. I make my brother, JOHN LE COUNT, and my brother-in-law, NICHOLAS STILLWELL, and my wife, executors.

Witnesses, JACOB BILLOW, JAQUES POILLON, ABRAHAM COLE. Proved, June ~~13~~ 18, 1729. Unrecorded will   WNYHS XI:137

In the name of God, Amen. I, **WILLIAM LEGGETT**, of the Borrough Town of Westchester, Esq., being indisposed in body...... I leave to my daughter MARY, wife of RICHARD LAWRENCE, of Staten Island, my negro wench "Jane" who now liveth with her, also a negro boy and £100............ I make my son ABRAHAM and my son-in-law, RICHARD LAWRENCE, executors. Dated December 8, 1762.
Liber 24:69   WNYHS VI:243

In the name of God, Amen, May 7, 1764. I, **JONATHAN LEWIS**, of Richmond County, "being sick, but having my usual understanding". All debts and funeral expenses to be paid. "I give and order to my beloved wife ABIGAIL a decent maintainance in such manner as my executors may think reasonable", "also the bed and furniture belonging to it that we lie on". I leave to my two unmarried daughters PHEBE and MARY all the rest of the bedding. All my lands and meadows in Richmond County to be sold by my executors, and ½ of the money to be paid to my son JONATHAN. All the movable estate to be sold, and the money and the other half from the sale of the farm, after paying debts, to be divided as follows: To my daughter PHEBE £40. To my daughter MARY £40. To my daughters HANNAH, wife of BENJAMIN BRITTAN £10, and to ELIZABETH, wife of JAMES LATOURETTE, £25. To my two grandchildren, SARAH and ANNE, daughters of my daughter BATHSHEBA MERSEREAU, deceased, each £30. Of the rest I leave 1/5 to the children of my deceased daughter SARAH, wife of JOHN SCOOBY, and to my daughters, PHEBE, MARY, and ELIZABETH each 1/5, and 1/5 to be put at interest for my daughter HANNAH during the life of her husband BENJAMIN BRITTAN. I make JOSEPH BEDELL, SILAS BEDELL, and BENJAMIN SEAMAN, executors.

Witnesses, PAUL MICHEAU, JOHN MICHEAU, ANTHONY STOUTENBERGH. Proved, March 9, 1765.
Liber 25:49   WNYHS VI:377

In the Name of God, I, **JONATHAN LEWIS**, of Staten Island, Richmond County, being sick and weak. I will that my Executors shall dispose of all my goods, chattels, lands, mills, and tenements as they in their discretion think fit within two years after my decease except such articles as shall hereinafter be bequeathed, and I give them full power to sell all my lands, mills, and tenements within the County of Richmond to any persons and their heirs forever by all such lawful ways as to my Executors or their Council learned in the law shall seem fit. To my dearly beloved wife MARY, my best horse and riding chair, two of my best cows of her own choosing, with sufficient of my household furniture to furnish her room together with the sum of £100 to be first taken out of my estate, and that in lieu of her dowry or power of thirds upon my estate. Also she to have the use of my negro wench and the yearly interest of £50 for life or while my widow. I will that my Executors use £10 for the further education of my son JOSEPH. After my debts, funeral charges and the above legacies are paid, the remainder of my estate shall be divided among my children in manner following: To my son

JONATHAN, one eighth of my estate, to my son DAVID one eighth, to my son JAMES one eighth, to my son ISRAEL one eighth, to my son JOSEPH one eighth, to my daughter, SARAH DEGROOT, one six-teenth part; to my daughter CATHARINE HUTCHINSON, one six-teenth; to my daughter MARY LEWIS, one sixteenth; to my daughter, FRANCES LEWIS, one sixteenth; to my daughter, ELIZABETH LEWIS, one sixteenth; to my daughter, PHEBE LEWIS, one sixteenth; none of the said legacies to be paid to any of my children till they are twenty-one years old, but if my Executors have money on hand and shall think proper to make a dividend thereof amongst those of my children that are of the above mentioned age, those of them that are under that age shall have the interest of their dividend yearly for their support till they arive of full age to receive such dividend or their full legacy. If any of my children die under age their part to be devided among my surviving children. I recommend my Executors at the sale of my houses and lands to reserve such part as they think convenient for the reception and continuing of my family together during the life or widowhood of my beloved wife MARY, and after her decease or discontinuance of widowhood such house or land reserved shall be sold as also my Negro wench and the money divided as aforesaid. I appoint my wife Executrix, my trusty friend and brother-in-law, DAVID LATOURETTE, my sons JONATHAN and DAVID, all of Staten Island, Executors.

Dated October 28, 1785. Witnesses, JOHN LATOURETTE, ABRAHAM VAIL (weaver) and EDWARD HALL (schoolmaster). Proved, Richmond County, January 5, 1786.
Liber 38:282   WNYHS XIII:251

"In the name of God, Amen. I, **PHEBE LEWIS**, of Richmond County being very sick. I order all debts to be paid. I leave to my brother, JONATHAN LEWIS, my house and land, with all buildings, now in possession of Dr. SAMUEL BURROWS, and rented to him for four years. I leave to my Niece, ELIZABETH ADLINGTON, two years' rent of said place, which amounts to the sum of £34, to be paid to her when eighteen years old. I leave to my Niece, PHEBE LATOURETTE, daughter of JAMES LATOURETTE, my bed and bedding. All the rest of my estate I leave to my sister ELIZABETH, wife of JAMES LATOURETTE, and to my niece SARAH, daughter of JAMES LATOURETTE, and to my niece SARAH, wife of NATHANIEL JOHNSON. I appoint DAVID LATOURETTE, executor."

Dated April 20, 1780. Witnesses, PAUL MICHEAU, HENRY LATOURETTE, ~~PETRUS~~ CATHREN BEDELL. Proved, April 29, 1780.
Liber 32:247   WNYHS IX:110

In the name of God, Amen. The 1st day of February, 1785. I, **JAMES LISK**, of the County of Richmond, being at this time very sick and weak. I leave to my son DANIEL, my Bay mare and the colt she is now with fold of and a new saddle to the value of three pounds ten shillings, and my wareing apearel and all my tools and line and tackling and £20 in cash. The remainder of my estate shall be sold and my debts and funeral charges paid after I am buried in a decent manner, and the remainder shall be equally divided between my loving wife (not named) and my four children, that is to say, my wife a share, and my son WILLIAM a share "if he is justly discharged from the charge he is now confined for and returns", and my son DANIEL a share, and my daughter CATHARINE a share, and my daughter ELIZABETH a share. I ordain my friend, RICHARD CONNER, and my son DANIEL, executors.

Witnesses, NATHANIEL BRITTEN, cooper; JOHN MARTENNO, RICHARD CONNER, Jr. Proved, Richmond County, March 3, 1785.
Liber 37:414   WNYHS XIII:106

In the name of God, Amen, September 14, 1767. I, **THOMAS LISK**, of Richmond County. I leave to my wife ELSIE my bed and furniture (except one rugg belonging to my first wife), and a chest of drawers, and tables, and a hive of bees. I leave to my son JOHN £5. All the rest of my personal estate to be sold by my executors, and I leave all the rest to my son JOHN and my daughters, CATALINA, MARGARET, MARY, MARTHA, ANN, and RACHEL, and to my granddaughter, ELIZABETH VANDERBEEK. I leave to my wife the use of my house and land for life, and then to my son JOHN. I make my friends, PETER HAUSMAN, JOHN LISK, and my son JOHN, executors.

Witnesses, PETER HAUSMAN, EDWARD BUSH, PETER ~~ZELOFF~~ ZELUFF. Proved, October ~~30~~ 31, 1767.

Liber 25:234 WNYHS VII:153

In the name of God, Amen, March 12, 1759. I, **ABRAHAM LOCKERMANS** of Staten Island, yeoman, being sick. I leave to my son ABRAHAM a sorrel horse and a gun. I leave to my son WALTER the 14 acres of land I purchased from the executors of PETER PERLIEU, Also the 16 acres purchased of JOHN GRANDINE, the easternmost part of it joining the said 14 acres. All the rest of the land, which is about 19 acres, and 4 acres bought of JONATHAN LEWIS, and the home lot in Fresh Kills, and my salt meadow in Fresh Kills, and my lot of meadow in Great Kills, the same are to be sold with my personal property, at the discretion of my executors, for the bringing up of my children, and then to be divided among all my children, except my sons ABRAHAM and WALTER. My wife SARAH is to be in full possession "and to be Mistress during her widowhood". I make BENJAMIN SEAMAN, Esq., and HENRY LA TOURETTE, and my wife executors.

Witnesses, JAMES POILLON, BARENT SLAGHT, JOHN JONES. Proved in Richmond County before BENJAMIN SEAMAN, Surrogate, April 14, 1760.

Liber 22:78 WNYHS V:392

Whereas, **BARTHOLOMEW LOTT**, of Richmond County, lately died intestate, Letters of administration are granted to his only son, ENGLEBERT LOTT, April 10, 1708.

Liber 7:486 WNYHS II:1

ABRAHAM LUTINE "Richmond County, December ye 2, 1702. I, ABRAHAM LUTINE, being in perfect memory, Praised be God for it". I give to my loving wife ANN LUTINE, one lot of land whereon I now live, joining to ISAAC BELLIN, with all the rights thereto belonging. I give to JOHN ASKING, Jr., my sister's son, one lot of land being near ye Isenberg, with all the rights thereto belonging. I leave all my lands in East New Jersey to the children of my two sisters, MARY and HESTER. I leave to my loving mother £2. I leave to JOHN ASKING Jr., two horses and to ABRAHAM ~~CROCHERAN~~ CROCHERON, son as JOHN ~~CROCHERAN~~ CROCHERON, one cow. Makes his wife executor.

Witnesses, JOHN STILLWELL, DAVID DE BON REPOS. Proved, December 22, 1702.
Liber 7:75   WNYHS I:357

Inventory of the estate of ~~WALNOVERS~~ **WALRAVEN LETIN**, of Dover, Staten Island, who hath lately deceased, taken by GIDEON MARLETT, constable, in presence of PETER ~~BELEW~~ BALEN, SIMEON CORNE, TYS BARENSON "and many others then present". Dated January 16, 1671/2. One lot and housing £1,000. Whole estate £2,592.
Liber 1-2:93   WNYHS I:23

-M-

In the name of God, Amen. I, **AENEAS MACKENZIE**, of Richmond County, clerk, being sick. After all debts are paid, I bequeath all my real and personal estate and whatsoever in right doth belong unto me, within Great Britain or in America, to my dear and well beloved spouse, ELIZABETH MACKENZIE, to her and her heirs and assigns. And for as much as the purchasing of the land, and building of the house, wherein I now live, hath layed me under the Difficulty, incurring and necessity for putting myself under obligations, for considerable sums of money, for accomplishing my desire, for the use and benefit of ye minister of St. Andrew's Church for the time being, my executors shall transfer and convey all my title to said land and house to the Church wardens and vestrymen of said St. Andrews Church, Provided they, within one year, shall pay to my executors such sums as have been actually expended, on the said house, and which must be paid out of my estate by such obligations.

Dated ~~February~~ January 7, 1722/3. Witnesses, EDWARD VAUGHAN, PHILIP TILLYER, J. GARREAU. Proved, August 29, 1723. (This will is in testator's own handwriting.)

[Note.-Rev. AENEAS MACKENZIE was sent to this country in 1704 as a missionary by the Society for the Propagation of the Gospel in Foreign Parts. He was the first pastor of St. Andrew's Church, on Staten Island. During the first seven years of his ministry, his church services were held in the French Church, through the charitableness of its officers.- W.S.P.]

Unrecorded will   WNYHS XI:94

In the name of God, Amen. I, **ELIZABETH MACKENZIE**, of Staten Island, being in weakness of body, I leave to my sons GEORGE and WILLIAM FRASER, all my estate, real or personal, in America or Europe. "They making a Porch and Tomb for the Church", and I make them executors.

Dated July 23, 1723. Witnesses, WILLIAM ~~FILLYER~~ TILLYER, MARY ~~BRAISEAU~~ RAISEAU, MARGARET TAYLOR.

William Burnet, Esq., Captain-General and Governor. To all etc. The will of ELIZABETH MACKENZIE, widow of ENEAS MACKENZIE, was proved before Isaac Bobin, December 3, 1723.

Liber 9:431   WNYHS II:280

June 19, 1759. I, **CHARLES McLEAN**, of Staten Island, Esq., being very sick. I leave to my wife MARY all my messuages, lands and tenements, and all goods and personal estate, until my youngest son CHARLES is of age, and after that I leave all my said lands and messuages to my sons WILLIAM and CORNELIUS,

and they are to pay to their sisters MARY and
CATHARINE £100, and to my son CHARLES £200
within 2 years after the death of my wife. I
leave to my wife a negro girl "Bell" and the
use of my negro "Ben" during her widowhood,
and she is to have the produce of 1/3 of my
lands for life, and such part of my dwelling
house as she shall choose. I leave all the
rest to my children, WILLIAM, CORNELIUS, MARY,
CATHARINE and CHARLES. I make my wife MARY
and brother - in - law CORNELIUS CORSEN,
executors.

Witnesses, GERARDUS BEEKMAN, PETER
CORSEN, DANIEL CORSEN.

Codicil, October 5, 1759. My executors
may sell all lands if necessary, and pay the
money to my sons WILLIAM and CORNELIUS, and
they are to pay all legacies.

Witnesses, MARY JENNER, DANIEL CORSEN,
{add JOHN JENNER}. Proved April 23, 1760
before GOLDSBROW BANYER.
Liber 22:15   WNYHS V:375

In the name of God, Amen. I, **DANIEL
McSWAIN**, of the County of Richmond, being weak
in body. My fast and movable estate to remain
as it is, until my son JOHN is of age, for the
purpose of bringing up the children. Unto my
loving wife, the use of one third of my fast
estate during her natural life; Also, a room
in the house during life; likewise to have a
cow and feather bed, bedstead and bedding.
Unto my son JOHN, the northernmost half of my
land, to have an equal proportion of woodland
with my son VINCENT; also to have one half of
my moveables when he comes of age; he to pay
to my daughter CATHARINE £60, and one cow;
also to pay to my daughter SARAH £60 and one
cow; also to pay to my daughter MARY £10.
When VINCENT is of age, my son JOHN must pay
one half of all my lawful debts. To my son
JOHN, 8 shillings. Unto my son VINCENT, the
southermost half of my land, including the
house that I now live in; likewise, one half
of my moveables when JOHN comes of age. When
VINCENT comes of age, then the house is to be

111

valued by two men, they each choosing one, and the one half of such valuation VINCENT is to pay to his brother JOHN. At his majority, VINCENT is to pay to my daughter ELIZABETH £60 and one cow; to my daughter MARY £70 and one cow; likewise he must pay one half of my lawful debts. Should any of the stock or moveables be stolen or taken away, then the heirs are to lose in proportion as the executors shall think proper to settle it. I make my loving wife and my true and loving friends, GEORGE BARNS and STEPHEN BEDELL, executors.

Dated, February 9, 1782. Witnesses, ANTHONY NEILL, farmer, DAVID DAY. Proved, November 11, 1782.
Liber 35:131   NYHS X:303

"In the name of God, Amen. I, **ABRAHAM MANY**, of Richmond County, being very weak. After paying all debts, the rest of estate to be sold by executors at public vendue. I leave to my four grandchildren, the children of my son ABRAHAM, deceased, viz., ABRAHAM, RICHARD, JOHN, and ISAAC, 1/4 of all my estate. To my son JOHN, 1/4. To my five daughters, ANN, MARY, CATHARINE, wife of JOHN GOULD, RACHEL, wife of HENRY JOHNSON, and SARAH, wife of JOSEPH SPRAGG, 1/4. The part of my son JOHN is to be put out by my executors for his support and that of his daughter ELIZABETH. The part of my daughter SARAH is also to be in the hands of my executors. I make my friends, PAUL MICHEAU, JOHN MICHEAU, JOHN JOURNEY, executors."

Dated August 29, 1777. {Witnesses JOHN MARSHALL, DANIEL VAN CLEFE and ISAAC MANEE}. Proved, March 11, 1780.
Liber 32:278   WNYHS IX:119

PETER MANETT. In the name of God, Amen. I, PETER MANETT, of Staten Island, yeoman. I leave to my wife MARY all houses, lands, and goods during her life, and after her decease to my eldest son ABRAHAM, and he shall pay to his three brothers, PETER, JOHN, and ISAAC,

112

£50 when of age. If my son ABRAHAM die without issue, then my house and lands where I now dwell, and the tract of lands in the woods, which is mentioned (though yet undivided) in a Patent, jointly with my neighbor ANTHONY TICE, are to go to my second son PETER, he paying to the rest £75. I make Captain JAMES POILLON, and Mr. JOHN LATOWRETTE, executors.

Dated ~~June~~ January 19, 1707. Witnesses, J. BILLOP, ANTHONY TYCE, TYCE ~~WILLIMSE~~ WILLIAMSON, {add JOHANNES JOHNSON}. Proved, April 8, 1712.

Liber 8:271   WNYHS II:121

In the name of God, Amen, September ~~3~~ 30, 1760. I, **JOHN MARSHALL**, of Richmond County, being sick. All my negro slaves and as much of my movables as my executors think best are to be sold. I leave to my wife MARTHA the use of all my estate, real and personal, during her widowhood. If she marries, she is to have a bed and furniture and £50. I leave to my three sons, JOHN, THOMAS and ~~BENJAMIN~~ ABRAHAM, all my lands and meadows in Richmond County. But my son THOMAS is to have the house and barn where he now lives, over and above the rest, in consideration of his having built them at his own expense. I leave to my daughter FRANCES, wife of PAUL MESEREAU, £80. To my daughter, MARY MARSHALL, £100. To my daughter, MARTHA MARSHALL, £100. To my daughter, CATHARINE MARSHALL, £100. All to be paid at the death or marriage of my wife. I leave all the rest of movables to all my children. My son ABRAHAM and my unmarried daughters are to live in my house with their mother. "If they marry, they are to move out, and have no further privilege". I make my wife MARTHA and my son ABRAHAM and my friends, HENRY LA TOURETTE and BENJAMIN SEAMAN, executors.

Witnesses, JOHN MORGAN, MARY PARLIER, MARTHA COLE. Proved, July 5, 1770.

Liber 27:455   WNYHS VII:381

In the name of God, Amen. The thirtieth day of August, 1778. I, **MARTHA MARSHALL**, widow of JOHN MARSHALL, of the County of Richmond, being very sick and weak in body. All my just debts and funeral charges to be paid. I leave to my daughter CATHARINE, two milch cows. Unto my son ABRAHAM, one milch cow. All my wearing apparel to be equally divided between my two daughters and my granddaughter, MARTHA MERSEREAU. My bed, bedstead and all the furniture which belonged to my daughter MARY, deceased, unto my granddaughter, MARY MARSHALL, daughter of my son ABRAHAM. Unto my said daughter CATHERINE, one bed and its furniture, which she now has in possession. Each of my grandchildren that bear my name, both of my sons's daughters, shall have as much money out of my estate as will buy each of them a gold ring, leaving the value of the same to my executors. The remainder of my estate to go as follows: One third part to my daughter MARTHA, wife of DANIEL VAN LEIFT; a like part to my daughter CATHERINE; the remaining third part to the children of my daughter FRANCES, deceased, in the following manner: £15 to my granddaughter, MARTHA MERSEREAU; £5 to my grandson, DAVID MERSEREAU; the remainder of said third part to be equally divided between my four grand children (children of my said daughter FRANCES), namely: MARTHA, abovenamed, JOHN, PAUL and DAVID. I make my trusty friends, BENJAMIN SEAMAN and JOHN MICHEAU, Esq., executors.

Witnesses, JOHN BEDELL, Jr., ferryman, BORNT PARLEE, PETER PARLEE, farmer. Proved, May 16, 1783.

Note.-BENJAMIN LAZALERE, of County of Richmond, farmer, was granted Letters of Administration on May 22, 1783.
Liber 35:256   WNYHS XII:51

In the name of God, Amen. December 20, 1740. I, **MARY MARSHALL**, widow, of Richmond County. I leave to my son, JOHN MARSHALL, all my lands, houses, and tenements. I leave all my movable estate to my daughters, MARY EGBERTSE, widow, ELEANOR, wife of ISAAC CANON, RACHEL, wife of JACOB ~~LEE~~ SEE, and my granddaughter, MARY JOHNSON, daughter of ROBERT JOHNSON, deceased. Her share is to be in the hands of my executors till she is of age. I make my son JOHN and JOHN LE CONTE, executors.

Witnesses, ABRAHAM COLE, ISAAC COLE, ESTHER COLE. Proved, March 18, 1740/1.
Liber 14:37   WNYHS III:322

In the name of God, Amen. September 17, 1768. I, **THOMAS MARSHALL**, of Richmond County, being sick. I leave to my son JOHN my gun and sword. My executors may sell any part of my estate, and after paying debts, the rest to be for my wife and my three children. If my wife marries, she is to have ¼, and the rest to my children, MARTHA, JOHN, and ELTIA. If my wife SARAH does not marry, she is to have the use of all till my youngest child is of age. I make my father, JOHN MARSHALL, and my friend, PAUL MICHEAU, executors.

Witnesses, JOHN MORGAN, ABRAHAM PARLEE, BENJAMIN DRAKE. Proved, November 28, 1768.
Liber 26:459   WNYHS VII:221

FRANCIS MARTENSE. In the name of God, Amen, this 1st day of October, 1706, I FRANCIS MARTENSE, of Staten Island, yeoman, being in health of body. I leave to STEPHEN MARTENSE, son of my son STEPHEN, late of Staten Island, deceased, £300 when he is of age. I leave to my wife ~~HANNAH~~ HESTER all the rest of estate during her life, but if she remarries, then only the use of one-third. After my wife's decease I leave all the estate, one half to my grandson, STEPHEN MARTENSE, and the rest to my grandson, VINCENT FOUNTAIN, Jr., son of VINCENT FOUNTAIN, Sr. I make my wife HESTER, and Mr. MARK DUSASOA, Jr., Mr. STEPHEN RICHARDS, and Mr. ABRAHAM LAKEMAN, executors.

Witnesses, D. VAN BRUGH, JOSEPH HUDDLESTONE, WILLIAM HUDDLESTONE. Proved before THOMAS WENHAM, Esq., August 5, 1707.
Liber 7:415   WNYHS I:446

115

"In the name of God, Amen. I, **STEPHEN MARTINE**, of Old Town, on Staten Island, April 13, 1779. I leave to such children as are single and live with me at the time of my departure the use of all my estate for two years, and then to be sold by my executors. I leave to my son STEPHEN £40. To my two daughters, CHARITY and ELIZABETH, £20 each. To my three sons, CORNELIUS, ABRAHAM, and BENJAMIN, £30 each, and the same to my three daughters, ELEANOR, CORNELIA, and SARAH. All the rest I leave to my eleven children, ANN, MARY, CHARITY, ELIZABETH, CORNELIUS, ABRAHAM, BENJAMIN, SUSANAH, ELEANOR, CORNELIA, and SARAH. I make my four sons, executors."

April 13, 1779. Witnesses, JOHN WILSON, CHRISTIAN JACOBSON, MARY VANDERBECK. Proved, August 4, 1779.

Liber 32:119   WNYHS IX:73

"The will of **STEPHEN MARTINO** recorded in Liber B of Wills, Page 119, &c."

The above entry is made on the margin of page 185, Liber 34. Search has been made in the Hall of Records and in the New York County Clerk's office; inquiry has also been made in Richmond County, where the will was probated, August 4, 1779. CORNELIUS MARTINO, BENJAMIN MARTINO, and STEPHEN MARTINO, were named as executors, and subsequently qualified.

Liber 34:185   WNYHS X:79

In the name of God, Amen. I, **STEPHEN MARTINS**, of Old Town, on Staten Island, being sick and weak in body this 13 day of April, 1779. I direct all debts and funeral charges to be paid. It is my will and desire, that such of my children as are single, and live with me, at the time of my departure shall have the whole use of all my estate, real and personal, for two years after my decease, they making no waste or destruction, and the estate is then to be sold by my executors, and the money to be divided as follows. To my son STEPHEN £40. To my two daughters, CHARITY and ELIZABETH, £20 each. To my sons, CORNELIUS,

ABRAHAM, and BENJAMIN, £30 each. To my daughters, ELENOR, CORNELIA, and SARAH, £30 each, and the remainder to my eleven children, ANN, MARY, CHARITY, ELIZABETH, CORNELIUS, ABRAHAM, BENJAMIN, SUSANAH, ELENOR, CORNELIA, and SARAH. I make my sons, STEPHEN, CORNELIUS, ABRAHAM, and BENJAMIN, executors.

Witnesses, JOHN WILLSON, CHRISTIAN JACOBSEN, MARY VANDERBEECK. Proved, August 4, 1779, before BENJAMIN SEAMAN, Esq.

(See Vol IX:73 WNYHS or p. 116 above)
Unrecorded will   WNYHS XI:199

MERRILL, includes MERIL, MERRELL, MERELL, etc.

In the name of God, Amen, July 25, 1730. I, **JOHN MERIL**, of Staten Island, being very sick, I leave to my wife CHARITY, all my estate during her widowhood. After her death I give to my son JOHN all my lands and tenements, and ½ the mill and appurtenances. I leave to my four daughters, SUSANNAH, CATHARINE, ANNE, and CHARLOTTE, £200 each, to be paid by my son JOHN in installments. I make my brother, RICHARD MERIL, and AERTE SIMSON, my brother-in-law, executors.

Witnesses, JAN RAL, JACOB ~~BENNIT~~ BENNET, RICHARD ~~MERIL~~ MERREL. Proved before WALTER DONGAN, Esq., April 11, 1743.
Liber 15:45   WNYHS III:391

In the name of God, Amen. April 14, 1758. I, **JOHN MERRELL**, of Richmond County, being in perfect health. I leave to my three daughters, GERTRUY, WEINTIA, and SARAH, each £35, to be paid by my three sons. I leave to my wife the sole use of all my estate, to enjoy so long as she remains my widow, and after that to my sons, JODIA, WILLIAM, and JOHN. JODIA shall have £5 more than the rest for his birthright. I make my wife ANN, and JACOB ROIZEAU, executors.

Witnesses, JOHN ~~KILLYER~~ HILLYER, RICHARD ~~BRITTAN~~ BRITTON, JOHN ~~MERELL~~ MERRELL. Proved, May 28, 1768.
Liber 26:343   WNYHS VII:187

In the name of God, Amen. I, **JOHN
MERRIL**, of Richmond County, carpenter, being
weak in body. All estate to be sold, and I
make BARENT SIMONSON and MOSES DE PEW,
executors. "Except the house that MARY
CLENDENING now lives in, and ½ of an acre of
land about the house, for which she has paid
£4 yearly rent". All the rest of personal
estate I leave to my wife LEANAH, and I leave
her £100 and a bed and a table. My executors
are to sell the rest of estate and pay the
proceeds to my nephew THOMAS, son of my
brother ~~MERILL~~ THOMAS MERRILL, and to CHARLES
DECKER, son of my sister, ~~MARY~~ MERCY DECKER.
Dated March 13, 1773. Witnesses,
NATHANIEL BRITTON, ELIAS THOMAS, ISAAC DOTY.
Proved, March 22, 1773.
Liber 28:415   WNYHS VIII:99

In the name of God, Amen, April 18, 1739.
I, **PHILIP MERELL**, of Staten Island, being in
perfect health. I leave to my wife ELIZABETH,
all my estate during her widowhood. I leave
to my eldest son, PHILIP, £25. To my son
NICHOLAS, £25. After my wife's decease, and
after payment of debts and funeral charges, I
leave all the rest to my children, PHILIP,
NICHOLAS, SUSANAH, CATHARINE, ELIZABETH, MARY
and ~~NELTIE~~ NELEY. I make my wife and my
brother, RICHARD MERELL, executors.
Witnesses, JAN RAL, ~~GREESSIE~~ GEESSIE
VANDER SCHUREN, ELIZABETH ~~BEACK~~ BUCH. Proved,
April 18, 1740.
Liber 13:373   WNYHS III:293

In the name of God, Amen, February 2,
1756. I, **RICHARD MERRELL**, of Richmond County,
being in good health. I leave to my wife ALSE
£20 a year during her widowhood in lieu of
dower, also my negro "Shelley". My son
RICHARD and my daughter ALSE are to pay the
said £20. I leave to my daughter ALSE a
plantation of 80 acres of land and 10 acres of
meadow, which is in PHILIP WELLS' Patent,
during her life, and then to her children.
Also a negro wench and a feather bed and

bedding. I leave to my son RICHARD all the rest of my lands and meadows, messuages and tenements, and make him executor.

Witnesses, JONATHAN ALLEN, JOHANES HUISMAN, PETER HOUSEMAN, JOHN MERRELL. Proved September 29, 1760, before BENJAMIN SEAMAN, Surrogate.

Liber 22:228   WNYHS VI:4

In the name of God, Amen, January 12, 1773. I, **THOMAS MERRILL**, of Staten Island, being sick. All debts to be paid. I leave to my son RICHARD £30. To my daughter SUSANAH my silver tumbler. To my daughter SARAH my silver salt cellar, and my bed and bedding. I leave to my sons, THOMAS and JOHN, all the rest of my estate, real and personal, and make them executors.

Witnesses, SAMUEL DE HART, TYON MERRILL, AARON VAN NAME. Proved, April 2, 1773.

Liber 28:418   WNYHS VIII:100

In the name of God, Amen. The thirteenth day of March, 1782. I, **WILLIAM MERRELL**, of Staten Island, Richmond County, yeoman, being in a low state of health, but in perfect senses. My funeral charges and other debts to be paid. I leave to MARY, my dearly beloved wife, all my estate, personal and moveable, except my gun and one pair of silver clasps. Them to my cousin, RICHARD DECKER, my sister MARGARET DECKER'S son. I make my dear and beloved wife MARY, executor.

Witnesses, JAMES GROVER GARRISON, CHARLES DECKER, farmer, RICHARD MERRELL. Proved, April 19, 1782.

Liber 34:505   WNYHS X:222

DANIEL MERSEREAU, yeoman, of Richmond County, New York, to my wife CORNELIA, £100; Also one milch cow, a riding chair, best bedstead and furniture, dining table, tea table furnished, one looking glass, six chairs, one chest, one spinning wheel, one tea kettle, two iron pots, 1 pair andirons, one iron trammell and some dishes and plates which she may select. To my grandson, AARON MERCEREAU, £60, to be put out at use within one year after my death, for his benefit, until he arrive at the age of twenty-one years; then to be paid with the interest; if he die before he is twenty-one years, the aforesaid monies shall be equally divided between such of my children as shall then be living and heirs of such as shall be deceased. To my wife, my sons JOHN, DANIEL and HENRY and daughter CATHARINE, £30 each; all to receive their shares within one year after my decease, excepting HENRY, whose share is not to be paid him until he shall attain the age of twenty-one years; in order that he may be further benefited, his share of £30 shall be put out at use until he is twenty-one years of age, the above moneys to be an equivalent for the outset I gave my daughter ELIZABETH at her marriage, and should either die before they shall be entitled to their respective share or shares and without lawful issue, the share or shares are to be equally divided between the survivors or their heirs. To my sons, JOHN, DANIEL and HENRY all my wearing apparel, to be equally divided among them. To my daughter CATHARINE, one chest and a spinning wheel. All the remainder of my estate, both real and personal, in Richmond County and elsewhere, not before mentioned, shall within one year after my decease be disposed of at public sale and after my just debts shall be discharged and the above legacies deducted, the remaining moneys arising from sale to be equally divided between my wife and children, JOHN, DANIEL, ELIZABETH, CATHARINE and HENRY; each to receive his share one year after my decease excepting HENRY whose share is to be put out for his benefit until he attain the age of twenty-one years; and should he or any of my heirs die before they shall be entitled to receive their share or shares, this share or shares to be equally divided among their heirs or to the survivors to be equally divided among them. My wife at her discretion shall be entitled to receive money from my executors to purchase necessary clothing for my son HENRY, while he is a minor; this money to be deducted from the interest arising from the moneys put out at use for his benefit. I appoint my brother JOHN MERSEREAU, my son JOHN, and ABRAHAM BANCKER.

Dated March 2, 1786. Witnesses, CORNELIUS CRUSER, W. HELMUS VRELAND, yeomen; ADRIAN BANCKER. Proved, April 7, 1786. Liber 39:17   WNYHS XIII:324

February 21, 1786. **DAVID MERSEREAU**, of Staten Island, Richmond County, New York. To my wife ELIZABETH, use or profits of my whole estate, real and personal, for bringing up and schooling my children for so long as she shall remain my widow; my executors to give to my wife immediately after her remarriage the choice of two negro wenches, either old or young SARAH, with so much of my household furniture as she shall choose, and to pay her £100 out of my estate in lieu of dower; to my son DAVID £200 when he shall arrive at the age of twenty-one years, with the silver bowl as specified in the will of my brother PAUL, the other articles being stolen cannot be delivered; to my son DANIEL £100, when he shall arrive at the age of twenty one years given to him in like manner by my brother PAUL; to my son PETER £100 out of my estate when he arrive at the age of twenty-one years; to my daughters, ELIZABETH, JUDE and MARGARET, each to receive £50 in lieu of an outset when they shall arrive at the age of eighteen or marry; the remainder of my estate shall be equally divided among all my children, namely, MARY, MARTHA, SARAH, NANCY, DAVID, DANIEL, PETER, ELIZABETH, JUDE and MARGARET; immediately after my daughter MARGARET shall arrive at the age of eighteen years or marry which shall first happen; in case any of my sons, DAVID, DANIEL or PETER, die under age and without issue that such share or shares given to them so dying shall be equally divided amongst the survivors or given to the survivor of my sons, and in case either of my

121

daughters, ELIZABETH, JUDE or MARGARET shall die before they arrive at age of eighteen or marry, without lawful issue, such share or shares of either of them so dying to be equally divided among the survivors or survivor of them above expressed; be it remembered that my daughter MARY has received £40, which is to be accounted by her out of such share as may become due to her out of my estate. I appoint GOZEN RYERSSE, DANIEL MERSEREAU, Sr., and JOHN MERSEREAU, executors. Dated February 21, 1786. Witnesses, CORNELIUS MERSEREAU, DAVID EDGAR, JOHN VAN PELT, all of Richmond County, ship carpenters. Proved, April 26, 1786.
Liber 39:62   WNYHS XIII:346

In the name of God, Amen, January 8, 1766. I, **JOHANES MERSEREAU**, of Richmond County, cooper, being in perfect health. I leave to my wife ELIZABETH one bed with the furniture. I leave to my eldest son, DANIEL, £10. My executors are to sell all my estate, real and personal, and pay all debts. All the rest I leave to my wife ELIZABETH and my four children, DANIEL, JOSHUA, JOHN, and PETER. I make my son DANIEL, and my loving friend, ~~DANIEL~~ DAVID MERSEREAU, executors.

Witnesses, LEWIS GRONDAIN, PETER GRONDAIN, PETER WILMURT. Proved, December 4, 1774.
Liber 29:281   WNYHS VIII:234

In the name of God, Amen. I, **JOSHUA MERSEREAU**, of Richmond County, yeoman, being in good health. My will is that my funeral be conducted with a frugal Decorum and in a Christian like manner. I leave to my beloved wife ESTHER, my negro girl TEANER, also one cow, one bed and furniture for the same, decent furniture for one room with the privilege of chusing one room belonging to the house I own with the use of the cellar, wintering and summering for one cow, firewood at the door for one fire; Also £7 per year, which sum I direct my sons, JOHN and DAVID, to

122

pay equally between them, provided she relinquishes her right of Dower, the above privileges to be good provided all relinquishment of Dower is made; and as long as she remains in a state of widowhood. To my daughter ABIGAIL, £50. To my son DAVID, my negro boy SAM, also one of my best horses, saddle and bridle. To my son JOHN, my negro woman named BET. To my granddaughter MARY WINANT, £25. To my grandson, PETER LA TOURETTE, £25, with my negro boy JACK, should my grandson die without issue the said negro boy to my son JOHN. All the rest of my estate, real and personal, to my two sons, JOHN and DAVID. My desire is that my estate be divided as soon as convenient to my executors. I appoint JOHN MERSEREAU and DAVID MERSEREAU, my two sons, executors.

Dated September 13, 1784. Witnesses, JOHN SIMONSON, shoemaker; ANTHONY STOUTENBOROUGH. Proved Richmond County, January 5, 1785. Confirmed, New York, January 21, 1785.

Liber 37:365   WNYHS XIII:83

"In the name of God, Amen. I, **PAUL MERSEREAU**, of Staten Island, shipwright. {June 4, 1773}. I leave to my cousin *[nephew]*, DANIEL MERSEREAU, son of my sister ELIZABETH, a bond of £55 which is due from him. I leave to my cousin, JOHN LA TOURETTE, £10. To my cousin, MARY LA TOURETTE, daughter of my sister MARY, deceased, £10. To my cousin, DAVID MERSEREAU, son of my brother ~~DANIEL~~ DAVID £200 when 21; Also my watch and silver bowl, and ½ dozen silver spoons for tea, and my gun and silver shoe buckles. To my cousin, DANIEL MERSEREAU son of my brother DAVID MERSEREAU, £100 when of age. To my brother DAVID MERSEREAU, whom I make executor, all the rest of my estate."

Witnesses, HENRY LA TOURETTE, JOHN LA TOURETTE. Proved, December 10, 1777.

Liber 31:77   WNYHS IX:15

In the name of God, Amen, I, **PAUL MICHAUX**, of Staten Island, being in perfect health. I leave to my wife ANNE the interest on £500 for life, and a negro woman, and my riding chair and a good chair horse. I leave to my son, JOHN MICHAUX, all that farm or plantation I now live on, and 33 acres of the woodland I lately bought of Mr. JAMES POILLON, and all the salt meadow I have on Carls Neck, all being on Staten Island. I leave to my son PAUL all that tract of land that I lately purchased of JOHN JOURNEY, which is ½ of said Journey's Plantation, and adjoining to BENJAMIN SEAMAN's farm, with the salt meadow belonging to it, and 20 acres of woodland next adjoining, being the remaining part of that woodland I bought of the heirs of JAMES POILLON; I also give him £500. I leave to my daughter CATHARINE £500, and a negro girl. All the rest of my estate I leave to my 3 children, JOHN, PAUL, and CATHARINE. I make my wife and my trusty friend, THOMAS BILLOP, and my two sons, executors.

Dated July 12, 1748. {Witnesses, DAVID LA TOURRETTE, BARNT SLAGHT, and JOHN MERRELL}. Proved, September 5, 1751.
Liber 17:424   WNYHS IV:348

In the name of God, Amen, October 19, 1754. I, **LAURENCE MORE**, of Richmond County, being sick. I leave to my wife SARAH my best bed and furniture. To my son JOHN, £50 and my wearing clothes. My executors are to sell all the rest of real and personal estate at public vendue and pay the proceeds to my wife and children, JOHN, LYDIA, and RACHEL. I make my wife, and my friend DAVID LA FARGE, executors.

Witnesses, DANIEL STILLWELL, LEWIS ~~GRANDAIN~~ GRONDAIN, AUGUSTUS DU BOIS. Proved, December 19, 1754.
Liber 19:188   WNYHS V:48

THOMAS MORELL of Staten Island leaves to ROBERT SEMSON of Gravesend, Long Island, "a colt, now in the hands of CHRISTIAN WOOLF of

124

Gravesend". To Mr. NICHOLAS STILLWELL of Staten Island "all other things and goods that belong to me". Dated 2 May 1670. Witnesses, OBADIAH HOLMES, JOHN KINGDOM.
Liber 1-2:65 WNYHS I:16

In the name of God, Amen, July 14, 1770. I, **JOHN MORGAN**, of Richmond County, "being very low in body". I leave to my wife DEBORAH the use of the lot of land I bought of NICHOLAS LARZELERE, Jr., "commonly called the Douglass Lot", until my son CHARLES is of age. "She making no waste of timber, nor cut any, only for the necessary use of the Plantation". Also the use of that portion of my farm I dwell on, with the houses, lands, and improvements adjoining to NICHOLAS LARZELERE, and adjoining the land before mentioned, until my son JESSE is of age. She making no waste. I also give her, in consideration of her bringing up my children and giving them Schooling, until they are fit to be put to trades, the following articles: one bed and furniture, "one bed which the children lyeth on", 2 cows, 2 horses, farming utensils, waggon, horse and chair, tea kettle, and tea ware, linnen wheel, woolen wheel, and a negro boy, and all my library books. "My large Bible I leave in the house for the use of my family, so long as my wife continues in it, and then to my son CHARLES". I also leave her all kitchen utensils. I leave to my daughter ANN a bed, 2 cows, a negro girl, and £20, when she is 18. I leave to my son CHARLES the lot I bought of NICHOLAS LARZELERE, called Douglass Lot, after the death of my wife. With the meadow ground thereto belonging, "And 6 acres of meadow, which was Sweems", lying between Larzeleres land and the upland, except a parcel bounded as follows: West by ~~ROBERT~~ RICHARD HARRIS, south by JOHN ~~JOURNY~~ JOURNEY, east by a deep gully, "and extends down said gully to a white oak tree stump, broken off by the wind, pretty well up, and standing near the place where we cross the gully with the waggons", and then north a straight line to a

125

white wood tree standing near the Harris fence, at the brow of the hill. And he is to pay to my son JOSEPH £100, when of age. I leave to my son JESSE the lot of land and meadow I now live on, with the house and barn; and lies between the land of NICHOLAS LARZELERE and the land given to my son CHARLES. Also the piece of wood land reserved. And he is to pay to my son JOSEPH £100. I order that the wood lot of land where my son JOHN now lives, with the salt meadow thereto belonging, be sold by my executors, and 1/3 of the money to be put at interest for my son JOHN, "and the other 2/3 to my two sons, JAMES and PETER BILLIEW, to be put at interest for them till they are of age". I leave to my grandson, JOHN CORNELL, £10. To my grandson, JOHN MORGAN, £10. All the rest of movable estate to my daughters, "first giving to my daughter FRANCES, wife of AUTER SIMESON, a negro girl SARAH, provided the said AUTER SIMESON pay a bond of £40 to JOHN WATTS, for which I am bound. I leave to my daughter CATHARINE, widow of BARENT CHRISTOPHER, a negro girl, now in her possession. I leave to my daughter ELIZABETH, wife of DAVID LA TOURETTE, a negro girl. {Mentions daughters MARTHA, RACHEL and LEAH, wife of MOSES DEPUE.} My wife is to have the use of a room in my house, and two cows and her fire wood and garden, and fruit, "and two barrels of cider a year". I leave to my son CHARLES a loom and tackling. I leave to my sons, JAMES and PETER BILLIEW, each a gun and a sword. I make my son-in-law, DAVID LATOURETTE, and my friend and kinsman, ~~DANIEL~~ DAVID LAFARGE, and my friend, JOSHUA ~~WILET~~ WRIGHT, executors.

Witnesses, ~~COLIN~~ CORNELIUS COLE, blacksmith, BENJAMIN SEAMAN, BENJAMIN DRAKE. My wife is to have all the grain and cloth for the use of the family. Proved, August 28, 1770.

[Note.-JAMES and PETER BILLIEW were probably stepsons.-W.S.P.]

Liber 27:462   WNYHS VII:383

"In the name of God, Amen. I, **ELIZABETH MOTT**, of Richmond County, widow, being sick. All debts to be paid. I leave to my grandson, RICHBELL MOTT, son of my son RICHARD, deceased, £160, when he is 22. I leave to my granddaughter, ELIZABETH SEAMAN, daughter of my daughter ELIZABETH, my bed and furniture, and my cupboard and my silver shoe buckles. All the rest of my estate, let the same consist of what it may be and where it may be, I leave to my daughter ELIZABETH, wife of BENJAMIN SEAMAN. I make my trusty friend, JOHN MICHEAU, and my grandson, RICHARD SEAMAN, executors."

Dated January 20, 1777. Witnesses, PAUL MICHEAU, Esq., MARY POILLON, widow, BENJAMIN SEAMAN, Jr. Proved, April 2, 1778.
Liber 31:118   WNYHS IX:22

-N-

In the name of God, Amen. I **ELIAS NEAU**, of New York, merchant, being sick...........To ANDREW ECERT and DANIEL MERCHEROW, both of Staten Island........, the ballance due to me from them.

Dated, August 15, 1722. Proved September 17, 1722.
Liber 9:329   WNYHS II:254

CORNELIUS NEFFE. In the name of God, Amen. I, CORNELIUS NEFFE, of Staten Island, yeoman, being very sick. I leave to my wife AICHTE, the sole use and benefit of all estate during her life. I leave to my eldest son, JORAS NEFFE, a cow, before any division is made; I leave to my three youngest daughters, {TRENTIE or} KATHARINE, ~~MARITZE~~ MARITIE, and SARAH, each at the time of their marriage, a good bed and furniture, equal with my other children that are married, and a good suit of apparell answerable to them already married, and each a good cow. After my wife's decease all estate is left to my children JORAS, ~~JOHAN~~ JOHANNES, ARIANTIE, {TRENTIE or} KATHARINE, MARITIE, and SARAH, equally. My eldest son is to have the refusal of my lands if he wishes to buy them. I make my wife executor.

Dated April 27, 1711. Witnesses JOSEPH ARROWSMITH, DIRCK ~~KRUGA~~ KRUZA, OSWALD FOORD. Proved May 1, 1712.

Liber 8:106   WNYHS II:87

In the name of God, Amen, August 31, 1746, I, **RICE NICHOLAS**, of Staten Island, tailor, being very sick. I leave to my wife, LUCENA, all household goods, "and my will is that my dere wife shall have the youse of all my estate". I leave to my son, RICE NICHOLAS, all that money "that is due in nu ingland; the bond is in the hands of Mr. CLAMMEN MINER". The money is to be paid by ELIAS TOMSON, in the town of Westerly. I make my wife executor.

Witnesses, JOHN VANDEVOORT, HENRY ~~LEE~~ LEA TOURETTE, NICHOLAS ~~LARGELEIL~~ LARZELERE. Proved, before WALTER DONGAN, Esq., March 16, 1747/8.

Liber 16:231   WNYHS IV:158

Will of **THOMAS NOBLE**, of New York, merchant. Dated July 27, 1745. Mentions his friend, SUSANNAH, wife of ELIAS BURGER, of Staten Island.

Liber 15:508   WNYHS IV:67

-P-

In the name of God, Amen, November 2, 1760. I, **ABRAHAM PARLIER**, of Richmond County, being very sick. All debts to be paid. I leave to my wife MARY the use of all my estate during her widowhood. If she marry, she is to have the use of one-third, and she is to bring up my children and give them schooling suitable for them, and when of suitable age they are to be put out to trades. The rest of my estate I leave to all my children, ABRAHAM, JOHN, CATHARINE, JACOB, HENRY, BARENT and PETER, my executors to sell land at discretion. I make my son ABRAHAM and my

128

friend JOHN BEDELL executors.

Witnesses, PETER VAN WOGLOM, JOHN GOOLD, JOHN MARSHALL. Proved, December 8, 1760 before BENJAMIN SEAMAN, Surrogate.
Liber 22:286   WNYHS VI:19

CATHERINE PARLEAY, widow of JACOB PARLEAY, Richmond County, New York, to my daughter MARTHA, bedding and curtains; to my son ABRAHAM, bed and bedding, also linen; all my wearing apparel to my daughter; to CATHERINE MARSHALL, daughter of my brother, ABRAHAM MARSHALL, £2; to MARY PARLEAY, daughter of BARNET PARLEAY, £2. All the remainder of my estate to be sold, and the moneys arising to be equally divided between my two children, excepting that ABRAHAM shall receive £30 more than his sister MARTHA. I appoint BENJAMIN LARZELERE and BARNET PARLEAY, executors.

Dated August 12, 1786. Witnesses, JACOB MERSEREAU, DANIEL VAN CLEFE, blacksmith; ABRAHAM SLAGHT, yeoman. Proved, October 12, 1786.
Liber 39:350   WNYHS XIV:93

"In the name of God, Amen. I, **JACOB PARLEE**, of Richmond County, at present in good health. I leave to my wife CATHARINE and my children, ABRAHAM and MARGARET, all my estate. I make my wife and my friend, JOHN BEDELL, executors."

Dated August 19, 1776. Witnesses, BENJAMIN SEAMAN, BENJAMIN SEAMAN, Jr. {and JOHN SEAMAN}. Proved, August 19, 1778.
Liber 32:25   WNYHS IX:46

In the name of God, Amen, March 11, 1748, I, **PETER ~~PARLICA~~ PARLIEA**, of Staten Island, boatman, being very sick. I leave all my estate to my three children, "but if my wife is like for another child, then to my four children". My son PETER is to have £3 more than the rest. My wife MARTHA is to remain in possession during her widowhood *(other children not named)*. I make my wife and HENRY

129

LA TOURETTE, executors.
    Witnesses, SAMUEL HOLMES, JOHN ~~GRANDAIN~~
GRONDAIN. Proved, May 24, 1748.
Liber 16:270   WNYHS IV:171

    In the name of God, Amen.   October 28,
1723. I, **JOHN PERLE**, of Staten Island, being
very sick. I leave to my wife all my estate,
real and personal, during her widowhood.   I
leave to my son JOHN all my carpenter tools.
If it is necessary to pay debts, my wife shall
sell the salt meadow that I bought of JEROME
DESLIN. I leave to my sons, JOHN, PETER, and
ABRAHAM, all my lands and Plantation. I leave
all my movable estate to my six daughters,
ANN, ELIZABETH, MARY, SARAH, ESTHER, and
MARTHA. My sons shall pay to their sisters,
£100. I make my wife and my beloved friend,
JOHN LE COUNTE, executors.
    Witnesses, MARGARET LE COUNTE, CATHARINE
JANDINE, WILLIAM ~~HILLYER~~ TILLYER.   *(not
proved.)*
Unrecorded will   WNYHS XI:90

    In the name of God, Amen, I, **DANIEL
PERRINE**, of the County of Richmond, being
sick. All my movable estate is to be disposed
of and divided among my wife and children. My
wife is to have a share and a half, and my
eldest son is to have 10 shillings more than
the rest *(names of wife and children not
given)*.
    Dated November 13, 1748.   Witnesses,
DANIEL LAKE, BENJAMIN BRITTON, PETER ~~PULLEN~~
POILLON. Proved, December 13, 1748.
Liber 16:371   WNYHS IV:201

    "In the name of God, Amen, April 20,
1777. I, **EDWARD PERINE**, of Richmond County,
farmer, being very sick.   All debts to be
paid. I leave to my wife ANN the use of all
my estate till my youngest child is of age. I
leave to my son JOSEPH all the farm I now live
on, except 6 acres of salt meadow. And he is
to pay to his brother HENRY £450.   I also
leave him my bay mare. To my son HENRY £450

and a colt. I leave to my son EDWARD all that farm or Plantation I purchased of Captain STANTON, and 6 acres of salt meadow out of the farm left to my son JOSEPH, bounding on the rear of the land of LEWIS RYERZ, of the same width, and to extend southeast to make 6 acres. I leave to my four daughters, MARY, SARAH, ANN, and MARGARET, all my money in cash, and due to me, when they are of age or married. All the rest I leave to my wife ANN. I make my brother, HENRY PERINE, and my brother-in-law, RICHARD CONNER, Esq., executors.

Witnesses, ELISHA LAWRENCE, BENJAMIN SEAMAN, PATIENCE ROLPH, GEORGE TAYLOR, Jr. Proved, September 2, 1779. PATIENCE ROLPH was then the wife of CORNELIUS COLE.
Liber 32:121   WNYHS IX:74

In the name of God, Amen, March 10, 1752. I, **PETER PERINE**, of Richmond county, being in good health. "My wife MARY is to have that part of my real estate, as long as she lives, as the Law directs", and the use of the east room in my house, and the bed and furniture for the room, and two cows, and fire wood, and the use of £125. I leave to my son PETER my silver hilted sword. To my son JAMES £40. To my daughter MARY, wife of THOMAS ARROWSMITH, £50. To my daughter MARGARET, wife of JOHN POILLON, £50. These to be paid by my son HENRY. To my daughter SARAH, wife of JOHN ~~SEE~~ LEE, £50. To my daughter DINAH, wife of THOMAS LEE, £50, to be paid by my son EDWARD. I leave to my two youngest sons, HENRY and EDWARD, all my real estate on Staten Island, having formerly disposed of my lands in Middlesex County, East New Jersey, to my sons PETER and WILLIAM. My son HENRY is to have the east part of my farm with the buildings, and he is to pay to my son EDWARD £30 towards building and improvements. I leave to my son HENRY a gun, and a horse and saddle. I leave to my son EDWARD my long gun, and a horse and saddle. I leave to my three grand children, NICHOLAS, ANN, and MARY BRITTON, each £10.

131

All the rest to my children, PETER, WILLIAM,
JAMES, MARY ARROWSMITH, MARGARET POILLON,
SARAH SEE, DINAH LEE, and the children of
DANIEL PERINE. My executors are to sell
personal estate at public vendue, except my
apparell, which I give to my sons PETER,
WILLIAM, and JAMES. I make THOMAS ARROWSMITH,
JOHN POILLON, JOHN LEE, of Somerset, and HENRY
PERINE, executors.

Witnesses, DANIEL STILLWELL, ISAAC ~~MONE~~
MANE, JOHN MESEREAU. Proved, November 29,
1756.

Liber 20:131   WNYHS V:139

JAQUES POILLON. In the name of God,
Amen. Be it known that I, JAQUES POILLON, of
the County of Richmond, Gent., being weak in
body. I leave to my wife ADRIANCE all
personal estate, and the rooms I now live in
in the house, and the produce of the crops now
in the ground, "also her diett". Of the rest
of my personal estate, I leave one half to my
son JAQUES, one quarter to the children of my
daughter MARIA ~~DU CLURE~~ DU CHESNE, deceased,
and one quarter to the children of my daughter
CATHARINE OSBURN. I also give to the children
of my daughter MARIA ~~DU CLURE~~ DU CHESNE £360,
as they come of age. And to the children of
my daughter CATHARINE £150. I leave to my son
JOHN what he is now indebted to me, as also
all that my farm and Plantation which I have
purchased of Colonel ABRAHAM DU PEYSTER,
commonly called Barker's land, except such
part of the meadow as I have given to my son
JAQUES. Also 25 acres of meadow in Richmond
County near Cannons Island. And one half of
my woodland behind the Fresh Kills, being the
north part thereof. I leave to my son JAQUES
all that my farm and Plantation on which I now
live, Also that part of the meadow of the
land called Barkers land, "beginning at the
foot of the ditch nighest to the sea," Also
that meadow along Lachermans land. Reserving
the Chamber in the dwelling house for my wife
during her life. Also all my meadow nigh the
Fresh Kills, near TEUNIS EYTERS land, Also

the lot I purchased of Mr. ANTOINE, commonly called Fastmakers land, Also the south part of my woodland behind the Fresh Kills. I make my wife ADRIANA, and my sons, JOHN and JAQUES, executors.

Dated "at my dwelling house in Richmond County", November 1, 1718. Witnesses, PETER PERINE, OBADIAH HOLMES, ABRAHAM GOUVERNEUR. "I, JAQUES POILLON, do declare on the word of a dying man that I never did seal or execute any bond or obligation to ALEXANDER STEWART, late of Richmond County, deceased, and that at the day of his death I was in no manner of way indebted unto him". Witness my hand November 2, 1718. Proved, June 14, 1720.

Liber 9:180   WNYHS II:220

In the name of God, Amen, September 17, 1732. I, **JAMES POILLON**, of Richmond County, brewer, being very weak in body. "My will is that my dearly beloved wife JUDITH shall remain absolute mistress, and have the sole use and benefit of my estate so long as she remains my widow". I leave to my four sons, PETER, JOHN, ABRAHAM, and JAMES, all my houses, lands and tenements in Richmond County, except as hereafter stated. If either die, his share is to go to the rest. My four sons are to pay to my daughters, viz., CATHARINE, wife of DAVID LATOURETTE, ELIZABETH, ADRIANNA, and JUDITH, £400, when of age. I leave to my son PETER a good riding horse. All the rest of my estate I leave to all my children, viz., JOHN, ABRAHAM, PETER, JAMES, MARY, wife of DANIEL STILLWELL, CATHARINE, wife of DAVID LATOURETTE, ELIZABETH, ADRIANA, and JUDITH. My executors are to sell a certain house and lot in New York, which I have lately bought of WESSELL WESSELLS; and also 20 acres of salt meadow lying at the Fresh Kill by ABRAHAM CANON's point; and 40 acres of wood land lying back or at the rear of JAMES SEGUINE, and JOHN CASSON's plantation. I appoint my wife JUDITH, JOHN LE CONTE and NICHOLAS STILLWELL, executors.

Witnesses, ADRIAN LE FARGE, JACOBUS BEBANT, PAUL MICHAUX. Proved, May 3, 1733.
Liber 12:39 WNYHS III:114

In the name of God, Amen. I, **JAMES POILLON**, of Richmond County, being in a remarkable state of health. My executors to sell these parts of my real and personal estate: my back pasture (so called), containing 36 acres, bounded east, south and west by PETER POILLON, north by the new road (always reserving in the grant a road through the same to the aforesaid new road); Also, a part of my farm bounded on the west side of my farm to begin at the south-east corner of my orchard as the fence now stands and to run in parallel line with PETER POILLON, formerly LAKARMAN, to the Beach, or as far as my lands and meadows extend, and include all the lands and meadows south of my orchard, as also 4 acres of timber land; being part of my new Lands, to be bounded on the north by the land of JAMES SEGUIN and JOHN MORGAN, west by PETER VAN PELT, east by THOMAS TAYLOR, and be equal width each end to make up said quantity, with liberty to pass through my land from the Fresh Kill Road to said premises. They to sell said three tracts at discretion; and all my personal estate, except some particular things herein disposed of. Unto my son JOHN, all my wearing apparel; a horse, bridle and saddle (his choice in such as I leave), my watch, gun, pistols, holsters, and sword; Also, all my lands, meadows and improvements in said County of Richmond (except said three tracts), upon condition that he complys with my will as follows: said lands and meadows to be sold, and of the proceeds my executors to pay all just debts and charges that may occur in settling my estate. The residue to be equally divided between my beloved wife, FRANCES, and my four daughters, MARY, JUDETH, ELIZABETH, and ADAONTIA. The legacy to my wife to be in lieu of dower. Should my son die under age and without lawful issue all my lands given to him are to be sold by my executors, and the proceeds to go to my four daughters in equal shares. I make my trusty friends, CHRISTOPHER BILLOPP, Esquire, RICHARD SEAMAN, and my brother, JOHN POILLON, executors.

Dated February 6, 1778. Witnesses, DANIEL SIMONSON, tailor, JOSEPH McDANIEL, farmer, ISAAC DOTY.

Codicil. March 24, 1783. Whereas, I appointed CHRISTOPHER BILLOPP, Esquire, RICHARD SEAMAN, and my brother, JOHN POILLON, executors of my last will, and as two of them, Esquire BILLOPP and SEAMAN, have lately removed to the City of New York, it may not be convenient for them to assist in settling my estate, I make other two executors, namely: JOHN JOURNEAY, and my nephew, JAMES GUION, both of the County of Richmond, executors, to act with the three others.

Witnesses, HENRY PERINE, JOS. RICKIT, ISAAC DOTY. Proved, July 27, 1783.
Liber 35:278   WNYHS XII:60

In the name of Good, Amen, October 8, ~~1722~~ 1723. I, **JOHN POLYON**, of Staten Island, being sick and weak. I leave to my wife SARAH all my Plantation and lands and meadows during her widowhood, but if she come to marry, then she shall have only the movable estate. After her decease I leave to my two sons JAMES and JOHN all my Plantation, lands and meadows equally, and they are to pay to my daughter MARTHA FOUNTAIN £150, and to my daughter ALICE POLYON £150. I make my wife and my sons JAMES and DANIEL LAKE, executors. *(No witnesses' names recorded.)*

Proved, December 7, 1724.
Liber 10:7   WNYHS II:305

In the name of God, Amen, January 17, 1753, I, **PETER POILLON**, of Richmond County, being at this time in good health. I leave to my wife HILLITIE a bed and furniture and cupboard and Looking Glass, and all the silver ware that I had with her. I leave to my son

PETER all my wearing apparell, saddle, pistol and holsters and my silver hilted sword. I leave to my daughter HILLITIE all the wearing apparell that was her mother's, and a cupboard, a silver snuff box, a silver girdle buckle, and 5 silver tea spoons, all of which were her mother's. My executors are to sell that parcel of salt meadow that I have at the Fresh Kills, and all the wood that I have in a Large Swamp lying near ADRIAN ~~LAFORTS~~ LAFORGE, joining to his land. The rest of my movable estate I leave to my wife and three children, PETER, HILLITIE, and CATHARINE. I leave to my wife HILLITIE the use of my farm until my son PETER is 18, and she is to bring up the children with schooling and other things suitable for them. And she is to pay yearly to my brother, JAMES POILLON, £10, and £3 2s. 6d to my mother yearly. I also give to my wife £200. I leave all my lands and meadows to my son PETER, and he is to pay £200 to his mother and £200 to his sisters, HILLITIE and CATHARINE. My wife is to have the use of two bedrooms lying on the north side of my dwelling house, and her firewood, and two cows and a horse, and apples, peaches, and other fruit. I make my wife and brothers, JOHN POILLON and ABRAHAM POILLON, and my friend, BENJAMIN SEAMAN, executors.

Witnesses, PAUL MERSEREAU, BARENT SLAGHT, RHODA WINANTS. Proved, May 21, 1753.
Liber 18:303 WNYHS IV:435

Page 88. In the name of God, Amen. I, **PETER POILLON**, of Richmond County, being very weak. I leave to my wife MARGERETT my best bed and a cupboard and looking glass, and all other household furniture and other things that was given her by her father, and all the hanging pictures about my house, and all silver spoons and China ware, and my riding chair and sorrel horse branded D, and four cows and £400. And the use of all lands till my eldest son, ABRAHAM, is of eighteen years of age. And my wife is to maintain, educate, and support my three sons, ABRAHAM, JOHN, and

PETER, in decent cloathes and proper education. I leave to my son ABRAHAM all my wearing apparell, and my riding saddle and long gun. I leave to my son JOHN my silver-hilted sword, pistols and holsters, and my carbine with all accoutrements. I leave to my son PETER my silver shoe, knee, and stock buckles, and a pair of gold sleeve buttons. All the rest of personal property to be sold, and all debts paid. My wife is to have charge of all my negroes until my son ABRAHAM is eighteen years old. I leave all my real estate to my three sons, and my executors are to make a just and equal division among them without favor or affection. I make my trusty friend, JOHN MICHEAU, and my two brothers-in-law, PETER REZEAU and WILLIAM LAKE, executors.

Dated October 3, 1780. Witnesses, PAUL MICHEAU, JAMES POILLON, Jr., AMOS ROOK. Proved, January 22, 1781.
Liber 34:88   WNYHS X:30

In the name of God, Amen, "the 31 day of 8ber, 1750." I, **GERRITT POST**, of Staten Island, Gent., being very weak. I leave to my wife FRANCYNTIE, during her life, all my messuages, lands, and tenements, goods and chattels. After her death I give all my lands and messuages where I now dwell unto my two sons, GERRITT and PETER POST, and they are to pay to their brother and their sisters £300, viz., to my son JOHANES, and my daughters, GEESIE, CATHARINE, and RACHEL, and to my two grand children, SARAH and LEAH POST, the daughters of my son, ADRIAN POST, deceased, £150, And my son PETER is to pay to my daughter ANTYE, ~~KLAARTISE~~ KLAARTJE, wife of PETER DE GROOT, JANETTIE, HELENA, and MARITIE, £150. I leave to my son JOHANES, and to my daughters, and my two grand children all that lot of land and tenements situate in Achquechtinock, in Essex County, New Jersey, adjoining the land of HARMAN GERRITTSE. I give to each of my daughters, to whom I have not given one, a milch cow. All the rest of my personal estate to my children and grand

137

children. And whereas I have given to my son JOHANES £25, that amount is to be deducted from his part. I make my wife FRANCYNTIE, and AARON VAN NAME, and DANIEL CORSEN, executors.

Witnesses, ~~GERRIT~~ GUSTAVUS CLAUSON, BENJAMIN ~~KELDY~~ KELSY, THOMAS LISK. It is my will that my son PETER shall be instructed and learn some trade or occupation.

Codicil, March 25, 1756. Whereas in my will I have ordered that my son PETER pay £150 as therein directed, he is discharged from the same.

Witnesses, JOHN LA TOURETTE, PETER VAN PELT, CHRISTOPHER GERBRANTS. Proved, August 13, 1756.

Liber 20:56 WNYHS V:121

In the name of God, Amen, February 23, 1773. I, **ABRAHAM PRALL**, of Staten Island, being in perfect mind. All debts to be paid. I leave to my wife ALEDA the best room in my house, and the best bed and bedstead, and all furniture thereto belonging, and her choice of my negro wenches, and her choice of two cows, with pasture and hay, and the best cupboard and chest, and her firewood brought to her door, and as much as she shall want. And my three sons, BENJAMIN, PETER, and ABRAHAM, shall pay her each £6 yearly. I leave to my 3 sons all my lands and tenements, woodland and meadows. "And they shall each of them separately pay to JOSHUA MERSEREAU, son of my daughter ~~MARIA~~ MARY, £10, when he is of age, and £10 to each of his brothers, ABRAHAM and JOHN MERSEREAU, and £10 to their sister, ~~ALIDA~~ ALLEDE MERSEREAU, to whom I also give a negro wench, when she is of age". I leave the rest of my movable estate to my three sons, and I make my sons, BENJAMIN and ABRAHAM, executors.

Witnesses, DAVID CANNON, ABRAHAM CANNON, AARON VAN NAME. Proved, October 4, 1775, before BENJAMIN SEAMAN.

Liber 30:7 WNYHS VIII:307

In the name of God, Amen. I, **ARENT PRALL**, of Richmond County, being sick and

138

weak. All my house and lands, and moveable estate, are to be sold. I leave to my eldest son, PETER PRALL, £10 in full of all claim as heir-at-law; I having heretofore sufficiently provided for him. I leave to my wife ~~MACKELENOR~~ MADLENOR £4, 10s, and one cow. I leave to my son, ARENT PRALL, my wheelwright tools, also 115 acres of land, situate at Cuckolds Town, in the County of Richmond. I leave to my son, JOHN PRALL, £200, which is intrusted to my son ARENT, and ~~ORECK HOPPER~~ TWARFE/HAFFER/or HEIFER, and my son in law, STOEFEL CHRISTOPHERS, and the interest to be used for him, and his support during his life. If he dies, then it is to go to my children, ARENT, MARY, wife of JOHANES LE COMPT; ~~BORACHE~~ BARNECK, wife of ORECK HOPPER; and FRANCES, wife of CHARLES MORGAN, "and the children of my daughter MATTHEWS". I leave to my daughter SARAH £10, and to her two children, LENOR and MARY, that she had by TICE SWAIM, her first husband, £10 each. To the children of my daughter FRANCES £40; To my daughter MARY, {wife of JOHANNES LE COMPT £60. To my daughter BARNECK,} wife of HOPPER, £60; To my daughter MATTHEW'S children £60. I make my son ARENT, and my son in law, ORECK HOPPER, executors.

Dated October 14, 1721. Witnesses, PHILLIP MERALL, ABRAHAM ~~SHAFFNELL~~ SHAFFWELL, RICHARD MERALL. Proved, November 4, 1725.

[Note. In the above will, the name given here as "ORECK HOPPER", is spelled apparently in so many different ways as to make the true name uncertain. In one place it seems to be "Onke Horbe", in another "Heifer", W.S.P.]

[The Swaim-Tysen Family of Staten Island, NY, Joseph F. Mullane, Lloyd B. Swaim, Marjorie Decker Johnson, 1984, pp. 56-60, presents evidence that the correct name of "Daughter Matthew" was Martha and that she married Johanes Swame whose will is Liber 9: 160, (see II:214/p.165 above). These authors also believe that the name Johannes Le Compt was misread and should be Johannes De Camp. The Prall Family, Richard D. Prall, 1990, p.

23, states that Martha (Prall) Swame had married (2) Stoeffel Christopher who d. 1727 intestate, as he is called 'son-in-law' in the above Prall will. Letters of administration of Christofell Christophers, see WNYHS II:328, /p. 29 above. C.M.H.].
Liber 10:98 WNYHS II:323

In the name of God, Amen. I, **ISAAC PRALL**, of Staten Island, being in perfect health. All debts to be paid. I leave to my wife MARY the interest on £300 yearly, and the furniture of a room, and two feather beds, and the use of two bedrooms, and my negro woman "Hagor", and 2 cows and a horse, and her firewood, "so long as she lives on my farm or lot called No. 5"; Also the pasturing on Lot No. 6. I leave to my son PETER, a negro boy. I leave to my son LEWIS all my farm and Lot No. 6, and ½ of my meadow within the bounds of Woodbridge, New Jersey, "at the Sunken Marsh"; Also a negro boy and a silver cup. "I leave to my son ISAAC all my Farms or Plantation known as Lot No. 5, on Staten Island". And ½ of my salt meadow at Woodbridge, New Jersey, "in Sunken Marsh"; Also a negro boy and silver tankard. All the rest of my estate I leave to my 5 daughters, MARY, ESTHER, CATHARINE, ALTIE, and MARGARET. "But the share of my daughter MARGARET is to be left at interest for her, so long as she remains the wife of JAMES FORREST; but after his death she is to have her part". After the death of my wife I leave the £300 to my daughters. I make BENJAMIN SEAMAN, JOHN MICHEAU, and CHRISTOPHER ~~BILLINGS~~ BILLOPP, executors.

Dated August 15, 1770. Witnesses, JOHN HILLYER, Jr., PAUL MICHEAU, DAVID LA FARGE. Proved, February 7, 1774.
Liber 29:194 WNYHS VIII:208

In the name of God, Amen. I, **PETER PRAAL**, of Richmond County, being in good health. Having by deeds already provided for my sons, JOHANES, AARON, PETER, and CORNELIUS, they are to have none of my present estate, except that JOHANES, my eldest son, shall have a negro woman and my large Dutch Bible. I leave to my son ISAAC all that Plantation which I bought of JOHN CRECHERON and DAVID CONGER CONGAR, in Woodbridge, and where he now dwells. I leave to my son ABRAHAM, all lands and meadows on Staten Island, and he is to pay £500. I leave to my wife ELIZABETH, £200 in lieu of dowry, as by an agreement before marriage, and a room in my house or some other small dwelling house, and she is to have a cow. I leave to my grand daughter ALIDA, daughter of my son AARON, £50. My son ABRAHAM is to pay £250 to his brothers and sisters, JOHANES, AARON, PETER, IRENE ISAAC, CATHARINE, and ANNE. I leave my apparell to my sons, and the rest of my movable estate to all my children. I earnestly recommend my children to live amicably together as brethren and friends. I make my sons PETER and ABRAHAM, executors.

Dated January 8, 1742/3. Witnesses, PETER VAN NAME, MARY WRIGHT, ANDREW WRIGHT. Proved, November 25, 1748.
Liber 16:364   WNYHS IV:199

In the name of God, Amen. The 22nd day of January, 1782. I, **PETER PRALL**, of Staten Island, Richmond County, being sick and weak of body. For the payment of my debts my Executors are to sell the necessary part of my movable estate, and with the same and with what monies I shall have, or be owing to me at my decease, to pay my said debts. My wife ABIGAIL shall have the benefit and income of all my land during her life or widowhood for the maintenance of my children during their minority, but if she die or marry then my land to be sold and the proceeds to be divided amongst my three daughters, MARY, ELIZABETH and ABIGAIL, viz: to ELIZABETH £100 more than to her two sisters, to be paid them as they shall severally arrive at the age of eighteen. My wife to have the furniture of her room for life, but if she marry then it to be sold and divided among my three daughters or the survivors of them. I make my wife and ISAAC PRALL, Executors.

Witnesses, JOHN TOTTEN, JOSEPH TOTTEN (yeoman) ISAAC PRALL. Proved, Richmond County, January 4, 1786.

Liber 38:303   WNYHS XIII:262

Inventory of the estate of **WOLFORT** ~~TRALL~~ **PRALL**. Taken October 9, 1709 by the constable of Richmond County, and 2 appraisers, namely EPHRAIM TAYLOR and JAMES LISKE. (Very small). Total £25. Exhibited, April 8, 1703 before Lord CORNBURY.

Liber 5-6:327   WNYHS I:312

Edward, Viscount Cornbury, Captain-General &c. Whereas, **WOLFERT PRALL**, late of the County of Richmond, planter, lately died intestate. His nephew PETER PRALL, his heir at law, is appointed administrator. October 3, 1702.

Liber 7:32   WNYHS I:344

In the name of God, Amen, I, **THOMAS PRICE**, of Richmond County, May 13, 1760. All my estate to be sold at discretion of executors and all debts paid, and my wife is to have the use of the overplus as long as she lives. {add wife ABIGAIL}. If anything is left, my daughter DILY is to have 5 shillings, and all the rest to my two daughters, HANNAH and SARAH PRICE. {Wife and RICHARD COLE, executors.}

Witnesses, JOHN HILLYER, Esq., WILLIAM HILLYER, and NATHANIEL HILLYER. Proved June 2, 1760.

Liber 22:110   WNYHS V:399

In the name of God, Amen, April 24, 1732. I **JACOB PRYOR**, of Richmond County, house carpenter, being very sick. My wife LEAH shall have power to sell my negro man, and as much goods as may be necessary to pay debts. I leave to my son JOHANES, 5 shillings for his heirship, as heir at law, when he is of age. My wife has power to sell my lot of land which

I now live on, also my tenement or dwelling house. After payment of debts, I leave 2/3 of the remainder, to be divided among my six children, JOHANES, SAMUEL, JACOB, ~~ANDRE~~ ANDREW, PETER and JOHANA, when they are of age. I make my wife executor.

Witnesses, RICHARD COLE, TUNIS BOGART, SIMON BOGART. Proved, April 18, 1733.

Liber 12:19   WNYHS III:109

In the name of God, Amen, September 24, 1751, I, **SAMUEL PRIOR**, of Richmond county, yeoman, being very sick. After payment of all debts, I leave to PETER PRIOR all my wearing apparel. I leave to my brother, JOHN PRIOR, 5 shillings. I leave to my sister HANNAH, and to SAMUEL PRIOR and JAMES PRIOR, each ¼ of the remainder. {Also mentions JACOB PRIOR}. I leave to my friend WINANT WINANTS all my real estate, lands and movables, to sell and dispose of as he shall think proper to pay legacies, "and to put the children out till they come of age." And I make him and ISRAEL DISCHAISON, executors.

Witnesses, JACOB RICKHOW, THOMAS JOHNSON, MATTHEW SHARP. Proved, October 31, 1751.

Liber 18:20   WNYHS IV:362

-R-

In the name of God, Amen. I, **JOHN RAY** of New York, being sick of body. I leave to my daughters MARY and KATHARINE, all my land upon Staten Island, when they are of age........

Dated January 21, 1688, Proved April 10, 1689.

Liber 14A:205   WNYHS II:405

I, **MARY RAY** of New York, spinster, being not well in body, do make this my last will. I leave to my sister WINIFREDE all my wearing apparel, I leave all the rest of my estate to my sister KATHARINE ~~PORTER~~ POTTER, and make her executor.

Dated December ~~4~~ 9, 1701. Witnesses,

JOHN BASFORD, ELISHA PARKER, ISAAC GOVERNEUR.
Liber 14A:405   WNYHS II:405

"Whereas **PAULUS** ~~RICHARDS~~ **REGRENIER**, late
of Staten Island, dyed. and in his will
bequeathed the greatest part of his estate to
PAULUS RICHARDS of this city, merchant, friend
and countryman, and there not being any of his
near relatives in this country", upon his
petition, the said PAULUS RICHARDS is made
administrator November 8, 1676.
Liber 1-2:151   WNYHS I:40

PETER REZEAU. In the name of God, Amen.
I, PETER REZEAU, of the County of Richmond,
mason, being sick and weak, I leave to my
dearly beloved wife DORCAS, all my estate of
houses and lands, and household goods, during
her widowhood, or until my eldest son PETER,
comes of age. I leave to my sons PETER,
JACOB, and JAMES, all my estate and Plantation, and all tenements thereto belonging, to
be equally divided between them from front to
the rear. I leave to my son PETER, a pin and
a sword, "and a little horse which he useth to
ride". I make my wife DORCAS, and JOHN
PORTER, and JOHN LE CONTE, executors.
Dated September 14, 1723. Witnesses,
CHARLES TAYLOR, LEWIS DU BOIS, Jr., LEWIS
GITONE, S. BEVINS. Proved, October 8, 1723.
Liber 9:410   WNYHS II:274

In the name of God, Amen, the 29 of
September, 1733. I, **PETER REZEAU**, of Richmond
County, being very sick. After the payments
of debts, all lands, tenements, and grounds
are to be equally divided between my brothers,
JACOB and JAMES REZEAU, and they are to pay to
my sister SUSANAH, £20. I make JOHN LE COUNT
and JACOB REZEAU, executors.
Witnesses, GEORGE PERSONETT, PETER RESOE,
DE BERRIS, LEWIS DUBOIS, Jr. Proved, November
19, 1733, before WALTER DONGAN, Esq.
Liber 12:107   WNYHS III:130

RINIER REZEAU. In the name of God, Amen.

February 18, 1719. I, RINIER REZEAU, of the County of Richmond, mason. I leave to my son PETER one half of all my Plantation situated at the Fresh Kills. All the rest I leave to my daughters, ANN ~~PORTER~~ PARLER/PARLIER and MARY REZEAU. I leave my daughter MARY £20 and all that belongeth to her, "that is to say, bed, furniture, chest, and several other things." I leave to my {grand}children, JOHN, ISAAC, PETER, SUSANAH, ELIZABETH and MARIAN BLANCHER, each 20 shillings. To my grand daughter, HESTER BILYOU, 20 shillings. The rest of my movable estate to my children, PETER, ANN ~~PORTER~~ PARLER/PARLIER and MARY, and I make them executors.

Witnesses, ELIZABETH HOOPER, ISAAC CASPER, CHARLES ~~TYLER~~ TAYLOR.

WILLIAM BURNET, Esq., Captain-General and Governor in Chief of the Province of New York and New Jersey, to all, etc., know ye that at New York, the 3d day of October, 1720, the last will of RINIER REZEAU was proved, etc.
Liber 9:207   WNYHS II:225

Will of **MARY RICKETTS**, of New York, widow. To RICHARD WALTON, of Staten Island, £25. Calls JACOB and WILLIAM WALTON, of New York, merchants, kinsmen. Her maiden name was WALTON. Dated May 16, 1740.
Liber 14:344   WNYHS III:379

WILLIAM RICKETTS, Gent. late of Island of Jamaica, but now of New York, mentions in will his farm on Staten Island which he left to his daughter ELIZABETH RICKETTS. 1734.
Liber 12:410   WNYHS III:188

In the name of God Amen, September 11, 1770. I, **JOSEPH RIDGWAY**, of Richmond County, "having at this time my usual senses". I leave to my wife ~~MARGARET~~ MARY £100. I leave to each of my daughters £100 and all my plate and household goods. I leave to my oldest son THOMAS £10, "and the Books entitled 'Thomas Chaukley' and 'Thomas ~~Morey~~ Sorey'", and my Billsted chest. I leave to my son JOSEPH the

145

book entitled "Josephus", and my watch and my red chest in which my papers are kept. I leave to my two sons, THOMAS and JOSEPH, all my real estate which I have in Richmond County or elsewhere, and all the rest of my movable estate, and they are to pay the legacies. If either son die, one-half of his part is to go to the survivor, and one-half to all his sisters [not named]. I make BENJAMIN SEAMAN, Esq., ABRAHAM JONES, and RICHARD LAWRENCE, ship carpenter, executors.

Witnesses, JOHN HILLYER, Jr., RICHARD ~~CONOVER~~ CONNER, ADRIAN BANCKER, Jr. Proved, March 8, 1771.
Liber 27:565   WNYHS VII:412

Whereas **WILLIAM RODNEY** late of this city, Gentleman and Surveyor of Customs, being bound for this place from the island of Nevis, dyed on board a certain vessell named "Lovell" in the Sound near unto New Haven, and leaving no will in writing. Yet as a nuncupative will did declare that he left the care of his concerns in these parts to Captain JOHN FOWLER of Staten Island. Upon application Letters of Administration were granted to him January -, 1678.
Liber 1-2:228   WNYHS I:56

"In the name of God, Amen,. I, **JOSEPH ROLPH**, of Richmond County, Esquire, being in perfect health, May 10, 1764. My executors are to sell enough personal property to pay debts and discharge what may remain unpaid of the sums of money charged by my father-in-law, HENDRICK ~~KRAESSER~~ KROESEN, on the lands devised by him to his daughter NEALTIE. I leave to my son LAWRENCE the land I bought of Mr. DONGAN, lying on the south side of the mill brook, excepting the mill lately erected and the stream, reserving for the mill the privilege of digging and damming where necessary, and as much land as may be necessary for a log yard and for a road to said mill; And he shall pay to his sisters, MARY and ANN, £200. I also leave to my son

146

LAWRENCE a sufficient road from the northeast part of said land, crossing the mill brook where it is now used, and from thence northeast to the Clove road; Also four acres of salt meadow which I bought of FREDERICK BURGER, together with a right which I purchased of Colonel DONGAN for four acres to be taken up where most convenient. I leave to my son ABRAHAM all those lands and tenements on the north side of Staten Island at present in my possession; Also those several pieces of meadow lately devised by HENDRICK ~~KRAESSER~~ KROESEN to his daughter NEALTIE. But his mother NEALTJE is to enjoy the same for life. And he shall pay to his sisters, CORNELIA and ELIZABETH, £400. My old wench LYDIA is to have a good support for life. I leave to my son ABRAHAM my silver tankard, and the rest of my personal estate to my four daughters, MARY, ANN, CORNELIA, and ELIZABETH. I make my friends, DAVID MERSEREAU and JOSHUA MERSEREAU, Esquires, executors.

Witnesses, RICHARD LAWRENCE, DANIEL SALTER, HANKEY ELLISS.

Codicil, October 26, 1765. "My son ABRAHAM has power to sell so much wood land as will raise £400, to be paid to my two daughters. I leave to my sons, LAWRENCE and ABRAHAM, all my reserved rights in my saw mill, and six acres of land on the north side of the mill brook."

Witnesses, RICHARD LAWRENCE, shipwright, WILLIAM FRASER, ~~LAWRENCE MURRAY~~ MARY LAWRENCE and MARY LAWRENCE, Jr. Proved, October 6, 1777.

Liber 31:80   WNYHS IX:15

In the name of God, Amen. I, **LAWRENCE ROOME**, of Richmond County, N.Y., being very sick and weak. My will is that all my estate be sold within six weeks of my decease. To ELIZABETH PARKER, wife of Dr. BENJAMIN PARKER, £25 . My servant CATHERINE to be maintained for life. My negro man MICHAEL shall be free three months after my decease, provided he bring to my executors a sum sufficient in case

147

of casualities or old age. Rest of estate to
my daughter ANN, and my grandchildren,
LAWRANCE, CORNELIUS and MARY MERSEREAU,
equally divided, to be paid ANN at her return
to this Island, and to grandchildren as each
comes of age; but if ANN do not return before
youngest grandchild is of age, or if she die a
minor then estate to be divided between
surviving grandchildren.

Executors, friends, CORNELIUS CORSEN,
Esq., Dr. BENJAMIN PARKER and ARIS RYERSZ.

Dated August 23, 1785. Witnesses,
CORNELIUS VAN BOSKERK, yeoman; MARY PARKER and
JOHN BUTLER, Mason, of Richmond County.
Proved, August 31, 1785, Richmond County.
Confirmed, September 5, 1785, New York.
Liber 38:147   WNYHS XIII:194

In the name of God, Amen. February 11,
1728. I, **ALBERT RYCKMAN**, of Richmond County,
currier, being sick. I make my wife
CATERNICHIE, and my father, JOHN RYCKMAN,
GERRITT CHRISTOPHER, and PHILIP KEIZEAN,
executors. All estate to be sold. *(Will here
illegible and torn)*. I leave all the rest to
my wife.

Witnesses, LOUIS DUBOIS, Jr., ADAM MOTT,
-- -- *(illegible)*. Proved, August 30, 1729.
Unrecorded will   WNYHS XI:159

"In the name of God, Amen. I, **ADRIAN
RYERSE**, of Richmond County, farmer, being in
perfect health, February 16, 1773. I leave to
my wife ESTHER the use of one-third of all my
estate during her life, and all the rest to my
three sons, GOZEN, LEWIS, and AURIS, only
GOZEN is to have £50 of New York money more
than the rest. And they are to pay to their
sister FAMETYE £150 per annum for three years,
and they are also to support her for one year
after my decease. I make my three sons,
executors."

Witnesses, JOHANES SIMONSON, CORNELIUS
CORTELYOU, JOANA SIMONSON. Proved, February
22, 1780.
Liber 32:196   WNYHS IX:93

In the name of God, Amen, May 15, 1745. I, **CHRISTOPHEL SCHARS**, of Gowanus, in the town of Brookland, in Kings County, Island of Nassau, being at present very well. After payment of debts and funeral charges, I leave to my loving cousins, TEUNIS VAN PELT, ALEXANDER VAN PELT, PETER VAN PELT, JOHANES VAN PELT, JACOMINTIE, wife of SAMUEL BERRIE and GRIETIE, wife of JACOB BERGEN of Staten Island, all my estate, both real and personal, in Brookland, and all my real estate in Neversink, in East New Jersey. I make my cousins PETER VAN PELT and JOHANES VAN PELT, executors.

Witnesses, WILLIAM HOOGLAND, JOHANES LOTT, ABRAHAM LOTT. Proved December 22, 1755. Liber 19:343   WNYHS V:86

Inventory of the estate of **JOHN** ~~SHEDINE~~ **SHADINE**, of Richmond County. Appraised by JOHN STILLWELL and ALEXANDER STEWART, public appraisers. May 17, ~~1706~~ 1708. 7 head young cattle, £7; 1 waggon, £2; negro man and 1 Indian man, £60; 4 hives of bees, £1. Exhibited before Lord CORNBURY. October 27, 1708 by MARY ~~SHEDINE~~ SHADINE, widow. Liber 5-6:478   WNYHS I:330

In the name of God, Amen, May 6, 1747, I, **AERT SIMONSON**, of Staten Island, husbandman, being very sick. I leave to my wife MARGARET the use of all lands, houses, and tenements in Richmond County, until my son ISAAC is 21. Then I leave all my said lands to my sons, SIMON, HANS, ARTHUR, CHRISTOPHEL, DANIEL, BARENT, CORNELIUS, and ISAAC. I leave to my son SIMON 20 shillings before any division. I leave to my daughters, CATHARINE, wife of JOHANES HUISMAN, and ANNA, wife of HENRY COCHERON, £120. I leave to my wife my Dutch Bible and brass kettle. All the rest to my wife and sons. I make my sons CHRISTOPHEL and DANIEL, executors.

Witnesses, PETER ~~DOLER~~ DECKER, JOHN

CROCHERON, DANIEL ~~CORSON~~ CORSEN. Proved, March 5, 1753.

[*In 1959, Elmer Garfield Van Name obtained a facsimile of the original will of AERT SIMONSON which states "Item I give & bequeath to my Daughter CATHARINE, WYNTIE the wife of JOHANNES HUISMAN, & ANNA the wife of HENRY CROCHERON, the sum of One Hundred & twenty Pounds curr^t money of New York, to be paid them out of my Estate by my Executors herein after named, before such Division be made as before mentioned in equal Proportions, Share & Share alike, that is to say, Forty Pounds to Each, to them their Heirs & Assigns forever". The Simonson Families of Staten Island, New York, (1959), page 7. This proves that AERT SIMONSON had three daughters, and not two, as shown in the above NYHS IV:424 abstract. C.M.H.]*

Liber 18:242   WNYHS IV:424

"In the name of God, Amen, April 25, 1777. I, **FREDERICK SIMONSON**, of Richmond County. I leave to my wife HELITYA all the estate I had with her, including negroes, Horses, cattle, etc., and £100. I leave to my eldest brother, SIMON SIMONSON, £5. To his daughter, ANN MacLEAN, £50. To CATHARINE, daughter of JOHN BEDELL, Jr., £20. To FREDERICK, son of JAMES SEGUIN, £20. All the rest, real and personal, to my brother, JEREMIAH SIMONSON, and he is to pay all debts, and I make him and my nephew, GOERSZ (?) SIMONSON, and my trusty friend, HARMANUS GARRISON, executors."

Witnesses, ISAAC SIMONSON, ~~HELEKE~~ HELECHE SIMONSON, BENJAMIN SEAMAN. Proved, June 12, 1777.

Liber 31:64   WNYHS IX:13

In the name of God, Amen. The fourth day of April, 1781. I, **JEREMIAH SIMONSON**, of the County of Richmond, and Colony of New York, will and direct that all my just debts and funeral charges shall be paid in such manner as shall be hereafter directed. I leave to my nephew, ISAAC SIMONSON, the son of my brother ISAAC, deceased, all my land and meadows with houses and all the improvements thereon which was "separated and divided" to me in the division between me and my brother FREDERICK, deceased, with my waggon, two horses, a plow, two harrows, all the "geers" and all my farming utensils, he paying and discharging all my just debts which I do owe on my own account, and exclusive of any debts of my aforesaid brother, and my funeral charges. Whereas my brother FREDERICK by his last will and testament duly executed, bearing date, the 25 April, 1777, did give and devise to me all his plantation lands, meadows, mesuages and ferry, subjecting the same to the payment of his just debts, funeral charges and certain legacies specified in said will, as by said will may more fully appear. My will is that all that part of my estate willed to me by my brother, as aforesaid, shall be sold by my executors and monies arising therefrom, and all my other moveable estate not before disposed of, I give and dispose of in the following manner, if any there be after paying the debts and legacies as aforesaid, to wit: One fourth part thereof to the children of my brother SIMON, deceased; one fourth part to my nephew, GOZEN SIMONSON; one fourth part to the children of my brother JEHONAS, deceased; the remaining fourth part to the children of my brother RAM, deceased. I make my friend, HAREMONAS GARRISON, my nephew, GOZEN SIMONSON, and my nephew, JEHONAS SIMONSON, the son of my brother SIMON, executors.

Witnesses, BENJAMIN SEAMAN, Surrogate, CORNELIUS CORSON, yeoman, JOSEPH LAKE, yeoman. Proved, April 16, 1781.
Liber 34:150   WNYHS X:62

"In the name of God, Amen. I, **JOHANNES SIMONSON**, of New Dorp, on Staten Island, yeoman, being weak and sick. I leave to my son JOHANES £200 when he is 21, the interest being applied to his bringing up. If he dies, it is to go to my wife CATHARINA. I leave to

my wife the house where I now live, with all lands, negroes, live stock, and household furniture, until my son JOHANES is of age, and then the whole to be sold, and the money to be divided among my wife and my son JOHANES, and the heirs of my daughter ANN and the heirs of my daughter ~~GERTRYE~~ GERTJE SIMONSON, and my daughters, ~~ALLIE~~ ALTJE, MARY, and ZENA ~~(or TENA?)~~, and my son ~~Hendrick~~ JOHANNES. I leave to my son JOHANES my silver Tankard. To my grandson, JOHN CRUSE, my silver watch. To my granddaughter, ANN ~~MARTIN~~ MARTINO, my negro wench. I make CORNELIUS VAN WAGENEN, AARON CORTELYOU, and DANIEL LAKE, Jr., son of DANIEL LAKE, Esq., executors."
March 15, 1777. Witnesses, SAMUEL THURSTON, CHRISTIAN JACOBSON, ANN LAKE. Proved, March 24, 1777.
Liber 31:28   WNYHS IX:7

In the name of God, Amen. The sixth day of August, 1776, I, **SIMON SIMONSON**, of the County of Richmond, being weak and in a low state of health. All my just debts and funeral charges to be paid. I leave to my eldest son, ISAAC, four acres of land and houses and barns beginning at the south-east corner of my land; Also, two acres of woodland at the south end of my land. Unto my three sons, namely: ISAAC, JOHN, and JEREMIAH. the remainder of my lands and salt meadows in equal shares; they paying to my daughter ANN, £150; each to pay £50. Should ISAAC die without issue, then the land devised to him is to go to my two other sons and daughter equally. My moveable estate to be equally divided amongst my four children. My son ISAAC's part to be at the south-east of my lot adjoining to the four acre lot to him before given; my son JEREMIAH's part to be at the north-west side of my lot fronting on the water; my son JOHN's part at the south-west end of my land at the Reer, and running across from fence to fence; ISAAC's part to have four acres of swamp and fresh meadow at the south side of the ditch. If the swamp or meadow shall fall in JEREMIAH's division, ISAAC must give up his land for meadow. I make my son ISAAC, my brother JEREMIAH SIMONSON, and GOYEN SIMONSON, executors.

Witnesses, JOHN TYSEN, farmer, THOMAS MILLER, THOMAS KINGSLY. Proved, February 25, 1783.

Liber 35:211   WNYHS XII:30

In the name of God, Amen, September 5, 1713. I, **ALEXANDER SIMSON**, of Staten Island, husbandman. I leave to my wife MARTHA the use of one-third of all lands and estate, and mill "as shall be appraised by two or three honest men". I leave to my son JOHN two-thirds of the remainder and one third to my daughter SARAH. I make my wife executor.

Witnesses, ABRAHAM COLE, HENRY ~~BARRY~~ BERRY, JOHN ~~MORGEN~~ MARGIN. Proved, September 28, 1721.

Liber 9:260   WNYHS II:240

SLAGHT includes SLEAGHT, SLEGHT

BARENT SLEAGHT. In the name of God, Amen, the 18 August, 1710. I, BARENT SLEAGHT, of Staten Island, yeoman, being very sick. I leave to my wife HELLITIE all estate during life, "but when it doth please God to call my wife out of this world," then my whole estate to my children, HENRY, BARENT, JOHN, CORNELIUS and CHRISTINA. And my eldest son HENRY shall have £5 above the rest.

Witnesses, ISAAC CORBET, REBECCA COLE, ABRAHAM COLE. Proved, September 28, 1712, and Letters of administration, with will annexed, granted to wife HILLITIE.

Liber 8:137   WNYHS II:92

In the name of God, Amen. I, **BARENT SLAGHT**, of Staten Island, being sick. I direct all debts to be paid. I leave to my nephew, HENRY PERINE, my desk. I leave to my niece, SUSANAH PERINE, wife of said HENRY PERINE, my bed, with its furniture. To HENRY PERINE, son of said HENRY, I leave "my gum

153

chest". To EDWARD PERINE, son of HENRY, my saddles and bridles. To my friend, ABRAHAM BRITTAIN, son of NATHANIEL BRITTAIN, "a gum chest, and my reddish broad cloth coat, and a striped vest, silk and cotton". I leave to my brother, JOHN ~~SLEGHT~~ SLAGHT, all the rest of my wearing apparell and a bond I have against him. All the rest of my estate I leave to SUSANAH PERINE, ABRAHAM COLE, ~~COLES~~ CORNELIUS COLE, STEPHEN COLE, JACOB COLE, ~~DANIEL~~ DAVID COLE, MARY, wife of WILLIAM LAKERMAN, all children of my brother, ABRAHAM COLE, deceased, and to CHRISTIAN, wife of HEZEKIAH WRIGHT, Esq., and to CATHARINE, wife of JAMES ~~LEQUIN~~ SEQUIN, and my nephew, PETER COLE, son of my brother, ISAAC COLE, deceased. I make PAUL MICHEAU, executor.

Dated October 26, 1772. Witnesses, HEZEKIAH WRIGHT, JACOB ~~RICKHAW~~ RICKHOW, JOHN SIMONSON. Proved, January 17, 1774.
Liber 29:50   WNYHS VIII:159

In the name of God, Amen. The 27th day of November, 1781. I, **BARNT SLEIGHT**, of the County of Richmond, yeoman, being at this time very weak and low in body, but of sound mind. All my just debts and funeral charges to be paid. I leave to ELIZABETH, my beloved wife, all my lands and all my stock of horses and cattle that is on my farm and my farmer's utensils and everything that belongs to me, so long as she remains my widow. If my wife marry then my three sons, HENRY, JACOB and BARNT, should divide my estate equally between them, excepting HENRY to have £5 more, and they to pay unto my wife £40 instead of her Right of Dower. My three sons each to have a negro boy; but not to be in their possession while my wife remains my widow. I make ELIZABETH, my wife, and my son HENRY, and my brother-in-law, JAMES SEGUINE, all of the County of Richmond, executors.

Witnesses, JOSHUA WRIGHT, yeoman, JOHN COLE, DANIEL PEATMAN, yeoman. Proved, February 21, 1782.
Liber 34:438   WNYHS X:197

In the name of God, Amen, May 26, 1757. I, **HENDRICK SLEGHT**, of Richmond County, being weak in body. I order all debts and funeral charges to be paid. I leave to my wife CATHARINE, the use of all estate so long as she remains my widow, If she marries, she is to have £60, and bed and furniture, and a negro girl, and she is to remove off from my estate. I leave to my son and heir, BARENT SLEGHT, the lot of land and the meadow thereto belonging where I now live, and he is to pay to his three sisters £200. I leave to my son JOHN the lot of land he now lives upon, and 9½ acres of salt meadow, with the apurtenances, and he is to pay to his sisters £100. I leave to my 3 daughters, MARY, wife of ABRAHAM ~~PORTIER~~ PARLIER, HELETYE, widow of PETER POILLON, and CATHARINE, wife of JAMES ~~LUEQUEER~~ SEGUIN, each £100, to be paid by their brothers. All the rest of my estate I leave ½ to my sons and ½ to my daughters. I make my son BARENT, and my two trusty friends, JOHN BEDELL and BENJAMIN SEAMAN, both of Richmond County, executors.

Witnesses, JOHN ~~GRANDAIN~~ GRONDAIN, JOSEPH ~~BONTILL~~ BEDELL, JOHN SEQUIN. Proved, May 10, 1758, in New York, before JOHN GODBY, Esq. Liber 21:8 WNYHS V:231

In the name of God, Amen. I, **SAMUEL SMITH**, of the County of Richmond, on Staten Island, yeoman, will and positively order all debts to be paid, and give to my well-beloved wife, ELIZABETH SMITH, my sons, SAMUEL ISAAC SMITH and GILBERT SMITH, all my estate. And as to the place whereon I now live at ye Morning Star on the North side of Staten Island is on redemption of mortgage, it shall be sold and the price equally divided amongst them also. I reserve for my loving wife out of the Movables towards her part of the same, two feather beds and the appurtenances, two cows, one looking- glass and ten silver spoons which shall not be sold. I make my wife executrix, and JOHN SIMONSON, of the north side of Staten Island, and WILLIAM TALMAN, of

Queens County, Nassau Island, executors. I do also (since the above) order that the estate whereon I live shall not be sold, but shall be left for my wife and children for their maintenance and learning, and to put them out to Trades, and also to be further kept till the said Redemption is paid, or they see a prospect of selling it advantageously. Also that the cows, two beds, be valued to the full worth and to be deducted out of the estate toward her part of the same. I order the ten spoons to be valued and kept for my two sons and also the estate on Long Island that is between me and my two brothers, GILBERT SMITH and TALMAN SMITH, my part to be sold and proceeds put at interest for the benefit of my said sons, and when my oldest son comes to age the money to be divided and the said son to receive his part and the younger one part, to be kept on interest till he comes to age, and then to be given to him. If either of them die before he comes to age his part of the estate to be given to his brother, and if they both die before they come to age their estate to fall to my brother TALMAN SMITH'S children, to be divided among them. If my said widow shall die before my children come to age, her part of said estate to be divided between them. I do also order my negro woman to be sold as my executors shall see most profitable for my heirs, by private sale or by vendue with the rest of the moveables, and the provisions that shall be in the house at my decease shall be kept for the use of my family.

Dated January 22, 1781, and in the twenty-first year of His Majesty's reign. Witnesses, GARRET ELLESS (ELLIS), yeoman, GARET POST, Jr., JAMES PRITCHARD (schoolmaster). Proved, March 30, 1781.
Liber 34:127   WNYHS X:49

In the name of God, Amen. I, **ABRAHAM SPEARS**, of Staten Island, give to my son ABRAHAM SPEARS my silver watch and my gold seal ring. To my wife, ANNA SPEARS, £25 to be paid her upon demand; also the whole of her effects that she brought with her into my house and all the "Difficiencys" of the same shall be justly made up to her, that being an agreement made between us before our marriage was instituted; also the rest of my whole real and personal estate I do bequeath amongst all my children, share and share alike, that is ABRAHAM, JOHN, HENDRICK, GITTY and MONOS, and CLOSON, with this Proviso that MONOS, CLOSON and HENDRICK to be maintained and educated out of my estate till they be fit to go to their trades or occupations, and all my debts and funeral expenses paid, then to be divided as above said. I make my son-in-law, DANL. CORSON and my sons ABRAHAM and JOHN SPEARS, executors, and overseers of this will to take and perform or see the same perform'd according to my true intent and meaning.

Dated October 17, 1780. Witnesses, DANIEL SALTER, yeoman, MOSES CLENDENNEY, blacksmith, WILLIAM EVAN HUGHS. Proved, March 30, 1781.

Liber 34:129 WNYHS X:51

In the name of God, Amen, November 13, 1745. I, **JACOB SPRAGG**, of Richmond county, victular, being very sick. I leave to my son JOSEPH, a certain tract of land which I bought of JOHN MUSSURULL (MESSEROLE?) containing 50 acres; Also a negro boy. All the rest of my real estate to my wife, and after her death or marriage to my son JOSEPH, and he is to pay to the rest of my children, viz., MARY, ABIGAIL, SARAH, MARTHA, JOHANNA, and PHEBE, £200. All my movable estate I leave to my wife and daughters. I make my wife DOROTHY and JOHN LE CONTE, Esq., executors.

Witnesses, NICHOLAS LAZALERE, NATHANIEL BRITTON, DANIEL STILLWELL. Proved, before WALTER DONGAN, Esq., March 18, 1745.

Liber 15:552 WNYHS IV:74

In the name of God, Amen. February 24, 1735/6. I, **JOHN STAATS**, of Richmond County, Gent., being very sick, I leave to my wife

CATHARINE all my estate, real and personal, during her natural life. After her death, I leave to my eldest daughter, MARIA, £50, before any division. I leave to my grand-son, JOHANES BREESTEDE, son of my daughter CATHARINE, deceased, my weaving-loom and my gun, and a young horse, and all my edge-tools. "My eldest daughter MARIA is to have the privilege to dwell in the house where I now dwell, with all reasonable comfort and privileges therein, and a room in the house so long as she lives". I leave all my real estate which I have on the north side of Richmond County, and all farming implements to my said grand-son, JOHANES BREESTEDE, and he is to pay £83, 6s.8d to each of my daughters, *viz*.: MARIA, CORNELIA, wife of JOHN VECHTE, ANNE, wife of Rev. CORNELIUS {VAN} SANTVOORD, JANETTIE, wife of DEWRY WOGLOM, REBECCA, wife of JACOB BACKHER. I make my wife CATHARINE and my brother-in-law CHRISTIAN CORSEN, Esq., executors.

Witnesses, JOHN ~~DUPUI~~ DUPUYS, JACOB CORSING, TEUNIS VAN PELT. Proved before WALTER DONGAN, Esq., June 18, 1737.
Liber 13:76   WNYHS III:223

In the name of God, Amen. I, **JEREMIAH STANTON**, of Richmond County, Gent., being in good health, "but reflecting on the many Casusalties to which Life is exposed". I leave to my wife, LOUISA TERESIA STANTON, ¼ of all my estate, real and personal. I leave to my wife during the non age of my children the use of all the rest of my estate for her support and that of my children. I leave to my son, GEORGE AUGUSTUS STANTON, and to my two daughters, DINAH MARIA STANTON and LOUISA STANTON, 3/4 of all my estate. I make my wife and my brother, JOHN STANTON, Captain in the Royal Navy, and my friend, GEORGE HARRISON, of New York, Gent., executors.

Dated October 3, 1767. Witnesses, PETER MARQUIS DE CONTY, Gent., JAMES LEADBEATER, RICHARD HARRISON, attorney at law.

Codicil. Whereas I devised to my

children, GEORGE AUGUSTUS, DINAH MARIA, and LOUISA, 3/4 of all my estate, And since making my will I have had another son born, named WILLIAM EDWARD STANTON, He is to have an equal share.

Dated June 19, 1769. Witnesses, MORLEY HARRISON, JAMES ~~LEADBEATER~~ LEADBETTER, RICHARD HARRISON. Proved, October 14, 1771.
Liber 28:98   WNYHS VII:451

Inventory of estate of **CORNELIUS STEENWYCK** by order of Mayor's Court, July 20, 1686... One farm on Staten Island at Smoakers Point, formerly of GEORGE LOCKHART, and now in tenure of RICHARD TATTERSHALL, £125....
Liber 19A:138   WNYHS II:444

In the name of God, Amen. I, **ALEXANDER STEWART**, of Richmond County, being sick. I leave to my son ALEXANDER, all the land where I now live with all housing, and £50 when he is of age. I leave to my daughter CATHARINE, the sum of £200 when she is 18 or married. I make my wife CATHARINE executor with power to sell, with the advice of JOHN JOHNSTON, DANIEL LAKE, and JOHN STILLWELL.

Dated February 11, 1716/17. Witnesses, LAMBERT GARRISON, HANS CHRISTOPHER, DUNCAN OLPHERTS. Proved, July 26, 1717.
Unrecorded will   WNYHS XI:35

In the name of God, Amen, February 14, 1760. I, **DANIEL STILLWELL**, of Richmond County, being sick. I leave to my wife CATHARINE the use of all my estate until my son ABRAHAM is of age, if she remains my widow. Also £100. I leave to my son and heir RICHARD STILLWELL, that part of my farm or Plantation which lyes below the road that leads from the Smoking Point to the Fresh Kill lands and meadow (except 3 acres of salt meadow, which I purchased of JOHN BROWN), and 5 acres of woodland lying next to the land of TUNIS VAN PELT, and he is to pay to his brother DANIEL £170. I leave to my son, NICHOLAS STILLWELL, all that part of my farm

159

that lies above or at the south side of the above-mentioned road (except 5 acres given to his brother RICHARD), and 3 acres of salt meadow which I purchased of JOHN BROWN, and he is to pay to his brother ABRAHAM £170. I leave to my daughter CATHARINE £100 and a negro girl. To my daughter HESTER £100 and a negro girl, and the same to my daughter MARY. The rest of my estate I leave to all my children. If my wife should marry before my son ABRAHAM is 21 she shall have her legacy of £100, and remove off from my estate. My executors may sell land to pay legacies. I make my wife and father-in-law, NICHOLAS LARZELEAR, and my son RICHARD executors.

Witnesses, BENJAMIN SEAMAN, SAXTON PARMAR, Sr., JOSEPH VAN PELT. {Proved December 10, 1760.}

Liber 22:290   WNYHS VI:20

August the 16 day, 1724. "I, **JOHN STILLWELL**, being in perfect memory and senses, Blessed be God". I leave to my wife my dwelling house in which I now live, and the lot on which it stands, during her life, and then to my two sons RICHARD and THOMAS, and I leave to them all my land in the County of Richmond. I leave to my son JOHN all my Plantation called Garratts Hill in the township of Middletown in New Jersey, and all my land lying near the said Plantation, with the Poplar Lots, and ½ of my meadows in said township. I leave to my sons JOSEPH and DANIEL all my land lying at a place called Parrassye in said township, and one house lot and orchard in Middletown, and the other ½ of my meadows in said township, and my son JOSEPH is to have his choice in the division. And I give my rights in all other lands in New Jersey to my sons JOHN, JOSEPH, and DANIEL. I give to my granddaughter, REBECCA SALTER, £5. To my daughter MARY STILLWELL, £80. I leave to my wife REBECCA, 1/3 of all the rest of my movable estate, and the other 2/3 to my 8 children above named. I appoint my wife and my brother RICHARD STILLWELL, and my two sons,

JOHN and RICHARD, executors, and Trustees for my three youngest children.

Witnesses, THOMAS WALTON, ~~MARTHA~~ MATTHEW RUE, RICHARD WALTON. Proved, January 17, 1725/6.

Liber 10:137   WNYHS II:329

NICHOLAS STILLWELL, Staten Island, "Husband-man", "being weak and sicke", leaves to youngest son JEREMIAH an iron gray mare. Leaves to "well beloved and affectionate wife ANNE", all lands, houses and estate and makes her executor.

Dated December 22, 1671. Witnesses, NICHOLAS DE MEYER, RICHARD CARLTON. Letters of Administration granted to wife June 17, 1672.

Liber 1-2:93   WNYHS I:24

GEORGE CLARKE, Esq., Lieutenant-Governor. Whereas, **NICHOLAS STILLWELL**, of Richmond County, died intestate, Letters of administration are granted to ADAM MOTT, as principal creditor, by WALTER DONGAN, Surrogate, and confirmed in New York, August 14, 1739. Widow MARYTIE having resigned her right.

Liber 13:243   WNYHS III:263

In the name of God, Amen, February 6, 1756. I, **NICHOLAS STILLWELL**, of Old Town, in Richmond County, being sick. I leave to my wife MARY the use of all estate, real and personal, during her life, or while she remains my widow, And after her decease my estate to be divided as follows: To my son NICHOLAS £10, and all the rest to my children, THOMAS, NICHOLAS, MARY, CATHARINE, SUSANAH, ANN, FRANCES, and SARAH. I make my wife MARY and my sons THOMAS and NICHOLAS executors.

Witnesses, THOMAS WALTON, JACOB BURGER, THOMAS PRICE. Proved in New York, before GOLDSBROW BANYER, March 20, 1756.

Liber 19:391   WNYHS V:100

Major RICHARD INGOLDSBY, Commander in

Chief &c. Whereas **RICHARD STILLWELL**, late of Staten Island, hath lately died intestate. Letters of administration are granted to WILLIAM DE MEYER of County of Ulster, and one of the principal creditors, October 30, 1691.
Liber 3-4:291   WNYHS I:192

Will of **RICHARD STILLWELL**, of Shrewsbury, New Jersey, November 17, 1742, names his cousin RICHARD STILLWELL, of Staten Island, executor.
Liber 16:89   WNYHS IV:114

In the name of God, Amen. I, **RICHARD STILLWELL**, of Staten Island, Gent., being at this time in New York, sick. I leave to my sister, MARY SEABROOK, widow, who lives with me, all my farm and Plantation on Staten Island with all lands, to her and her heirs and assigns for ever. And I make her and my esteemed friends, PAUL MICHAUX and DANIEL CORSEN, executors.

Dated March 25, 1748. Witnesses, JOHN VAN GELDER, JOSHUA ~~SLIDELL~~ SILDELL, JOHN CHAMBERS. Proved, August 11, 1748.
Liber 16:304   WNYHS IV:181

THOMAS STILLWELL. In the name of God, Amen. I THOMAS STILLWELL, of Staten Island, Esq., being sick and weak. I leave to NICHOLAS STILLWELL, son of my son, THOMAS STILLWELL, deceased, all that Plantation or farm, commonly called Wallbours' farm, lying on the east side of the Old Town, and also one half of the meadow belonging to it; that it to say, that part of the meadow that lies next to the ditch. And the said NICHOLAS is to pay to his two sisters, MARY and ANNE STILLWELL, £50 each, when they come to the age of eighteen. And he is to pay to MARTHA BRITTAN, daughter of BENJAMIN BRITTAN, £-. If he die under age, then the land is to go to his sisters MARY and ANNE, and they are to pay to MARTHA BRITTAN £100. I leave to my daughter FRANCES, wife of NICHOLAS BRITTAN, 60 acres of land joining to the land I now live on, as it is now in his

162

possession, during her life, and then to her son NICHOLAS BRITTAN, and he is to pay to his sister, MARY BRITTAN, £25. I leave to my daughters, ANNE and RACHEL STILLWELL, the messuage and tenement with all the housing and buildings and all the lot, and three quarters of a lot of land, with a lot of salt meadow at the Great Kill, marked No. 2, which is the land I now live upon, after my wife's decease, and they are to pay to my daughter, FRANCES BRITTAN, £50. I leave to my wife MARTHA, the use of all the estate I now live upon, for life, or during her widowhood, and make her sole executor, and my loving friends, JOHN STILLWELL and ABRAHAM TAYLOR, Esq., and RICHARD ~~STILLWELL~~ MURRELL/MERRILL, SR., overseers.

Dated May 21, 1704. Witnesses, NATHANIEL WHITMAN, ELLIS ~~DUSEBURY~~ DUXBURY, ALEX. STUART. Proved before THOMAS WENHAM, Esq., being duly authorized by Lord Cornbury, May 9, 1705.
Liber 7:240   WNYHS I:404

EDWARD, VISCOUNT CORNBURY, Captain-General and Governor, etc. Whereas **THOMAS STILLWELL** Sr., lately died intestate, Letters of administration are granted to his wife MARY, April 10, 1708.
Liber 7:484   WNYHS II:1

ROBERT HUNTER, Esq., Captain-General and Governor. Whereas **THOMAS STILLWELL**, of Richmond County, died intestate, Letters of administration are granted to his mother, MARTHA, now wife of DANIEL DE BONREPOS, In trust for NICHOLAS STILLWELL, an infant son of said THOMAS STILLWELL. October 25, 1711.
Liber 8:67   WNYHS II:77

In the name of God, Amen. I, **ANTHONY STOUTENBOROUGH**, of Richmond County, do make this will. All my just debts and funeral expenses to be paid. I leave to my daughter ELIZABETH, wife of EPHRAME JOHNSON, £60. Unto my daughter MARY, wife of JAMES LATURETTE, a like sum. Unto my grandchildren, born of my

163

daughter LEANAH, deceased, £60, to be equally divided among them, namely: ANN, ABRAHAM, JOHANNA, ISAAC, JACOB, ANTHONY, JAMES, AARON, and LEANAH, to be paid to each at the time of my death. Unto my wife MARY, the use of my whole estate, real and personal, while my widow, upon condition she makes no waste thereof. Unto my eldest son, JOHN, £25; unto my youngest son, STEPHEN, £50; to be demanded by them at the death or marriage of my wife. The remainder of the estate at her decease or marriage to be equally divided among my four sons, namely; JOHN, JAMES, ANTHONY, and STEPHEN. Should any die before the death or marriage of my wife, and without lawful issue, then the parts of them so dying are to be divided equally among my surviving sons. I make my dearly beloved wife MARY, and my two sons, JOHN and JAMES, executors.

Dated February 8, 1783. Witnesses, HENRY SEGINE, black-smith, and PETER ANDROVET, farmer, both of said County, and ISAAC DOTY. Proved, June 9, 1783.

[Note.-The executors above named having refused to qualify, ISAAC and CORNELIUS REMSEN, sons and legatees were granted letters of administration on July 18, 1783.]
Liber 35:267   WNYHS XII:56

Whereas **AMBROSE SUTTON** of Staten Island did in his last will, make OBADIAH HOLMES, of the same place, his executor, and proof having been made at Court of Sessions held at Gravesend in June last. The same is confirmed July 8, 1678.
Liber 1-2:196   WNYHS I:48

SWAIM, includes SWAME, SWEEN

In the name of God, Amen, December 29, 1772. I, **ABRAHAM SWAIM**, of Richmond County, being sick. I leave to my wife MARY the bed and bedstead, "as stands in the back room", and one cow, "the choice of the flock", and £50. I leave to my son JOHN £100, and my gun and sword. I leave to my daughter ELIZABETH the bed in the front room, with all the furniture. Executors may sell all the estate. I leave all the rest to my children, JOHN and ELIZABETH. If both die, then to the children of my three sisters *(not named)*. {Add AARON CORTELYOU and WILHELMUS FREELAND as executors}.

Witnesses, JOSEPH ROLPH, PETER HAUSMAN, JANE VAN PELT. Proved, February 22, 1773.
Liber 28:397   WNYHS VIII:94

ANTHONY ~~SWEENS~~ **SWEEM.** In the name of God Amen, June 16, ~~1717~~ 1719. I, ANTHONY ~~SWEENS~~ SWEEM, of the County of Richmond, being sick. I leave to my eldest son, JOHANES, £5, in full of any pretence as heir at law. I leave all the rest of my estate, real and personal, to my wife, NEALTIE, during her life or widowhood. I leave to my daughter ELIZABETH, £50 more than my other children. I leave to my daughters, ELIZABETH, MARY, HANNAH, RACHAEL, and LEAH, £30. To my grand son THOMAS WILLMOTH, £25. I leave all the rest of my estate to my sons JOHANES, MATHYAS and JACOBUS. If my son CORNELIUS is not deceased, and should ever return to this place, he shall share with the rest. I appoint Colonel THOMAS FARMER, and Dr. JOHNSON, of New York, and GOESEN ADRIANSE, of Richmond County, executors.

Witnesses, ABRAHAM EGBERTSEN, OBADIAH ~~VISTER~~ VINTER, JOHN DUPUIS. Proved, March 10, 1719/20.
Liber 9:150   WNYHS II:212

JOHANES SWAME. In the name of God, Amen. January 20, 1719/20. I, JOHANES SWAME, of Staten Island, being sick and weak. My whole estate is to be divided among my children, BARENT, MARY, LENA, MARTHA, TIES and ELIZABETH. I make SIMON VAN NAME and AARON PRALL, Jr., executors. {Witnesses, CLEMENT CHRISTOPHER, NICHOLAS DUPUY, WILLIAM TILLYER}. Proved, May 17, 1720.
Liber 9:160   WNYHS II:214

Page 119. In the name of God, Amen. I, **MATHIAS SWAME**, of Staten Island. I leave to my sons, JOHN, SIMON, MATISE, and BENJAMIN, all the piece of meadow called the Bock Meadow, to be equally divided, situate on Carl's Neck. The remainder of my lands and meadows shall be sold, and all my moveable estate, at the discretion of executors. After debts and funeral expenses are paid the remainder of the estate is to be equally divided amongst five sons; one share to be equally divided between my grandchildren, heirs of my daughter HESTER, deceased. If either of these children should die before they come of age the survivor is to have their share; if both should die before they come of age then that one part is to be divided equally amongst my five sons. I make my sons, SIMON SWAME and MATISE SWAME, executors.

Dated December 20, 1780. (Before signing and sealing I order that my son JOHN should have £50 over and above the other legatees.) Witnesses, ABRAHAM EGBERTS, cordwainer, ISRAEL BRITTEN, RICHARD CONNER. Proved, March 12, 1781.

Liber 34:119   WNYHS X:45

In the name of God, Amen. I, **MATTHIAS SWAIM**, of Staten Island, Richmond County, this second day of October, 1782. My just debts and funeral charges to be paid out of my personal estate. My executors to sell my lands and meadows (except the 9 acres of salt meadow fronting the land of JUSTIS BEDELL and the land that I have of Proall's patent; and all my personal estate). Unto my loving son, MATTHIAS SWAIM, the above excepted land; should he die without issue, the said meadow shall be equally divided between my surviving children. Unto my loving daughters, CATREN, MARY and ELISABETH, all my personal estate, or the proceeds of sale of it, together with proceeds of sale of land and meadow, in equal shares, payable as they respectively come of age. I make my loving brother, SIMON SWAIM, of said County; and my loving friend, ISRAEL

166

BEDELL, of the City of New York, executors. Witnesses, JOSEPH WOOD, yeoman; JOHN VAN PELT, cordwainer, both of Richmond County; JACOB REZEAU. Proved, December 20, 1783. Liber 36:154 WNYHS XII:140

EDWARD, VISCOUNT CORNBURY, Captain-General, &c. Whereas **TICE SWAN**, of Richmond County, died intestate, Letters of Administration are granted to his wife SARAH. March 24, 1707/8.
Liber 7:472 WNYHS I:458

-T-

In the name of God, Amen. I, **ABRAHAM TAPPEN**, of the County of Richmond, New York, Shipwright. To my nephew, DAVID TAPPEN, £5. Unto my dearly beloved wife LEAH the use of all my estate while my widow. After her death or marriage all my estate to my daughter MARY, wife of GARRET ELLIS. Should she die without issue then my estate to the two daughters of my brother, ASHER TAPPEN, namely ELIZABETH and ELLINOR, equally divided. I appoint my wife LEAH, Executrix and my son-in-law, GARRET ELLIS, Executor.
Dated February 24, 1783. Witnesses, JACOB SPRAGG, MARY SPRAGG and ISAAC DOTY. Proved, October 15, 1785.
Liber 38:270 WNYHS XIII:246

EPHRAIM TAYLOR. In the name of God, Amen. I, EPHRAIM TAYLOR, of Staten Island, leave to my son ABRAHAM, all that land that I have leased of the Earl of Limerick, until the lease has expired, he paying the rent yearly. I leave to my son JOHN £12, and all my clothing and my loom and tackling. I leave to my daughters, MARGARET, SARAH, and MARTHA, each a cow when of age. I leave to my wife so long as she continues unmarried, all my farm and buildings, with all improvements, and after her decease to my sons and daughters. I appoint my wife and my son JOHN executors.
Dated December 11, 1713. Witnesses, FRA

WILLIAMSON, DANIEL ~~STILLWELL~~ SHOTWELL, NICHOLAS MANING. Proved, November 18, 1715.
Liber 8:423   WNYHS II:157

In the name of God, Amen, December 31, 1770. I, **OLIVER TAYLOR** of Richmond County, being sick. I leave to my son THOMAS all my worldly estate, both real and personal, that is to say, all my land in Richmond County, with all buildings, and all my goods, "my negroes in Genrall, and my cattle in Genrall, and all in Genral", and he is to pay the following legacies. I leave to my grandson, OLIVER TAYLOR, all my lands in New Jersey; To my granddaughter, HANNAH COLE TAYLOR, £50 when of age, and a maple desk; "To my daughter ELIZABETH, who was the wife of NEHEMIAH SMITH, provided she do appear in Richmond County personally and living", £20. I make my son THOMAS and my trusty friend and neighbor, JOHN HILLYER, Jr., executors.

Witnesses, RICHARD COLE, innkeeper, JOHN BEDELL, Jr., THOMAS TAYLOR, Jr. Proved, August 27, 1771, before BENJAMIN SEAMAN.
Liber 28:55   WNYHS VII:439

In the name if God, Amen, December 1, 1738. I, **WILLIAM TILLYER**, of Richmond County, Esq., being very sick. I leave to my wife MARY, her bed and furniture, also the use of all my estate of lands and houses, during her widowhood. After her death or marriage I leave all my houses and lands to my son PHILIP, also my negro boy. All the rest of my estate is to be sold at public vendue, and the proceeds are to be divided among my children and grand children, "that is to say to my daughter ELIZABETH TILLYER, *alias* JOB, her part to be divided among the children that come of her body, and the son of her daughter MARY TILLYER, *alias* PRIME, {her portion to BENJAMIN BRITTEN."} "My daughter ANN TILLYER, *alias* CHRIPS, {should be ANNE TILLYER *alias* TAYLOR}, her part to be put at interest, and if her husband dies, she is to have the same." {MARTHA TILLYER, *alias* CHRIPS}, DIANA TILLYER *alias* DEY, her part to be at her own disposal. The children of my son WILLIAM, deceased, are to have an equal share, viz., WILLIAM, JOHN, MARGARET, and MARY. My son PHILIP is to pay to the said WILLIAM and JOHN £7 each. I make my wife MARY and my son PHILIP, and JOSEPH BEDELL, executors.

Witnesses, SAMUEL MOORE, RICHARD COLE, MATTYS SWEEM. Proved, March 7, 1739.
Liber 13:349   WNYHS III:287

In the name of God, Amen. I, **JOHN TOTTEN**, of the County of Richmond, being in a low state of health. I will to my son, JOSEPH TOTTEN, all my Buildings with five acres adjoining taken in such form as he, JOSEPH, shall see fit. To my wife ANNA £3 per annum as long as she shall remain my widow to be paid in manner hereafter mentioned. The residue of my estate to be sold and the money arising to be divided in six shares in manner following, that is my son GILBERT three shares, he paying to my wife three pounds per annum, to my son THOMAS one share, to my son JAMES half a share, to my daughter MARY half a share, and the other share equally divided between my grandson, JOHN TOTTEN, and my two granddaughters, MARY, daughter of THOMAS TOTTEN, and MARY BROWN. I appoint my sons, GILBERT and JOSEPH, and my worthy friend, GILBERT JACKSON, executors.

Dated March 7, 1785. Witnesses, ZEBEDEE TOTTEN, JACOB RICKHOW, yeoman; BENJAMIN DRAKE. Proved, Richmond County, April 4, 1785. Confirmed, New York, April 9, 1785.
Liber 37:461   WNYHS XIII:130

In the name of God, Amen. I, **MARY TYSON**, of Richmond County, widow of BARNET TYSON. I leave to my youngest daughter, MARY, wife of WILLIAM LAKE, my bed and chest. All the rest I leave to my three daughters, SARAH, wife of BENJAMIN PRATT; MARTHA, wife of AARON DEPEAW, and MARY, wife of WILLIAM LAKE. I make my son-in-law, WILLIAM LAKE, executor.

Dated May 5, 1779. Witnesses, JAMES

GUYON, JOSEPH GUYON, ISAAC DOTY. Proved, January 22, 1781, before BENJAMIN SEAMAN.
Liber 34:79   WNYHS X:28

-V-

In the name of God, Amen. I, **JOHN VANDERBEAK**, of Richmond County, "knowing the certainty of death and the uncertainty of the time". My executors are to sell all my estate, reserving to my good wife HANNAH one cupboard, one bed and furniture, and 5 chairs. I leave to my son, REM VANDERBEAK, £5. All the remainder to be divided between my wife HANNAH and my children *(not named)*. I make my good friend, ~~DOLPH~~ DANIEL LAKE, and STEPHEN MARTIN, {Jr.} executors.

Dated September 26, 1754. Witnesses, WILLIAM WALTON, THOMAS STILLWELL, GILBERT WHITE. Proved before JOHN GODBE, in New York, November 12, 1754.
Liber 19:181   WNYHS V:46

In the name of God, Amen. "I, **JACOB VANDERBILT**, of Staten Island, Gent., being infirm and weak, do this 10 day of May, 1759, make this my last Will and Testament". All debts and funeral charges to be paid and satisfied. I leave to my wife NEELTIE one of my negro women slaves, she is to have her choice, also a horse and chaise, and two good cows, and such part of my household goods as my said wife shall think fit, to choose and accept. I leave to my wife and two sons JACOBUS and CORNELIUS, all my lands, messuges, and tenements on Staten Island, or elsewhere, with all appurtenances, and I make them executors. And at the end of six months they are to sell at public vendue all my lands and personal estate, and collect all debts due to me. From the proceeds I leave to my wife £300, also a bond of DENNIS VANDERBILT for £300. All the rest I leave to my children, DENNIS, HELLITYE, JACOBUS, HELENA, JOHN, CORNELIUS, ANNE, PHEBE, and NEELTIE, except 1/10 which I give to my 5 fatherless

170

grandchildren, the sons and daughters of my son ADRIAN, deceased, viz., CORNELIA, CATHARINE, JACOB, JOHN, and ARIS. I make my wife and my sons JACOBUS and CORNELIUS executors.

Witnesses, MARY CORSEN, ~~ABRAHAM~~ ANN SMITH, DANIEL ~~CORSON~~ CORSEN. Proved, January 9, 1761.

Liber 22:345   WNYHS VI:31

Page 52. In the name of God, Amen. I, **JACOB VANDERBILT**, of Richmond County, innkeeper, "being sick and weak, but of sound mind, Blessed be God for it, and knowing that it is appointed for all men once to Dye, do this 22 day of August, 1768, make and publish this my last will and Testament". "My body to be buried in a decent like and Christian manner". "In the first place, my executors are to sell the land below the road, except the land I gave my wife a deed for", And as much movable estate and other land as will pay all debts. I leave to my wife MARY the land below the road which I gave her a deed for, being 4 acres; Also my bay mare and riding chair, and my best bed, and her choice of my Looking Glasses. I leave to my eldest son JACOB £25, "as in full bar to his pretence as being Heir at Law to my estate". I leave to my wife MARY the use of all my estate during her widowhood, and then to be sold. I leave to my children, JACOB, JOHN, DOROTHY, OLIVER, JOSEPH, and CORNELIUS, £25 each. If there is any remainder, I leave it to my children, JACOB, ELENDOR, JOHN, DOROTHY, OLIVER, JOSEPH, and CORNELIUS. I make my wife, and my son JACOB, and TUNIS EGBERTS, clerk, executors.

Witnesses, RICHARD CRIPS, shoemaker, ABRAM BARBANK, JOHN WATTS. Proved, February 24, 1769, before BENJAMIN SEAMAN.

Liber 27:52   WNYHS VII:261

Page 25. "In the name of God, Amen. I, **JOHN VANDERBILT**, Sr., of Richmond County, blacksmith, being very weak this September 8, 1776. I make my friends, EDWARD BATY

(BEATTIE) and JACOB VANDERBILT, executors, and they are to sell all my estate and pay debts and funeral charges. The remainder to be put to interest to best advantage for my children until they are of age, viz., CATRIN, JOHN, AARON, BALITIE, and EDWARD."

Witnesses, TUNIS EGBERTS, JOHN BEATTY, RACHEL BODINE. Proved, September 14, 1776, before BENJAMIN SEAMAN. Confirmed by Governor WILLIAM TRYON, May 10, 1777.
Liber 31:25 WNYHS IX:6

In the name of God, Amen. I, **MARY VANDERBILT**, of Staten Island, in the County of Richmond, widow, being weak in body, do this twelfth day of December, 1781, make and publish this will and testament. I leave to my son CORNELIUS my house I now live in, with all my lands I now possess, on condition he paying six months after my decease to my [son?] JOHN VANDERBILT, £100; unto my son OLIVER £100. Unto my two daughters, ELONER JOHNSON and DORETEA GARRISON, all my wearing apparel to be divided between them, share alike. Likewise, to my said two daughters and my grandson, JACOB VANDERBILT, all my movable estate (my funeral expenses first being paid). I make my two sons, OLIVER and CORNELIUS, and my son-in-law, NATHANIEL JOHNSON, my executors.

Witnesses, CHRISTIAN JACOBSON, yeoman, JOHN BARBANK, yeoman, MARY BARBANK. Proved, December 18, 1781.
Liber 34:401 WNYHS X:180

February 13, 1786. **CORNELIUS VAN DE VENTER**, of Staten Island, in Richmond County, New York, to the Rev. Mr. GAMBOLD, £10, to be paid to him six weeks after my decease; the lands and chattels that have been possessed by me and my brother ABRAHAM, deceased, which was intended to have been divided between us, but as there has been no division made I give to my two sisters, CATHARINE and ANN, now ANN JACOBSON, my one-half part of all the said lands and improvements on the same, with my

172

one half of all the live stock, negroes, farming and fishing utensils, and my one half of all such furniture as has been held and used in common between me and my late brother, with all my wearing apparel and private effects for them and their heirs; the other one half, belonging to my late brother, shall be and belong to my said brother's daughter ELIZABETH or her heirs (excepting her mother's dowery right), excepting all such privileges as have been reserved by my sisters above named, such as the vault on the land, is always to be reserved for the heirs and offspring of Van de Venter's family to bury in, with a free passage to and from the same, and the liberty of the Beach reserved for the use of fishing. I appoint LEWIS RYERSON, ISRAEL BEGALL, executors.

Witnesses, RICHARD CONNER, Esq., JOHN HERTTELL, JOHN JACOBSON, gentleman. Proved, September 2, 1786.
Liber 39:238   WNYHS XIV:54

In the name of God, Amen. I, **JOHN** ~~VANDEWATER~~ **VANDEVENTER**, of Staten Island, yeoman. I leave to my son CORNELIUS as heir at law, £20. To my son ABRAHAM, £10. It is my will that my wife ELIZABETH and my two daughters, CATHARINE and ANN, and my son ABRAHAM, shall have one part of my dwelling house to live in, and my son CORNELIUS the other part, as long as they jointly think proper or mutually agree. I leave to my wife a negro girl. All the rest of my estate to my children, and they are to provide my wife ELIZABETH sufficient meat and drink, "or in other words, a comfotable maintaince", And my children are to give bonds to my loving friends, CHRISTIAN ~~FROLICK~~ FROLICH and HENRY VAN VLEECK, of New York, and PETER ~~CORTILYOU~~ CORTELYOU, of Long Island, for the support of my wife. I make my children executors.

Dated August 25, 1758. Witnesses, CORNELIUS ~~MARTINSE~~ MARTINO, NICHOLAS STILLWELL, SAMUEL THURSTON. Proved, July 6, 1759.

In the name of God, Amen. The twenty-fourth April, 1780. I, **ZACHEUS VAN DYKE**, of the County of Richmond, being weak in body. All my just debts and charges to be paid and satisfied out of my moveable estate. I leave to my beloved son JOHN all the lands and meadows that I now possess, together with two horses and one waggon, plows, harrows, and tackling belonging thereto; and two negro boys named JACK and BOB; he is to full possession at the age of twenty one. If he die without lawful heir, then his portion is to be equally divided to my two daughters, ELIZABETH and CATHARINE. Unto the said daughters, all my moveable estate (except the above mentioned) to be equally divided when my son JOHN is twenty-one; my daughters to have their option to make their home with my son JOHN on the homestead during his non-age. My two daughters' portions shall not be sold immediately after my decease, but shall remain on the farm until my son JOHN is of age, and then be delivered to them in equal shares agreeable to the inventory that shall be taken at my decease. My daughters shall so share with my son JOHN in all the increase of my stock and every other emolument that may arise from the place during the same period. Should either of my daughters marry, then the executors to pay unto her one equal half of what money there may be at my decease. If ever my beloved brother, CORNELIUS VAN DYCKE, should return, my son JOHN shall maintain him during his life with victuals and Cloath upon the homestead farm. In case the lands should be confiscated, my son JOHN shall share equally with my beloved daughters ELIZABETH and CATHARINE to the contrary notwithstanding. I make CORNELIUS COLE, ISAACK PRAUL, and my son JOHN, executors.

Witnesses, JACOB COLE, JOHN MARSHALL (farmer), OBADIAH BROWNE. Proved, May 31, 1782.

In the name of God, Amen. March 26, 1739, I, **NICHOLAS VAN** ~~GILDER~~ **GELDER**, of Richmond county, carpenter, being sick. I leave to my wife, FAMETIE, during her life, all houses, lands, and tenements. I leave to EPHRAIM VAN GELDER all my wearing apparel. After the death of my wife I leave all estate in New York, or Richmond County, to my four children, EPHRAIM, HANAH, SOPHIA JOHNSON, and LYDIA JOHNSON. I appoint my son EPHRAIM, and my son-in-law, WILLIAM JOHNSON, executors.

Witnesses, JACOB RACHOW, ADAM MOTT. Proved, May 17, 1740.

Liber 13:385   WNYHS III:296

In the name of God, Amen. I, **ANN VANHORN**, of the County of Richmond, being weak in body, doth this fourth day of February, 1774, make this my only last will. I leave to my brother HENDRICK DEMOTT's daughter, MARGARET, £25 (living in Morris County and Province of East New Jersey). To the eldest daughter of my brother-in-law, JOHN and MARY VAN WAGENIN, whose name is MARGARET, £25, to the second oldest daughter of the aforesaid, whose name is ANN, all the remaining part of my estate. If she should die without issue, then that part of my estate shall be divided equally among the surviving children of my aforesaid brother-in-law and MARY his wife. I make my loving brother-in-law, JOHN VAN WAGENIN, and MARY his wife, together with my trusty friend, JACOB FREELAND, executors.

Witnesses, JOHN JACKS, ANTHONY FOUNTAIN, yeoman, VINCENT FOUNTAIN. Proved, February 21, 1782.

Liber 34:435   WNYHS X:195

In the name of God, Amen. I, **CORNELIUS VAN HORNE**, son of GERRITT VAN HORNE, late of New York, merchant, at present of Richmond town in the County of Richmond, "being in an infirm state of health". "I leave to my brother GERRITT VAN HORNE as a mark of my regard for him and on account of the particular notice, attention and Friendship,

175

that he has given, paid and shown to me, the sum of £25". All the rest of my estate, real and personal, I leave to my said brother, GERRITT VAN HORNE, and my sisters, JOANNA, ANN, ALADA, and MARY. If either die under age, then to the survivors. I make my uncle, AUGUSTUS VAN HORNE, and JOSEPH READE, and my brother GERRITT, when 21, executors.

Dated November 30, 1774. Witnesses, JOSEPH LESTER, MATUS (MATTHIAS?) SWEME, HANNAH SWAIM. Proved, August 28, 1775.
Liber 29:537   WNYHS VIII:298

In the name of God, Amen. I, **PETER VANAME**, of Staten Island, Richmond County, being weak in body, April 8, 1780. I leave to my brother, JOHN WRIGHT, £100 in lieu of a Mortgage on my place, see deed given me by GARRIT ELIS for 4 acres May 15, 1779. To wife, HANNAH VAN NAME, the whole of said place for life or while my widow, and after "if she marye a discreat person that will improve the place and make no waste upon it, but that shall be left to the Judgment of my brother, JOHN WRIGHT". After death of wife said land, house and out houses to THOMAS VAN NAME, son of JOHN WRIGHT, and after his decease to JOHN WRIGHT, Jr., son of said JOHN WRIGHT. Burial to be "desent and without pomp or state".

Executors, wife, and brother, JOHN WRIGHT.

(Signed)   PETER VAN NAME
Witnesses, WILLIAM HUGHS, DANIEL SALTER, Innholder. Proved, Richmond County, July 2, 1785. Confirmed, New York, July 7, 1785.
Liber 38:84   WNYHS XIII:172

In the name of God, Amen. I, **SIMON VAN NAME**, of Staten Island. I leave to my wife ELIZABETH, all goods that were her own before marriage; also her choice of rooms in my house, and a bed. "And she is to have yearly ¼ of a fatted cow or steer, and ½ of a well fatted hogg". I leave all lands and meadows to my two sons, AARON and MOSES, but my eldest son, AARON, is to have that part of my land next to the church land; also my two boats. I leave to my daughter SARAH, wife of JOHN QUIN, £100. I make my son AARON, and BARENT ~~MATTEYS~~ MARTLING, executors.

Dated October 4, 1740. Witnesses, JOHN ~~DAY~~ DEY, WILLIAM ELLSWORTH, ANDREW WRIGHT. Proved, December 9, 1740.

Liber 14:12

In the name of God, Amen, October 1, 1748, I, **HANS VAN PELT**, of Richmond County, husbandman, being sick. My executors are to sell all houses and lands. I leave to my wife SOPHIA £10 in lieu of dower. Of all the rest of my estate I leave 1/3 to my son SIMON, 1/3 to my son PETER, and 1/3 to my three daughters, BLANDINA, wife of TITUS TITUS, CATRINA, wife of THOMAS HICKS, and ANNE, wife of HANS SIMONS. I make my sons SIMON and PETER, and my friend, JOHN LE CONTE, executors.

Witnesses, HARMAH BOWMAN, ~~ANNE~~ ARON VAN NAME, CHARLES McLEAN. Proved, September 18, 1750.

Liber 17:214

In the name of God, Amen, November 6, 1742. I, **HELENA VAN PELT**, of Staten Island, being weak in body. I leave to my grandson, JOHN VAN PELT, my small spotted trunk. To my grand daughter WIANCHE VAN PELT, my large round box. I leave all the rest of my estate to my son JOHN VAN PELT and make him executor.

Witnesses, LEWIS DUBOIS, Jr., ALEXANDER ANDERSON, PHILIP TILLYER. Proved before WALTER DONGAN, Esq., August 25, 1744.

Liber 15:289

In the name of God, Amen, This 11th of December, 1719. I, **JOHN TUNISEN VAN PELT**, of Richmond County, yeoman, being weak of body. I leave to my eldest son, TUNIS VAN PELT, all that my lot of land situate in the County of Richmond, next adjoining the land of RICHARD WOOD, and purchased by me from LEONARD BARREMAN. All the rest of my lands and

tenements, and goods, I leave to my beloved
wife, MARY VAN PELT, during her life, and
after her decease to be divided among my
children, TUNIS, PETER, JOHANES, HENDRICK,
JACOB, JOHN, DANIEL DE HART, ANN, MARGARET and
AERT VAN PELT. I make my wife MARY executor.

Witnesses, ~~LEONARD DE CHAMP~~ LAWRENCE DE
CHAMP, YAN BAL {or JOHN BALL}, ISAAC
WHITEHEAD. Proved, December 11, 1734.
Liber 12:253   WNYHS III:164

In the name of God, Amen. I, **JOHN VAN
PELT**, of Staten Island, being sick. "All my
real and personal estate is to be sold out of
hand, or at Publick Sale, by my executors". I
leave to my wife ALTYE £50, and my best bed
and furniture; and for her better support
during her life or widowhood as much as my
executors shall judge sufficient. I leave to
my grandson JOHN VAN TUYL, son of my daughter
MARY, ½ of what remains; and he is to pay to
my grandson, VAN PELT SYMONSEN, £50. The
other ½ I leave to the children of my daughter
SARAH VAN PELT, deceased, when they are of
age, viz., ALTYE SYMONSEN, VAN PELT SYMONSEN,
AKERT, MARYTIE, ELIZABETH, SYMON, JOHANES, and
EVERT. I make my son-in-law, EVERT BYVANCK,
and my cousin, DIRCK LEFFERTS, both of New
York, executors. Dated November 11, 1761.

Witnesses, JOSEPH ROLPH, LAWRENCE ROLPH,
ABRAHAM ROLPH. Proved, March 22, 1762.
Liber 23:282   WNYHS VI:141

In the name of God, Amen. I, **JOHN VAN
PELT**, of Staten Island, Richmond County,
weaver, being weak in body. All my just debts
to be paid. I leave to my son JOHN, ten
shillings. After my decease, within one year,
all my real and personal estate to be sold;
proceeds to pay debts, charges, and above
legacy. The overplus to be divided between my
son GEORGE and my four daughters, viz: MARY,
RACHEL, LUCRECE, and SARY, and my two
grandchildren, JOHN and MARY, children of my
daughter SUSANNAH, deceased; my son GEORGE to
have £6, to my daughters and two grand-

178

children, £2; and in like proportion for what there is. The share of any of said children dying under age and without issue to be equally divided between the survivors. I make my brother, ANTHONY VAN PELT, and JOHN MERSEREAU, son of JOHN MERSEREAU, deceased, executors.

Dated May 16, 1782. Witnesses, HENRY LATOURETTE, JOHN VAN PELT, farmer, JOHN VAN PELT. Proved, March 26, 1783.
Liber 35:223   WNYHS XII:36

In the name of God, Amen. I, **PETER VAN PELT**, of the County of Richmond, being in a reasonable state of health. My executors to take as much of my estate as shall discharge all my just debts and funeral charges. My wearing apparel to be equally divided between my two sons, TUNAS and PETER. Unto TUNAS, my fowling piece; unto PETER, my brass Barrel Frozee. All my goods to be sold at vendue or otherwise at the discretion of my executors for reasonable prices; the proceeds, with all the residue of my estate, to be equally divided among my five children, namely: TUNAS, PETER, ELIZABETH, PHEBE, and MARY; their respective shares to be paid as they are twenty-one, or marry. My estate to be subject to the support of my children in their minority, in case of sickness or other misfortune that may attend them. I make my said two sons, TUNAS and PETER VAN PELT and my trusty friend, RICHARD SEAMAN, merchant, of the City of New York, executors.

Dated October 2, 1781. Witnesses, JOHN BEDELL, ferryman, CATHERINE BEDELL, ISAAC DOTY. Proved, February 25, 1783.
Liber 35:203   WNYHS XII:26

RICHARD INGOLDSBY, Esq., Lieutenant-General, Commander-in-chief, etc. Whereas **SAMUEL VAN PELT**, of Richmond County, died intestate, Letters of administration are granted to his brother JOHANES VAN PELT, February 8, 1709.
Liber 7:567   WNYHS II:36

179

In the name of God, Amen, June 25, 1765. I, **TUNIS VAN PELT**, of Richmond County. I leave to my eldest son ANTHONY £5 and a fowling-piece that I bought for him, and all my wheelwright tools. All the rest of my estate, real and personal, to be sold at public vendue by my executors. From the proceeds I leave 1/8 to my grandsons, FRANCIS and JOHN FOY, children of my daughter MARY, deceased, and of this £10 is to be paid to their father, my son-in-law, JOHN FOY. All the rest of my estate I leave to my sons, ANTHONY, PETER, JOHN, JOSEPH, TUNIS, JACOB, and BENJAMIN, and I make them executors with my trusty friend, BENJAMIN SEAMAN.

Witnesses, LEWIS DUBOIS, LEWIS GRONDAIN, RICHARD ~~MESSEREAU~~ MERSEREAU. Proved, March 25, 1766.
Liber 25:210   WNYHS VI:435

In the name of God, Amen, January 14, 1768. I, **TUNIS VAN PELT**, of Richmond County, "having at this time my usual sences". I direct all just debts to be paid. I leave to TUNIS VAN PELT, son of my brother PETER, my watch. I leave to my brother PETER "my blew coat and black vest and blew briches". I leave to my brother JOSEPH my new coat and breeches. To my brother BENJAMIN my black coat and my stuff coat and two vests. To my brother JACOB my buckskin breeches. To my brother PETER's wife my shoe buckles. To my brothers, ANTHONY and JOHN, each £3. My ½ of my boat and looms and tackling to be sold. My executors are to have money to bring up my nephews, FRANCIS and JOHN ~~FOY~~ FEY. I make my two faithful friends, PETER WOGLOM and PETER VAN PELT, executors. Witnesses, PETER WOGLOM, JOHN WOGLOM, ABRAHAM ~~MERSEROLE~~ MARSHALL. Proved, August 4, 1772.
Liber 28:291   WNYHS VIII:56

Will of **CORNELIUS VAN SANTVOORD**, Minister of Reformed Dutch Church, Schenectady, NY.

...Whereas I am yet indebted for the land I heretofore bought of JOHN STAATS, my first wife's father, on Staten Island, as my children may inherit part of his estate, it and the money due to me are to go toward paying the same. I bequeath to my son, who is lawful heir, 5 Spannish dollars in full of all claim. To my son ~~TEGER~~ ZEGER my silver seal and silver shoe buckles, and one of my large silver spoons. I leave to my grand-child, ANTIE VELDSMAN, 4 large silver spoons, and the necklace of amber beads. I leave to my grand-child, ANN WENDELL, a large silver spoon, and to my sons, CORNELIUS and STAATS, each a large silver spoon. I leave to my daughter JACOBA my desk, table cloths and 4 napkins, and sheets and pillow-cases, "also a large silver spoon and 4 biggest thea spoons." I leave to the eldest daughter of GERTIE METZELAER, wife of RYCK VANDER BILT, on Raritan, 30 shillings. I leave the linnen belonging to my body to my son ~~TEGER~~ ZEGER, and my woolen clothes to my sons CORNELIUS and STAATS.... All the rest of my personal property is to be sold, and of the proceeds I give the same to my children, ~~TEGER~~ ZEGER, CORNELIUS, STAATS, and JACOBA, and the children of my daughter, ANN ~~CAMLING~~ COMEING. And whereas my late spouse (not named) desired that I should give to her sisters her golden finger and ear rings she had of her mother, and her clothes to them and ELIZABETH, daughter of PETER ~~CARMER~~ CORNU, and to my daughter JACOBA, I affirm the same. And my daughter JACOBA may give something to ANTIE VELDSMAN, but nothing to JOHN E. WENDALL, nor his wife or children. I make Mr. PETER GROENENDYCK, merchant in Schenectady, executor.

Dated March 6, 1746/7. Witnesses, JOHN SANDERS, GERRIT {A.} LANSING, GERRIT VAN ANTWERPEN. Proved, before MYNDERT SCHUYLER, Esq., in Albany, June 2, 1752. The executor resigned and CORNELIUS VAN SANTVOORD was made administrator.

Liber 18:238 WNYHS IV:422

In the name of God, Amen, July 5, 1735. I, **ABRAHAM VAN TUYL**, of Richmond County, Gent., being in health. I leave to my eldest son, DENNIS VAN TUYL, "my Great Dutch Bible and silver Tankard, in full for his pretence as heir at law". To my son OTTO, and to my daughters, GERTRUY, HELENA, and LEENTYE, £140 each. My son OTTO to have his part when he comes of age, the shares of my daughters are to be paid when my executors "think fit and reasonable". I leave to my sons, DENNIS, JOHANES, and ABRAHAM, all my real estate, and DENNIS is to have his choice of the 1/3 part of the land where I now live, and he is to have the choice of my negro slaves, or £50. My wife FEMITYE shall remain seized of all my estate, real and personal, and reap the benefits of the same during widowhood, and she is to bring up the children till of age. "If my wife should again happen to marry she shall be cut off of all my estate, and shall be maintained by her husband". I make my wife, and my sons DENNIS and JOHANES, executors.

Witnesses, JOHN VEGHTE, HENDRICK ~~KRASSON~~ KROESEN, JAN VAN PELT. Proved before WALTER DONGAN, Esq., September 29, 1735.
Liber 12:366   WNYHS III:181

In the name of God, Amen, "The 8 day of 9ber 1750." I, **ABRAHAM VAN TUYL**, of Staten Island, I leave to my four children, MICHAEL, ABRAHAM, JANETTIE, and JANEKE, all my messuage and lands situate on the north side of Staten Island or elsewhere. I make my father in law, MICHAEL VREELAND, of Bergen, New Jersey, Gent., and my brother, OTTO VAN TUYL of Staten Island, yeoman, executors, with power to sell lands,

Witnesses, JOHN RALPH, WILLIAM GROOM, DANIEL CORSON. Proved, January 30, 1751.
Liber 17:304   WNYHS IV:321

In the name of God, Amen, November 30, 1738. I, **DENNIS VAN TUYL**, of Richmond County, being very sick. I leave to my eldest son, ABRAHAM, my silver Tankard, in full for all his pretences of birthright. I leave to the Elders and Deacons of the Reformed Dutch Congregation in Richmond County, £10, to pay part of the arrears of the salary due to Rev, Mr. CORNELIUS SANTVOORT. My wife, NEELTYE, is to remain in possession of all my estate, and also my part of the estate of my father, ABRAHAM VAN TUYL, deceased, which is to come to me with my brothers, JOHANES and ABRAHAM, by agreement made May 25, 1738 {by his mother FEMETJE VAN TUYL}. When my youngest child is of age the estate is to be sold, and my wife is to have £100, and the rest to my four sons, ABRAHAM, HENRY, DENNIS, and ISAAC. I make my wife, NEELTYE, and HENRY ~~CRASSEN~~ CROESSEN and REM VANDERBECK, executors.

Witnesses, JOHN DAY, OTTO VAN TUYL, C. VAN ~~SATRELL~~ SANTVOORD. Proved before JOHN ROBINSON, Esq., July 2, 1740.

Liber 13:401   WNYHS III:300

In the name of God, Amen, September 15, 1740. I, **JOHN VAN TYLE**, of Staten Island, yeoman, being in good health, I leave to my son ABRAHAM ½ of my farm or Plantation on the north side of Staten Island, with ½ the buildings, when he is of age. "I give and bequeath unto the Fruit of my Body, be it son or daughter, now in the womb of my wife BEELTIE VAN TUYL, the other half of my farm when of age". If both children die, then to my two youngest brothers, ABRAHAM and OTTO VAN TUYL. I make my brothers ABRAHAM and OTTO VAN TUYL, and NICHOLAS ~~VECHTE~~ VEGHTE executors.

Witnesses, JOHN BRESTEDE, AARON ~~TRALL~~ PRALL, Jr., JOSEPH ~~ANKENS~~ ANKERS. Proved June 26, 1744.

Liber 15:241   WNYHS IV:11

In the name of God, Amen. I, **OTTO VAN TUYL** of Staten Island, yeoman, being in sound mind. I leave to my eldest son ANDRIES £5 when he is of age or married, he being my heir at law. I leave to my wife, FRYNTIE, all my estate, real and personal, so long as she remains my widow, to bring up my children,

ANDRIES, ABRAHAM and FAMETIE. If she marries, she shall have £300 and the choice of my negro wenches. After her death or marriage, I leave all to my 3 children. I make CORNELIUS KRUSA, JACOB CORSEN and ~~REM SIMONSEN~~ BENJAMIN SIMMONS, executors.

Witnesses, JOHN KEEN, GERTRY SIMONSEN, NICHOLAS VAN DAM. Proved December 22, 1757. Liber 20:433   WNYHS V:209

"In the name of God, Amen. I, **CORNELIUS VAN WAGENEN**, of Richmond County, black-smith. I leave to my son JOHN all my real estate, viz., the place I now live on, and 5 1/2 acres of Woodland, and all my salt meadow lying on the Great Kill and on the New creek, and all my tools and horse and wagon. All the rest to be sold and turned into money, except one bed for my daughter GERTRUY. My negro woman SUSAN may live with any one of my children she may choose, but if she chooses to be sold to any other person it shall be at her option. I leave to my grandson ABRAHAM CROCHERON, £25. All the rest of my personal estate to my five daughters, ANNE, HANNAH, CATHARINE, HELENA, and GERTRUY. My son JOHN shall pay to his five sisters £250. I make my trusty and well beloved son-in-law, DANIEL LEAKE, SIMON SWAIM, and my son JOHN, executors."

Dated September 22, 1779. Witnesses, PETER CORTELYOU, JAMES ~~COLAN~~ COLON, JOHN BEATTY. Proved, December 23, 1779. Liber 32:174   WNYHS IX:87

In the name of God, Amen. I, **JOHN VAN WAGENEN**, of Staten Island, Richmond County, being in a reasonable state of health. I leave to my wife MARY all my real estate, houses and lands in Richmond County or elsewhere till my youngest son JACOB arrives at the age of twenty-one, on condition she remains my widow, also £300 paid at the same time, and my negro woman, MARY, and her daughter MARY; also the use of two rooms in my house, one with a fireplace, the other a bead room. I order my eldest son, JOHN, to pay his mother, my said wife, yearly during her widowhood £10, and to find her sufficient fire wood at her door and pasture for two cows and forage for them in winter, and all the furniture of every kind she brought me at the time or soon after our marriage. To my eldest son, JOHN, my homestead whereon I now live on the south side of the road that leads from the Narrows to Amboy, also a piece of land that contains 32½ acres "contegious thereto", with two lots and a half of salt meadow at the great Kills, the above on condition that he provides for his mother as directed. To my youngest son, JACOB, the lands and meadows which I bought of GERARDUS BEEKMAN on the north side of the road leading from the ferry, commonly called Simonsons, to Richmond town, the meadow lies at the great kills, eight acres; likewise £300 when of age and a negro boy named STEPHEN. To my eldest daughter, PEGGE, £350 when JACOB is of age, and a negro girl named JUDITH. To my second daughter, ANNE, ye wife of NICHOLAS JOURNEAY, £250 and a negro girl named PHILLIS. To my youngest daughter MARY, £300 and a negro girl named SUSANNAH. The residue of my estate, if any there be, to be divided between my two sons and three daughters as aforesaid, share and share alike; and as there is two aged black ones, slaves, the man named WILL, and DINAH ye woman, my executors to give them liberty to chuse their own masters. I appoint my wife MARY, my eldest son, JOHN VAN WAGENEN, and my trusty friend, JACOB FREELAND, executors.

Dated June 12, 1782. Witnesses, HARMANUS GARRETSON, HENRY KROUSE, both of Richmond County, yeomen, ISAAC DOTY, House carpenter, of Queens County. My will is further that my son JOHN to whom I have given the bulk of my estate in lands shall pay his said brother and three sisters £300 the first payment when my youngest son JACOB comes of age or at ye death of my wife MARY, which sum he shall pay in equal six payments, to each an equal share. And as I have a right by purchase in 500 acres of land in a Patent called "Brampt" which I purchased under the Province of New York, situate on ye "extier" part of Connicticut I give said tract to my five children. Proved New York, August 24, 1784; also Richmond County, May 21, 1784.

Liber 37:161   WNYHS XII:391

In the name of God, Amen. I, **GERRET VEGHTE**, of Staten Island, "being in advanced age, but of sound and perfect mind". My body is to be buried at the discretion of my son, JOHN VEGHTE, "and he is to pay the charge out of his share of my estate, and also pay all my debts, which are but few and trifling". I leave to my two grand sons, GERNET VEGHTE and GERRET LACKERMAN, all my silver or plate buttons. I leave to my daughter LUMMITIE, wife of ABRAHAM LACKERMAN, Jr., of New Castle, ½ of a certain tract of land and meadow, near Dutch Creek, in the County of New Castle, upon Delaware river, formerly purchased from one RICHARD CANTWELL, by myself and the said ABRAHAM LACKERMAN. I leave to my son JOHN 300 acres of that tract of land which I have at Milstone, in Somerset County, New Jersey, which I purchased from JOHN HARRISON, deceased, and are adjoining to ARIAN ~~KINCIS~~ KINNEIS land; Also ½ of all mines and minerals in said tract. The remainder of the tract and the other ½ of the mines and minerals, I leave to my daughter, LUMMITIE LACKERMAN, and also ½ of all bonds, bills, and book debts due to me. I leave to my son JOHN all that my farm or plantation on Staten Island, and all the rest of my estate, real and personal. "And whereas I have heretofore executed certain conveyances, or deeds of gift to my said children, which were drawn by Mr. WALTER DONGAN, which I have since thought fit to destroy and cancell, I do hereby declare the same unto my children, in order to prevent any trouble about them; as I desire they will doe Justice to each other, and rest satisfied with this my last will and Testament".

Dated November 28, 1732. Witnesses, WILLIAM CHAMBERS, JOHN CHAMBERS, PHILIP

186

GOELET, THOMAS ~~ELDE~~ ELDER.
Codicil, March 9, 1732/3. "To all to whom this present Codicil or writing shall come, The before written GERRET VEGHTE send Greeting in Our Lord God, Everlasting". Since the making of my will I have purchased from JONATHAN ROWLAND and MARY his wife, a certain farm or Plantation, on the northeast side of Staten Island, against Constable Hook, as by deed of February 21, last. I leave the same to my son JOHN, and he is to pay to my daughter, LUMITIE LACKERMAN, £215, as by an agreement made by my son and NICHOLAS VEGHTE. I leave to my grand son, NICHOLAS VEGHTE, son of my son JOHN, 2 lots of ground near or upon Golden Hill, in New York. I make my son JOHN, and NICHOLAS LASILLIER, executors.
Witnesses, FREDRICK PHILLIPSE, THOMAS ~~ELDE~~ ELDER, JOHN CHAMBERS. Proved, January 2, 1734/5.
Liber 12:256 WNYHS III:165

In the name of God, Amen. I, **JOHN VEGHTE**, of Richmond County, Gent., "at present laboring under some indisposition". All debts to be paid. I leave to my son NICHOLAS my silver hilted sword, sheath, and belt. I leave to my son GERRITT my silver Tankard. I leave to my said sons all my wearing apparell. I leave to my wife CORNELIA the use of all my estate while she remains my widow. I leave to my son GERRITT £25. To my daughter, CATHARINE VANDERBILT, £25. {Also mentions his grandson CHRISTOPHEL HOOGELAND and daughter JANITIE VEGHTE, deceased}. To my granddaughter, CORNELIA HOOGLAND, £25. To my granddaughters, CORNELIA VEGHTE and GERITIE VEGHTE, daughters of my son JOHANES, £25. All the rest of movables I leave to my children, NICHOLAS, GERRITT, and CATHARINE, and to my grandchildren, CORNELIA HOOGHLAND, CORNELIA and GERITIE VEGHTE. I leave to my wife CORNELIA the use of all lands and meadows during her life; then my executors are to sell, and from the proceeds I leave to my daughter, CATHARINE VANDERBILT, £300. To my granddaughter CORNELIA HOOGLAND, £300. To my granddaughter, CORNELIA MERSEREAU, £70. Whereas my son NICHOLAS, without my permission, has sold to WILLIAM GROOM 6 acres of land formerly part of the farm, now possessed by JOHN LAKE, for £70. And whereas I am indebted to him £70 for money expended by him on repairs at home. He is to release the same. I make my son GERRITT, and DANIEL MERSEREAU, and my son-in-law, CHRISTOPHEL HOOGLAND, of Long Island, executors.

Dated November 30, 1763. Witnesses, CORNELIUS ~~CROSWOIER~~ CROSUIVER, SAMUEL BRITTENE, RICHARD ~~HASNAN~~ HOUSEMAN.

Codicil. My son NICHOLAS being dead, I leave his legacy to all the rest of my children. October 5, 1765. Witnesses, ~~HELMOR~~ HELMUS VREELAND, ROBERT DE GROOT. {Add CORNELIUS CROSUIVER}. Proved January 18, 1773.
Liber 28:369   WNYHS VIII:88

-W-

Whereas Major RICHARD INGOLDSBY, Commander in Chief &c. Whereas **THOMAS WALTON** hath lately deceased, leaving goods and chatels, Letters of administration are granted to CORNELIUS COURSEN of Staten Island. Principal creditor. November 7, 1691.
Liber 3-4:299   WNYHS I:193

Inventory of estate of **THOMAS WALTON**, late of County of Richmond. Taken {by GERRIT VEIGHTEN and JEREMIAH BASS} March 12, 1689, and exhibited by CORNELIUS COURSEN, administrator. 1 White cow and calf, £2, 12. 1 Black cow and calf, £2, 5. 1 yoke of oxen, £11. Long list of articles of small value, £142.
Liber 3-4:310   WNYHS I:195

Quietus granted to CORNELIUS COURSEN administrator of estate **THOMAS WALTON**, granted by Governor Richard Ingoldsby, May 6, 1692.

In the name of God, Amen.   February 19,
1727/8. I, **THOMAS WALTON**, of Richmond County,
Gentleman, being very sick.   Whereas it has
pleased God to give unto me 6 children,
THOMAS, RICHARD, MATTHEW, WILLIAM, MARTHA, and
JOHN.   My wife MARTHA is to continue is
possession of the farm or Plantation, where I
now live, during her widowhood. I leave to my
son THOMAS, a negro boy, and to my daughter,
MARTHA, a negro girl.   I leave to my three
older sons, ½ of all my estate real and
personal, and ½ to my wife and my three
younger children. I make my wife and my son
THOMAS, and RICHARD STILLWELL, executors.
    Witnesses, JOHN MITCHELL, MATTHEW REEV,
CATHARINE REEV.   Proved, November 26, 1728.
Unrecorded will   WNYHS XI:71

    Inventory of the estate of **FERDINAND
WAMSLEY**, of Richmond County.   Exhibited by
JOSEPH BILLOP February 9, 1703.   Consists of
articles on a small farm.   Total £57.
Liber 5-6:373   WNYHS I:317

    In the name of God, Amen.   I, **ANTHONY M
W. WATERS**, Jr., of Staten Island, farmer,
"being at present in a very languishing
condition". I order all debts paid.   I leave
to my dearly beloved wife SUSANAH my whole
estate, as well real as personal, to her and
her assigns forever, and make her executor.
Dated, April 16, 1770.
    Witnesses, ALTHIS CRIMSHIER, JOHN D.
CRIMSHIER,   {add   "Zacharis   Ouenmoufe"}.
Proved, July 13, 1770.
Liber 27:388   WNYHS VII:358

    In the name of God, Amen.   I, **ANTHONY
WHITEHEAD WATERS**, of Richmond County, Gent.,
being sick, this 4 of October, 1768.   I leave
to my daughter JOHANA, wife of JABEZ JOHNSON,
a negro girl, and a silver bowl, a silver
Tankard, silver Tea pot, sugar Pot, milk pot,
6 Table spoons, 10 tea spoons, Sugar tongs,

and silver skimmer. I leave to my daughters
JOHANA and ELIZABETH, wife of JOHN HALSTED,
Jr., the rings and lockets which belonged to
my deceased wife. "And as to all the rest of
my estate, lands, and houses, and goods, I
devise the same to my executors, TALLMAN
WATERS, Esq., and my son-in-law, JABEZ
JOHNSON, in Trust to sell and pay the money as
follows:" To my son, ANTHONY WHITEHEAD
WATERS, 1/5; To my son, EDWARD WATERS, 1/5; To
my son JOHN TREDWELL WATERS, 1/5, except £200,
which is to be paid to my daughter JOHANA; To
my daughter ELIZABETH 1/5; To my daughter
JOHANA 1/5. If any of my children shall claim
any sums as being due to them from me they
shall be excluded.
  Witnesses, JOHN BARD, JOHN KING,
ALEXANDER HAMILTON.
  Codicil, October 4, 1770. My son ANTHONY
WHITEHEAD WATERS having departed this life and
left no issue his share is to go to all the
rest of my children.
  Witnesses, JOHN DONINGTON, boatman,
WILLIAM CRANE, DAVID JEFFRIES. Proved,
September 23, 1771, before Governor WILLIAM
TRYON in person.
Liber 28:66   WNYHS VII:442

  In the name of God, Amen. I, **JOHN WATTS**,
of Staten Island, shopkeeper, "being well,
both in mind and body, Blessed be God." I
direct all debts to be paid. I leave to my
wife SUSANNAH my whole estate, both real and
personal and she is to pay to SUSANNAH CAMERON
£100. I make my wife executor.
  Dated January 30, 1772. Witnesses, JAMES
DUFFIE, school-master, ~~MINAGH BURGER~~ MINNAH
BURGER, mason, TERENCE REILLY, schoolmaster.
Proved, April 13, 1772, before BENJAMIN
SEAMAN, Surrogate.
Liber 28:243   WNYHS VIII:37

  Inventory of estate of **NATHAN WHITMAN** of
Staten Island made August 28, 1679. A house
and land and 4 erves, joining to the house,
and 40 acres of land in the Old Town, 27 acres

190

of land in the Close laid out by surveyor and 8 acres of Bogg meadow, adjacent to the Erves, and 10 acres of meadow at the Great Kills. £75.
Liber 1-2:259   WNYHS I:64

NATHAN WHITMAN late of Staten Island, husband-man, was about ye 28th of August accidentally drowned and died intestate leaving wife and 6 children. Wife SARAH made administrator January 6, 1679/80.
Liber 1-2:260   WNYHS I:64

ISAAC WILLETTS, Richmond County, New York, to my wife SUBMIT, all my estate, both real and personal; Also the property that may be given to me by the will of RICHMOND WILLETS, deceased, late of New York.

Dated July 8, 1785. HENRY PARLEE, of Westfield, Richmond County, New York, yeoman; REBECCA PARLEE, HENRY PERINE. Proved, September 8, 1790.
Liber 40:409   WNYHS XIV:180

In the name of God, Amen, February 21, 1734/5. I, **CORNELIUS** ~~WINANS~~ **WINANT**, of Richmond County, being very sick. I leave to my wife MARY 1/3 of my movable estate and the rest to be sold by my executors, or so much as they think needful; Also my wife is to have the use of the real estate during her widowhood. If she marries, then all to be sold, and from the proceeds my two daughters, ELIZABETH and MARY, are to have £50 each. "And whereas my dear wife is now with child; if it shall please God to give her a daughter, then £50 is to be put at interest for her". I leave to my son CORNELIUS "one Fowling piece or Gun, as heir at law". All the rest of my estate is left to my sons CORNELIUS and ABRAHAM, "and to the child my wife is now bigg with, if a son". My executors may bind my children to learn trades, if they think proper. I make my wife and my friend ADAM MOTT, executors.

Witnesses, SIMEON BOGART, ROBERT SLEIGHT, ABRAHAM COLE. Proved before WALTER DONGAN, Esq., April 8, 1735.
Liber 12:314   WNYHS III:173

In the name of God, Amen. February 25, 1734/5. I, **CORNELIUS WINANT**, of Richmond County, yeoman, being sick. All debts to be paid. I leave to my wife MARY, one third of all movables, and the rest to be sold by my executors. I leave to my wife the use of all my lands, during her widowhood, but if she see cause to marry then as follows: To my daughters, ELIZABETH and MARY, £50 each. And whereas my wife is now with child, if it be a daughter, she is to have £50. I leave to my son CORNELIUS, one fowling piece or gun, as my heir at law. All the rest of my estate to my sons, CORNELIUS and ABRAHAM, and the child unborn, if it be a son.
Witnesses, ABRAHAM COLE, SIMON BOGART, BARENT ~~SCHUYLER~~ SLAGHT. Proved, April ~~6~~ 8, 1735. — *See III:173, p.191 above.*
Unrecorded will   WNYHS XI:126

In the name of God, Amen. I, **DANIEL WINANT**, of Richmond County. I leave to my eldest son, DANIEL, five shillings; to CATHARINE WISER, my youngest daughter, all my money and goods and chattels (except Bonds); to ELIZABETH WINANT, my granddaughter, £5, to be paid out of the Bonds when the money is called in; to ANN WINANT, my granddaughter, £10 out of said Bonds; to my granddaughter, MARY WINANT, the daughter of CATHARINE WISER, £10 out of the said Bonds, to my daughter, CATHARINE WISER, two equal shares out of said Bonds, with my grandchildren, viz., DANIEL BUTLER, JOHN BUTLER, PETER BUTLER, CATHARINE BUTLER, CHRISTIAN BUTLER, RACHEL BUTLER, MARY MACMOE, DANIEL WINANT, GEORGE WINANT, MOSES WINANT, ZEDEKIAH WINANT, REBECKAH WINANT, ELIZABETH WINANT, MARTHA WINANT, PETER WINANT, CORNELIUS WINANT, GEORGE WINANT, ISAAC WINANT, JANE WINANT, ANDEZIAH WINANT, MARY WINANT, each one equal share out of said Bonds. I make JOHN MERSEREAU, Esq., and my daughter, CATHARINE WISER, executors.

Dated November 19, 1780. Witnesses, GILBERT TOTTEN, farmer, JACOB RICKHOW, farmer, ISAAC DOTY. Proved, March 7, 1781.
Liber 34:114   WNYHS X:43

In the name of God, Amen, January 23, 1754. I, **PETER WINANT**, of Richmond County, being in good health. My body to be buried in Christian-like and a decent manner. All debts and funeral charges to be paid. I leave to my son WINANT 6 shillings, "as his heirship at law". "My good will and desire is that HENDRICK SLEIGHT shall have my silver-headed cane, plain marked with P. W." I leave to MARGARET, wife of JOHN SLEIGHT, my silver spoon. I leave to my grandson PETER, son of JOHN WINANTS, deceased, £25, when of age. To my son DANIEL, 3 shillings. To my daughter ~~CASTERN~~ CATHARINE, wife of HENDRICK SLEIGHT, 3 shillings. All the rest of my estate to my grandchildren, "shear and shear alike, and not one to have more as the other". I make JOHN LECONTE and TUNIS VANPELT executors.

Witnesses, MICHAEL HART, MATHIAS VANBROCKLE. Proved in New York before JOHN GODFREY, October 9, 1759.

JAMES DeLANCEY, Esq., Lieutenant Governor. Whereas PETER WINANT of Richmond County, farmer, made his will January 23, 1754, and appointed JOHN LECONTE and TUNIS VANPELT executors; and whereas JOHN LECONTE is now dead and TUNIS VANPELT has resigned, Letters of Administration are granted to his grandson, DANIEL WINANTS. July 25, 1760.
Liber 22:222   WNYHS VI:2

"In the name of God, Amen, August 29, 1772. I, **PETER WINANTS**, son of DANIEL WINANTS ~~(son of DANIEL WINANTS)~~, of Richmond County, being very weak and low in body. I leave to my wife CHRISTIAN my best bed and one set of Chinces, and a horse, saddle and bridle, and one set of silver teaspoons, marked S. W. C., and £150. And she is to live on my Plantation

and reap the benefit thereof until my youngest
child is of age. If she marries, she is to
quit my farm, and all my real estate is to go
into the hands of my executors for the use of
my children. And my wife shall keep and
maintain my children, and give them suitable
schooling, fitting and necessary for them.
All the rest of my estate, both here and in
New Jersey, is to be sold when my youngest
child is of age. And they shall sell my boat
and other personal estate at their discretion,
and they are to pay the proceeds to my three
sons, PETER, CORNELIUS, and GEORGE. I make my
trusty friends, JOHN MICHEAU and HENRY PERINE,
executors."
    Witnesses, BENJAMIN SEAMAN, ANTHONY
STOUTENBURGH, JOHN STOUTENBURGH.
    Codicil. "Whereas since making my will I
have had another son born, viz. ISAAC WINANTS,
he is to have an equal share, and if my wife
CHRISTIAN should be with child, the same shall
have an equal share."
    Dated July 11, 1778. Witnesses, EPHRAIM
JOHNSON, JAMES STOUTENBURGH, BENJAMIN SEAMAN,
Jr. Proved July 27, 1778.
Liber 32:26   WNYHS IX:46

    In the name of God, Amen. September 28
22, 1773. I, **WINANT WINANTS**, of Richmond
County, being weak in body. I leave to my
wife RHODA £100 forever, likewise my best bed
and furniture belonging to it in the house,
and the privilege of living in the house with
my grandson, WINANT WINANTS; Also the use of
household goods, and my grandson is to furnish
her with meat and drink sufficient, so long as
she remains my widow, and also her firewood.
I leave to my eldest son, PETER, 10 shillings.
To my son DANIEL, £150. I leave to my
grandson, WINANT WINANTS, son of ABRAHAM
WINANTS, deceased, ½ of all my lands in
possession, "And the land of Mombrens, in
partnership with his cousin, JACOB WINANTS.
His part along the line of PETER VAN PELT,
from front to rear, each half, clear land and
woodland," "And likewise my long piece of salt

194

marsh lying in Sunken Marsh along Smith's Creek in the Province of East New Jersey", Also all my stock of horses and cattle, and a negro boy. I leave to my grandson JACOB, son of WINANT WINANTS, deceased, the other half of all my lands, "and that of Mombrens, his half to be along the line of ABRAHAM TAPPEN"; "Also a piece of salt marsh lying in Sunken Marsh, being 1¼ acres, lying in a field of meadow belonging to HEZEKIAH WRIGHT." I also leave him my desk and a cow, and £200. I leave to my son DANIEL my three houses and lots in Perth Amboy, that I bought of JOHN BURNET. I leave to my grandchild, CATHARINE WINANTS, daughter of my son ABRAHAM, £40. I leave to my grandchildren, WINANT and PETER WINANTS, sons of my son PETER, £50. I leave to my grandchild, LIDDA WINANTS, daughter of my son PETER, £15. I leave to the two youngest children of my daughter ELIZABETH, deceased, £20. "My negro boy 'MEAN' shall wait upon my wife so long as she remains my widow to make Fires for her and go of Arrents". I leave to my daughter ELIZABETH'S seven children (except RICHARD), £35. I leave to my grandson, WYNANT WINANTS, son of my son JOHN, £50. To the other 5 children of my son JOHN I leave £50, and all the rest to my children and grandchildren. {Add Son DANIEL WINANTS, grandsons JACOB and WINANT WINANTS as executors}.

Witnesses, HEZEKIAH WRIGHT, JOSHUA WRIGHT, ANDREW WRIGHT. Proved, November 23, 1773.
Liber 29:48   WNYHS VIII:158

"Richmond County, the 10 September 1721. I, **NATHAN WITMAN**, being in my perfect mind". I leave to my eldest son JOHN, a lot of land joining to NICHOLAS STILLWELL, and he is to pay to his sisters, SUSANAH, MARY and SARAH, £75. I leave to my son NATHAN my dwelling house, and one-half of the lot whereon it stands, and he is to pay to his sister CATHARINE, £25. My wife ANNE is to have the use of the house and land till my son NATHAN is of age. I leave to my wife two negroes and one-third of my movable estate and the other two-thirds to my 6 children. And my son JOHN is to live in the house until such time as he can build.

Witnesses, JOHN STILLWELL, VINCENT FOUNTAIN, JAMES KIERSTEAD, THOMAS ~~STARR~~ STORER. Proved, October 27, 1721.

Liber 9:262   WNYHS II:240

WOGLUM, includes WOOGLAM

JOHN ~~WOGLIM~~ WOGLUM, Jr. In the name of God, Amen. I, JOHN ~~WOGLIM~~ WOGLUM, Jr., of Staten Island, being very sick. I leave to my eldest son, ~~DAVE~~ DOWE ~~WOGLIM~~ WOGLUM, my gun and sword. I leave to my wife BLANDINA all estate and lands during her life. After her decease to my children ~~DAVE~~ DOWE, CORNELIUS, JOHN, CHRISTINA, SYTIE, and BLANDINA. My sons ~~DAVE~~ DOWE or CORNELIUS may have my lands if they pay £400 to the rest. I make my wife executor.

Dated, March 30, 1712. Witnesses, JACOB COURSON, JOEL VAN PELT, OSWALD FOORD. Proved, July 22, 1713.

Liber 8:217   WNYHS II:109

JOHN WOOGLAM. In the name of God, Amen. I, JOHN WOOGLAM, of the County of Richmond, being in good disposition of body. I leave to my beloved son ADRIAN, £50, "and my new North wester" [coat]. I leave to my grand son, DOWE WOOGLAM, the eldest son of my son JOHN, deceased, my lot of land lying on the north side of Staten Island, fronting to the Kill von Kull, bounded west by the land of the widow HOOGLANDS, east by the lot of JACOB CORSEN. Together with the half lot lying in the woods, in the rear of said lot, with all the meadow, houses, orchards and barns. Also all the meadow grounds by me purchased in New Jersey, lying at a certain place called the West Vly, within the bounds of Elizabeth town, and he is to pay to my executors the sum of £260. But he is not to enter into possession until his sister is 15 years of age, unless his mother BLANDINA should die before his sister {BLANDINA} comes to that age. But if my grand son DOWE WOOGLAM should die, then the lands are to go to his brother JOHN WOOGLAM. I also give to my grand son DOWE, my wearing apparell, and my gun and a copper vessell containing two barrels. I leave to my four grand children, DOWE, JOHN, CHRISTINA and BLANDINA, £250, and 6 pewter dishes, 6 plates, 5 iron pots, a gridiron, 2 flax hetchells, 4 augurs, 24 iron teeth for a harrow, 2 beetle rings, 2 hooks for thatching, cattle and horses, "and one negro man which I paid SAMUEL BAYARD for." I leave to my grand son JOHN WOOGLAM, my long gun, and to each of my grand daughters a feather bed. I make my brother PETER, and my son ADRIAN, executors.

Dated March 1, 1717. Witnesses, ~~MERCY~~ MARY BUTLER, ~~JAMES SIMPKINS~~ JANE C. JENKINS, AUGUSTUS GRAHAM. Proved, April 8, 1719. Liber 9:29 WNYHS II:185

In the name of God, Amen. This twenty-third day of March, [1781]. I, **JOHN WOGLOM**, senior, of Staten Island, Richmond County, yeoman, being very weak in body. I leave to my well-beloved wife, an out-set of my moveable estate, after my decease. Unto my son JOHN, a mare and £5 in token of his birth-right, and of my affection and good will. Unto my son ABRAHAM, £5. Unto my son PETER his Mare, which is taken as his property. All my estate in lands and goods to be divided equally among my children, JOHN, ABRAHAM, PETER, CORNELIOUS, BENJAMIN (and to MARY, £5 additional), ELIZABETH JOHNSON, CATHARINE STORY, SEILEY JOHNSON, and JANE WOGLOM. I make my wife CATHARINE, and my loving or beloved son JOHN, executors.

Dated, in the twenty-first year of our Sovereign Lord George III., A.D. 1781. Witnesses, PETER WOGLOM; ROBERT PIGGOT; ABRAHAM RICKHOW, of said County, vintner. Proved April 30, 1784. Liber 36:442 WNYHS XII:263

In the name of God, Amen, the 23 day of
October, 1724. I, **PETER WOGLUM**, of New York,
yeoman, being in health of body, I leave to my
wife ANNA all my estate for life. I leave to
PETER VANTOOGER HORN, living on Staten Island,
my negro boy, called "JOHN", and my gun and
silver hilted sword and cane. I leave to
ADRIAN WOGLUM, my brother's son, and to his
wife ZELITIE all the rest of my household
goods. My negro man JOHN, and my negro woman
MARY are to be free after the death of my
wife. I make my wife ANNA executor.
Witnesses, MATTLER HOCK, ABRAHAM MESSIER,
PETER MERSELISM. Proved, November 21, 1724,
and the widow ANNA WOGLUM, being dead, Letters
of Administration are granted to ADRIAN VAN
WOGLUM and his wife ZELITIE.
Liber 10:1   WNYHS II:304

In the name of God, Amen. I, **PETER
WOGLOM**, of Richmond County, March 17, 1762.
"My executors shall sell my half of the Boat
which I have in partnership with my brother,
ANDRIES WOGLOM, and enough of my movable
estate to pay debts and to raise £170". I
leave to my daughter MARY £50. To my daughter
ANN £50, and a cow and calf and a feather bed,
when she is 18. I leave to my daughter SARAH
£50 and a bed, when 18. I leave to my wife
the use of all the rest of my estate, real and
personal, during her widowhood. If she
marries she is to have £250, two cows and a
bed. After her death I leave all my estate to
my son PETER. I leave £20 to my granddaughter, MARY WOOD. I make my wife MARY and
my son PETER and my trusty brother, JOHN
WOGLOM, executors.
Witnesses, ANDREAS WOGLOM, ABRAHAM
WOGLOM, JACOB REZEAU. Proved, November 6,
1773.
Liber 29:9   WNYHS VIII:144

In the name of God, Amen. I, **EDMUND
WOOD**, of Staten Island, being in health. I
leave to my wife ANNE my best feather bed,
with pillows, curtains, etc., and all linnen

198

and woolen, and pewter, iron pots, side saddles, "and all setting cheres", and a negro girl, and all household furniture. I leave to my son DANIEL 6 shillings. To my son STEPHEN 5s. To my grandson PETER, son of DAVID WOOD, 5s. To my daughter, HANNAH CORNELL, 5s. To my son TIMOTHY a bed and 2 sheets, etc. To my son, EDMOND WOOD, a horse, waggon, and plow. All the rest to my wife for life, and then to my sons, EDMUND and TIMOTHY, and I make my wife and sons executors. Dated May 11, 1767.

Witnesses, DANIEL STILLWELL, JEREMIAH STILLWELL, ISAAC DOTY, carpenter. Proved, September 18, 1770.

Liber 27:446   WNYHS VII:378

In the name of God, Amen. I, **JAMES WOOD**, of Richmond County, February ~~19~~ 9, 1763. My executors are to sell all estate and pay debts. I leave to my wife EVE my best bed and 1/3 of the rest of my estate. The other 2/3 shall be for the benefit of my children, for their bringing up and education. I leave to my sons JAMES and ABRAHAM each 1/3 when of age. I make my brother, JOSEPH WOOD, and my brother, SILAS BEDELL, executors.

Witnesses, MATHEW DECKER, ISAAC ~~SIMSON~~ SIMONSON, JACOB ~~REZEAN~~ REZEAU. Proved, March 14, 1763.

Liber 23:619   WNYHS VI:222

In the name of God, Amen, May 10, 1763. I, **STEPHEN WOOD**, Sr., of Staten Island, cordwainer, being in good health. I leave to my wife SARAH £60 and my best bed and furniture and a cow. I leave to my son STEPHEN 25 acres of the land I bought of JOHN VAN ~~TELL~~ PELT, from the road in front upward, except the highways. and a road to and from the woodland for my sons. I leave to my sons, JOSEPH and JOHN, the remainder of the said tract, and they are to pay to my grandson, STEPHEN WOOD, son of my daughter, MARY WOOD, each £20 when he is of age. I leave to my son TIMOTHY 10 shillings. To my daughter PHEBE £10. To my daughter ELIZABETH £50. To my daughter SARAH £50. I leave to my two sons, JOSEPH and JOHN, 15 acres of wood land which I bought of the executors of my son JAMES, lying in the Manor of Castleton, bounding upon RICHARD CANNON and LAWRENCE HILLYARD, to the clear land, "and in a square". Also a road to and from it. And my son JOSEPH is to pay to my grandson, JAMES WOOD, £60. and JOHN is to pay to my grandson ABRAHAM WOOD £60, when they are of age. The remainder of the tract and 20 acres of fresh meadow adjoining are to be sold, and after paying debts, I leave the surplus to my son RICHARD. I make JOHN MORGAN, HENRY ~~LA TOUR~~ LA TOURETTE and my son JOSEPH, executors.

Witnesses, STEPHEN MESEREAU, ABRAHAM YATES, MATHIAS SWEEME. Proved, February 4, 1764.

Liber 24:323 WNYHS VI:301

In the name of God, Amen. I, **STEPHEN WOOD**, County of Richmond, cordwainer, being sick do this 20th day of November, 1781, make this will. I leave to my son JACOB 10 shillings; unto my son JOHN 5 shillings; unto my son JAMES £50. The remainder of my estate to be equally divided amongst my four children, namely, PHEBE, MARY, JOSEPH, and JAMES. Should JAMES die under age, or without issue, then his part is to be equally divided among the other three children after paying out the above legacies, all my just debts, and funeral charges. All my real and personal estate to be sold by my executors. I make my loving friend and brother, SILAS BEDELL, Jr., and STEPHEN BEDELL, both of Richmond County, executors.

Witnesses, TIMOTHY WOOD, shoemaker, JOHN WOOD, JAMES GROVER GARRISON. Proved, May 22, 1782.

Liber 35:12 WNYHS X:250

In the name of God, Amen, I, **ANDREW WRIGHT**, of Richmond County, school master, being weak in body. My executors are to sell all my estate, and after paying debts and funeral charges, the rest is to be for the maintainance of my wife MARY, and my two children, JOHN and JANE, when of age. I make my friend, PAUL MICHAUX, executor.

Dated December 5, 1747. Witnesses, ABRAHAM YATES, BENJAMIN ~~BRITTAINE~~ BRITTEN, STEPHEN MERCEREAU. Proved, before WALTER DONGAN, March 16, 1747/8.

Liber 16:232 WNYHS IV:158

In the name of God, Amen. December 22, 1739. I, **ANTHONY WRIGHT**, of Staten Island, yeoman, being in perfect health. I leave to my wife ELIZABETH 1/3 of my movable estate "and the little room wherein we now lye." I leave to my daughter, TABITHA ~~RANDALL~~ BANDAT/BONDET?, £50. To my daughter, JUDITH WRIGHT, £30, to be paid 12 months after my son ANTHONY is of age. To my daughter, ELIZABETH WRIGHT, a negro girl, "DAPHNE". My two daughters, ZEBORAH and MARY, are to be maintained out of my estate till they are 18, and then my sons, HEZEKIAH and ANTHONY, shall pay to each of them £40. All the rest of my estate I leave to my sons HEZEKIAH and ANTHONY; my son HENDRICK is to retain the whole till my son ANTHONY is of age. I make JACOB PHITZ RANDALL (FITZ RANDOLPH) and HEZEKIAH WRIGHT, executors.

Witnesses, BARNET SLAGHT, THOMAS CHURCHWARD, ANDREW WRIGHT. Proved, December 10, 1746.

Liber 16:58 WNYHS IV:105

LETTERS OF ADMINISTRATION

Name of Intestate	To Whom Granted	Date
Wyntie Barcklow, Richmond Co. widow............	Nicholas Stillwell Richmond Co., yeoman a creditor..	Aug 11, 1786 WNYHS XIV:343
Robert Beek........	wf Sarah....	Sep 14, 1763 WNYHS VI:447
Thomas ~~Beale~~ Blake............	Wf Margaret..	~~Sep 11, 1753~~ Sept 4, 1753 WNYHS V:431
Isaac Bogart carpenter........	Edmund Seaman, NY merchant....	May 20, 1784 WNYHS XII:409
Catharine Brestede, {widow of John}...	bro ~~Englebert Hawkins~~ Egbert Haughwout...	Apr 15, 1761 WNYHS VI:444
Benjamin Brittin...	Jonathan Lewis.......	Dec 20, 1769 WNYHS VII:468
Samuel ~~Britor~~ Briton...........	Richbell Mott, SI....	Mar 10, 1744 WNYHS III:428
Abraham Buskirk, Captain in the British Service, Richmond Co.......	Widow, Ann, Richmond Co.........	Jan 19, 1785 WNYHS XIII:383

```
Edmund
  Butterfield.......  Joseph
                      Bedell......Sep 18, 1747
                                  WNYHS IV:484
Richard Caner,
  clerk............  wife Jane.....Mar 6, 1746
                                  WNYHS IV:483
Moses Glendening
  Moses
  Clendenning.......  Wife, Mary...Sept 7, 1782
                                  WNYHS IX:325
Moses Clandenny,
  blacksmith........  Brother
                      Walter,
                      Bergen, NJ..Mar 13, 1784
                                  WNYHS XII:406
Walter Glendenne
  Clendenne.......  wf Nelly,
                      son Jacob...Sep 24, 1775
                                  WNYHS VIII:375

Solomon Comes......  Joseph
                      Royall......Oct 31, 1750
                                  WNYHS IV:486

Dan'l Cursen.......  wf Mary......Feb 25, 1761
                                  WNYHS VI:444

Daniel Corson......  Abm Spear
                      {& Mary
                      Corsen,
                      widow of
                      deceased}....Apr 9, 1764
                                  WNYHS VI:448

Daniel Corsen......  Wife,
                      Charity.....Sept 7, 1782
                                  WNYHS IX:325

Jacob Cuesen
  Cursen...........  dau Mary
                      Simonson &
                      Catrina
                      Cornelia
                      Duffee.......Oct 9, 1772
                                  WNYHS VII:472
```

```
Richard Corsen..... Wife, Clesha
                    Clashe......Dec 18, 1782
                              WNYHS IX:326

Richard Crips...... Paul
                    Micheau......Dec 9, 1745
                              WNYHS IV:483

Matthias Decker.... wf Mary......Mar 30, 1771
                              WNYHS VII:470

Peter Decker....... son Matthew..Dec. 1, 1772
                              WNYHS VII:473
Mark Disosway...... John Bedell
                    {& John
                    Poillon}....Aug 28, 1766
                              WNYHS VI:450
Walter Dongan,
 Gent.............. eldest son
                    Thomas
                    Dongan.......Aug 2, 1749
                              WNYHS IV:485
Moses Doty,
 carpenter......... Benjamin
                    Larzelere,
                    yeoman.......Apr 21 1785
                              WNYHS XIII:385
Catherine Dubois,
 widow, Lewis
 Dubois............ Johanes
                    Zacheus
                    Van Dike
                    her eldest
                    son.........Jan 27, 1761
                              WNYHS VI:443
Lewis Dubois,
 farmer............ Sons Lewis
                    & Charles
                    of Richmond
                    Co, farmers,
                    upon
                    renunciation
                    of Lucy
                    Dubois,
                    widow.......Apr 14, 1783
                              WNYHS XII:404
```

Barent Du Puy...... wf Elsie.....May 14, 1778
                                 WNYHS VIII:376

Abraham Egberts.... Wf
                    Elizabeth...Apr 27, 1756
                                 WNYHS V:433

Tunis ~~Sybert~~
  Egbert............ eldest son
                     Anthony
                     ~~Sybert~~
                     Egbert......Apr 6, 1778
                                 WNYHS VIII:376

Thomas Field
  "clerk"........... Wife,
                     Elizabeth...Apr 24, 1781
                                 WNYHS IX:322

Patrick Fleming.... John Van Pelt
                    son Peter
                    Van Pelt....~~Jul 20, 1757~~
                                Jun 20, 1757
                                 WNYHS V:434

Thomas Glentworth
  mariner........... Cousin, John
                     Breath, Jr.,
                     and friend,
                     John
                     Mersereau....Apr 2, 1799
                                 WNYHS XV:258

Jacob Glendenen.... wf Anne......Oct 21, 1775
                                 WNYHS VIII:375

Philip Guyon....... wf {Addrie
                    Guyon} &
                    Stephen
                    Guyon.......Dec 14, 1761
                                 WNYHS VI:445

Hannah Hand........ Phebe
                    Vanderbilt..Nov 12, 1798
                                 WNYHS XV:254

Abraham Harris,
 Richmond Co,
 yeoman............ Brother-in-
                    law Joshua
                    Mersereau
                    Richmond Co,
                    Esquire.....Jan 17, 1786
                                WNYHS XIV:337

Nicholas
 Hogerwert......... Joseph
                    Christopher,
                    brother-in-
                    law, and
                    Peter
                    Hogerwert,
                    nephew......~~Mar 19, 1781~~
                                Mar 10/13
                                WNYHS IX:322

John Housman....... son Peter....May 10, 1777
                                WNYHS VIII:376

Thomas Karl........ Isaac Jones,
                    SI {father-
                    in-law}.....24 May 1745.
                                WNYHS III:428

John Kierstead..... brother
                    Samuel......Aug 13, 1751
                                WNYHS IV:486

William Lake....... Wf Sarah.....Sep 21, 1758
                                WNYHS V:434

{Solomon Langdon... Thomas
                    Mannering...Mar 2, 1753}
                                WNYHS XIV:197

Peter Latourette... Son Peter....Jan 22, 1754
                                WNYHS V:432

Margaret ~~Le Compte~~
 Le Conte.......... sister
                    Margaret, wf
                    Abraham
                    Poillon.....Nov 14, 1750
                                WNYHS IV:486

```
Dr Arnest Linde....  James Duffee,
                     Gent. who m.
                     the widow...Feb 21, 1772
                                 WNYHS VII:472
Abraham Lockerman..  wf
                     Elizabeth...Jul 21, 1775
                                 WNYHS VIII:375
Charles McLean,
 New York City,
 grocer.....         Brother,
                     Cornelius and
                     brothers-in-
                     law, Jeremiah
                     Simonson
                     and Joseph
                     Lake, all
                     of Richmond
                     Co.........Apr. 2, 1794
                                 WNYHS XIV:360

Barent Martin......  Wf
                     Susannah....Sep 19, 1760
                                 WNYHS V:436

John Merill.......   wife Altie...Oct 19, 1747
                                 WNYHS IV:484

Martha Mesereau....  husband
                     John........Mar 16, 1752
                                 WNYHS IV:487

John Mersereau,
 merchant.........   Widow,
                     Elizabeth and
                     brother-in-
                     law, John
                     Breath......Dec 20, 1800
                                 WNYHS XV:266
Mary Mersereau
 late wf
Joshua Mersereau..   son Joshua...Nov 23, 1774
                                 WNYHS VIII:373

Adam Mott.........   wife
                     Elizabeth....Mar 8, 1750
                                 WNYHS IV:485
```

```
Wm Nicholls........ John Hillyer..Apr 9, 1761
                                 WNYHS VI:445

Samuel Norris...... wf Elizabeth
                    and eldest
                    son Samuel
                    of Essex,
                    NJ..........Jul 18, 1751
                                 WNYHS IV:486

Abraham Poillon.... John Poillon
                    & James
                    Poillon.....May 31, 1757
                                 WNYHS V:433

James Pillion...... Widow Sarah..May 29, 1783
                                 WNYHS XII:404

Rachel Prior,
 widow Jacob
 Prior............. Wynant
                    Wynants......Apr 27, 1753
                                 WNYHS V:431

Jacob Rezeau....... f                      a
                    Jacob........Mar 9, 1764
                                 WNYHS VI:448
Joseph Ridgway,
 Richmond Co,
 yeoman............ Widow, Sarah
                    same place..Sep 18, 1786
                                 WNYHS XIV:344

John Roll.......... ~~John Mersereau~~
                    Jacob
                    Mersereau,
                    grandson....Jan 21, 1763
                                 WNYHS VI:447

Andrise Roman...... Augustus
                    DuBois......Apr 14, 1760
                                 WNYHS V:436

Silvanus Seaman.... Wf Mary......Aug 21, 1759
                                 WNYHS V:435
```

```
Rem Simonson....... Widow Gurtie,
                      now wf
                      Peter
                      Corson.......Oct 9, 1761
                                    WNYHS VI:445
John Sleight
  Sleght............ Hezekiah
                      Wright......May 14, 1770
                                    WNYHS VII:469

John Stillwell..... Bro-in-law
                      Dan'l
                      Corsen......Oct 26, 1757
                                    WNYHS V:434
John Sunderland.... Paul
                      Michaux.....Apr 26, 1760
                                    WNYHS V:436
Isaac Swaim........ bros
                      Benjamin
                      & Martinus..Mar 18, 1778
                                    WNYHS VIII:376
Matthias M. Swaim,
  grocer............ Father,
                      Mortimes,
                      of Richmond
                      Co..........Nov 7, 1799
                                    WNYHS XV:260

Gerritt Thorpe..... Wf Clasie....Aug 15, 1760
                                    WNYHS V:436

Samuel Thurston.... Nephew, John
                      Montross
                      Thurston,
                      farmer of
                      Dutchess
                      Co.........May 23, 1783
                                    WNYHS XII:403
Samuel Thurston,
  weaver............ Nephew, John
                      M. Thurston
                      yeoman,
                      Charlotte
                      Precinct,
                      N.Y.........Nov 23 1785
                                    WNYHS XIII:391
```

Thomas Trott....... Joseph
                    Stragg......Aug 18, 1758
                                WNYHS V:434

David Tysen........ bro John.....Nov 19, 1771
                                 WNYHS VII:471

Cornelius
 Vanderbilt,
 farmer........... wf Neltie....May 13, 1768
                               WNYHS VII:465

Ephraim Van
 Gelder........... John
                   Mersereau...Nov 21, 1774
                               WNYHS VIII:373

Hendrick Van Tuyl.. sister
                    Helena, wf of
                    Cornelius
                    Vanderbilt...Aug 4, 1761
                                 WNYHS VI:444

Wm. Ward........... Thomas Bartow,
                    Charles
                    McClean.....Oct 23, 1782
                                WNYHS IX:325

John Winants....... eldest son
                    John........May 2, 1778
                                WNYHS VIII:376

Hezekiah Wright.... wf
                    Christian...Jan 16, 1775
                                WNYHS VIII:374

ANDROVET, DANIEL, of New Brunswick, Middlesex Co., cooper. Inventory of personal estate.......mentions bonds in hands of JOHN and PETER ANDROVET on Staten Island. Feb. 4, 1740-1. Administration granted to HANNAH ANDROWVAT Feb. 12, 1740-1.
XXX:21   Calendar of wills II: 1730-1750

ANDROVET, JOHN, of Staten Island, Richmond Co., New York. [Note: See Liber 22:288, WNYHS VI:19, page 1 this volume. New Jersey Colonial documents add the following information to this will. C.M.H.] Dated Aug. 29, 1760, proved Sept. 10, 1765. Also at the same time, probate was granted to LEAH ANDROVET and MARY TAPPEN, late MARY ANDROVET. Lib. H:602
XXIII:18   Calendar of wills IV: 1761-1770

BAKER, LAWRENCE, of Richmond County., province of New York. Bond of JOHN BRASHEN, of New York City, as administrator: HENRY BERRY, fellow bondsman. Witness LAWRENCE SMYTH. Dated Nov. 28, 1737. Middlesex Wills, Lib. C:181.
XXX:31   Calendar of wills II: 1730-1750

BEBOU, JOHN, of Stattin Island, N.Y., brewer; will of. Wife METTE. Sons PETER, JACOBUS. Wife's "first-children" spoken of. "Worldly estate". No executor named. Witnesses JO^n MORGEN, CHARLES MARSHAL, ABRAHAM COLE. Dated Oct. 28,1710, proved before JAS. SMITH, Surrogate. See BIBOUT. Lib. A:16.
XXIII:32   Calendar of wills I: 1670-1730

BIBOUT, JOHN (endorsed as of Staten Island, N. Y.), Inventory of personal estate

of, £26, made by JOHN BORROWS and JOHN MOLLESON. See BEBOU. Middlesex Wills. Dated Oct. 27, 1716.
XXIII:36   Calendar of wills I: 1670-1730

BROUN, WILLIAM, of Woodbridge; will of. Friend GEORGE BROUN, principal heir and executor; legacies to JOHN BROUN, of Staten Island, and JOHN MOURS. Witnesses ADAM HUDE and GEORGE BROUN. Dated Dec. 28, 1698, proved Feb. 23, 1698-9. Middlesex Wills.
XXIII:63   Calendar of wills I: 1670-1730

BROWNE, WILLIAM, of Woodbridge; will of. JOHN BROWNE of Staten Island, JOHN MOORE, GEORGE BROWNE. Personal property. GEORGE BROWNE executor. Witnesses ADAM HUDE, GEORGE BROWNE. Dated Dec. 28, 1698, proved May 18, 1699. May 18, 1699, letters issued to GEORGE BROWNE of Woodbridge. E.J.D., Lib. G:2
XXX:557   Appendix-Certain omitted Abstracts

DE HART, JACOB, of Elizabeth Town, Essex Co.; will of. ....Mentions grandson JACOB MORRIS DEHART who was to receive ½ of the salt meadow on Staten Island which was patented to LAMBERT DORLAND by Governor ANDROS. Grandson JACOB DE HART, son of his son JACOB, was to receive the other ½ of the salt meadow on Staten Island. Dated Feb. 9, 1777, proved Sept. 18, 1780. Lib. 22:287.
XXXIV:136-7   Calendar of wills V: 1771-1780

DES MARETS, JOHN, of New Barbados, Bergen Co., "youman"; will of. Wife MAGDALENA. Children JOHN of Apoghquinimy, Penna., PETER of New Barbados, MARIA, wife of JACOBUS SHOT, who has son PETER, SARAH, wife of ABRAHAM CANNAN of Richmond County, who has son ISACK, RACHEL, wife of THOMAS HYER, of Apoghquinimy, who has son JOHN, JAQUEMINE, wife of JOHN STEWARD of Chester Co., LEA, wife of ABRAHAM

BROWER, MAGDALENA, wife of JEAMES CHRISTINSON, who has son JOHN, grandson DAVID, son of deceased eldest son DAVID. Real and personal estate. Executors sons JOHN and PETER. Witnesses JOOSE DE BAENE, SARAH DE BAENE, JOHN CONRAD CODWISE. Codicill of December 4, 1719, makes a few changes in devises to daughters CONAN and HEYER and substitutes son-in-law ABRAHAM BROWER as executor in place of son JOHN. Witnesses VOJJOR WEISEM (??), POULES VAN DER BEECK, JEAMES CHRISTYSON. Dated Mar. 29, 1714, proved November 10, 1719. Letters of administration issued to the executors "sometime in February 1719"-20. Lib. A:137.
XXIII:136   Calendar of wills I: 1670-1730

DISOSWAY, ISRAEL, of Staten Island. Int. Adm's CORNELIUS DISOSWAY, brother of said ISRAEL, of said place. Fellow bondsman NATHANIEL FITZ RANDOLPH, of Woodbridge, Middlesex Co. Lib. K:76. Dated Apr. 1, 1769.
XXXIII:118   Calendar of wills IV: 1761-1770

DUBOIS, SAMUEL, late of Staten Island, N.Y., now of Perth Amboy, Middlesex Co.; will of. JOHN THOMSON, husband of sister. MARGARET DUBOIS, sole heir and Executor. Witnesses ABRAHAM WEBB, JONATHAN DEARE and WILLIAM FONDRILL. Dated Oct. 15, 1759, proved Nov. 12, 1759. Lib. G:109.
XXXII:98   Calendar of wills III: 1751-1760

FITZ RANDOLPH, REUBEN, formerly of NJ, but now of Staten Island, Richmond Co., New York; will of. Wife ELIZABETH, 1/3 of real and personal estate. Son REUBEN, also 1/3. Daughter MARTHA, now wife of ELIAS MARSH, other 1/3. Executors wife ELIZABETH, and JOHN DOBS and ELIAS MARSH. Witnesses PETER ROZEAU, DAVID ALSTON. WILLIAM BURY. Dated Aug 6, 1784, proved May 7, 1785. Lib. M:287
XXXV:147   Calendar of wills VI: 1781-1785

FRAZEE (FRASER), GEORGE, of the Borough of Elizabeth, Essex Co., gentleman; will of. Body to be interred near my father and mother on Staten Island. GEORGE, son of brother WILLIAM FRASER, estate in Europe or America. Executors PHILIP KEARNY, of Middlesex Co., gent., and ELIAS GRAZILIER, of Elizabeth Town. Witnesses GERSHOM HIGGINS, JOSEPH HETFIELD, THO. JACKMAN. Dated Feb. 12 1740; proved Feb. 25, 1740. Lib. C:396.
XXX:187   Calendar of wills II: 1730-1750

HAMPTON, JONATHAN, of Rahway, Essex Co., will of.   Eldest son, ABRAHAM, of Staten Island, land joining lands of PETER TREMLEYS and GARRET POST.......... Dated Mar. 5, 1744-5; proved April 13, 1745. Lib. D:262.
XXX:215   Calendar of wills II: 1730-1750

KRUSE, ABRAHAM, of Richmond Co., New York, yeoman; will of.   [Note: This will is the same as liber 28:10, WNYHS VII:426, page 45 of this volume. C.M.H.]   Proved April 25, 1774, in NJ Lib. K:502.
XXXIV:291   Calendar of wills V: 1771-1780

LAROE, ABRAHAM, of Staten Island, yeoman; will of. Wife ALCHE, sole heiress. Children mentioned, but not by name.   Movable and immovable estate. Witnesses WILLIAM TILLYER, JEAN CASIER, LOUIS DE BOIS, SAMUEL GRASSET. Burlington Wills. Dated Sept. 21, 1702.
XXIII:283   Calendar of wills I: 1670-1730

LATOURETTE, SARAH, of Richmond Co., New York, widow; will of. To St. Andrews Church in Richmond Co., £25, To SARAH (wife of ABNER TUCKER), £25. To WINANT WOOD (son of TIMOTHY WOOD), £25.   To niece, RUTH (wife of CALEB WARD), £10, bed and bedding and ½ of clothes. To SARAH DEGROOT (daughter of WILLIAM DEGROOT), a bed and bedding.   To MARY

(daughter of brother-in-law JOHN LATOURETTE),
£10. To MARGARET GREEN, of the City of New
York and her daughter, SARAH MARY (both my
kinswoman), each £15. To MARY and ELIZABETH
(daughters of STEPHEN WOOD, son of ISAAC
WOOD), each 3 silver table spoons. To JOHN
COLE (son of PETER and SUSANNAH COLE), £50.
Remainder of estate to be divided between my 3
children-in-law, JOHN LA TOURETTE, PETER LA
TOURETTE and WILLIAM DEGROOT. Executors sons-
in-law JOHN LATOURETTE and WILLIAM DEGROOT.
Witnesses ISAAC VAN DOREN, WILLIAM S. HARRIS,
CATHARINE CASTELLI. Dated Nov. 6, 1805,
proved Feb. 9, 1806, at New Brunswick,
Middlesex Co. Feb. 6, 1806. Inventory
$2,438.11; made by ISAAC VAN DOREN and WILLIAM
HARRIS. File 10109 L.
XL:210   Calendar of wills XI: 1806-1809

MONEE, ABRAHAM, Jr., of Woodbridge,
Middlesex Co. Int. ELIZABETH MONEE, widow,
declined to administer; witness, ANDREW
HAMPTON. Adm'r ABRAHAM MONEE, of Richmond
Co., on Staten Island, yeoman, father of said
ABRAHAM MONEE Jr. Bondsman ANDREW HAMPTON, of
Woodbridge, yeoman. Witness THOMAS BARTOW.
Dated May 15, 1755. Lib F:201.
XXXII:99   Calendar of wills III: 1751-1760

NORRIS, SAMUEL, of Richmond Co.; Staten
Island, yeoman. Int. Adm'rs ANDREW CRAIG and
SAMUEL WILLIAMS, both of Essex Co., yeomen.
Witness THOMAS BARTOW. Lib. F.:548   Dated
Sept. 25, 1751.
XXXII:237   Calendar of wills III: 1751-1760

SIMONSON, SIMON, of Hackensack Precinct,
Bergen Co.; will of. Eldest son, VAN PELT, £1
for his birthright. (Grandson) HENRY MARSH,
son of HENRY MARSH, £100. (Granddaughter)
SARAH MARSH, daughter of HENRY MARSH, £100.
Daughter, JOHANNA, £200; also all household
goods her mother brought when I first married.

215

Son VAN PELT, daughter JOHANNA, and daughter, ELIZABETH, wife of HENRY MARSH, to remain and stay in possession of real and personal for 7 years before division is made. After sale of estate; sons VAN PELT, JOHN, AERT and SYMON, and daughter ELIZABETH, each a double share; and daughter, MARYA, wife of JONES HUYLER, and daughter AELTIE, wife of THUNIS BOGERT, each a single share. Executors sons VAN PELT [SYMONSE] and JOHN [SYMONSE], and daughter, ELIZABETH MARSH. Witnesses CORNELIUS BANTA, ROELOF P. BOGERT, JOHANNES DEMAREST. Dated June 20, 1782, proved Mar. 19, 1792. Lib. 34:12, file 2192B.
XXXVII:320   Calendar of wills VIII: 1791-1795
    New Jersey Post-Revolution Documents
[Note: This will is identified by ELMER GARFIELD VAN NAME in his "The Simonson Families of Staten Island, New York, 1959", page 8, as that of SIMON SIMONSON, son of AERT SIMONSON, Liber 18:242, WNYHS IV:424, p. 150 this volume. C.M.H.]

INDEX

Abigail, 22(2)
Adam, 28
Ambo, 56
Bell, 111
Ben, 93, 111
Bet, 123
Beth, 96
Betty, 22, 48, 59
Bob, 174
Brennus, 28
Carlos, 28(2)
Catherine, 147
Daphne, 201
David, 22
Dina, 49
Dinah, 57, 185
Elisah, 50
Ephraim, 99
Francis, 29
Ginney, 22
Hagor, 140
Harry, 49
Jack, 56, 59, 97,
  123, 174
Jane, 100, 104
Jenny, 57
John, 22, 198(2)
Judde, 50
Judith, 185
Lydia, 147
Margaret, 102
Martha, 51
Mary, 22, 51, 94,
  102, 184(2), 198
Mean, 195
Michael, 147
Mink, 61

Nan, 28
Peg, 57
Peter, 49
Phebe, 28, 57
Phillis, 185
Pine, 102
Polly, 79
Rachel, 51, 78
Sada, 47
Sam, 22, 49, 123
Samuel, 22
Sans, 51
Sarah, 48, 66, 97,
  121, 126
Shelley, 118
Stephen, 185
Suck, 85
Susan, 184
Susannah, 185
Teaner, 122
Tenah, 9
Titus, 28
Warrick, 93
Will, 185

-A-

ADLINGTON
  Elizabeth, 107
ADRIANS
  Gosen, 96
ADRIANSE
  Goesen, 165
ALINGTON
  Arthur, 23
ALLEN
  Jonathan, 119
ALLICOCKE
  Joseph, 85(2),
  86(2)
  Martha, 85, 86

ALSTON
David, 213
ALSTYN
John, 73
AMERMAN
Peter, 15
ANDERSON
Alexander, 177
ANDREVET
Peter, 39
ANDREWENT
Peter, 30
Rebecca, 30
ANDROS
Governor, 212
ANDROVET
Andrew, 2
Ann, 2
Anne, 2
Catharine, 1
Daniel, 211
Elinor, 1
Elizabeth, 2(3)
John, 1(4), 2(2),
3, 31, 211(2)
Leah, 1(2), 211
Lewis, 1(3), 2(2)
Mary, 1(2), 211
Peter, 1(3), 2(3),
3, 164, 211
Rachel, 2
Rebecca, 1, 2(3),
31
Susanah, 2(3)
Susannah, 1
Tabitha, 2
ANDROVETTE
John, 36
ANDROWVAT
Hannah, 211
ANKERS
Joseph, 183
ANTOINE
Mr., 133
ARMSTRONG
Martin, 99

ARROWSMITH
Joseph, 128
Mary, 131, 132
Thomas, 131, 132
ASKING
John Jr., 109(2)
AYRES
Benjamin, 43
Mary, 43

-B-

BACKHER
Jacob, 158
Rebecca, 158
BADGLEY
Cornelius, 44
BAKER
Ann, 4
Catharine, 3, 4(2)
Elizabeth, 4
Ephraim, 3
Jacob, 3(2), 4(3)
Lawrence, 211
Neelkie, 4
Nicholas, 3(3)
Rebecca, 3
BALDERIDG
Adam, 54
BALEN
Peter, 109
BALL
John, 178
BALLION
James, 103
BANCKER
Abraham, 57, 121
Abrm, 47
Adrian, 4, 47, 121
Adrian Jr., 146
Adrn, 47
Anna, 4
Catharine, 4
Elizabeth, 4
Evert, 4(2)
Hendrick, 4

Richard, 4(2)
William, 4
BANTA
Cornelius, 216
BANYER
Goldsbrow, 111, 161
BARBANK
Abram, 171
John, 172
Mary, 172
BARCKLOW
Abraham, 34
Wyntie, 202
BARD
John, 190
BARENSON
Tys, 109
BARKELO
Abraham, 4, 5(2)
Catharine, 5(2)
Cornelius, 4, 5(2)
John, 4, 5(2)
Nicholas, 4, 5(2)
Sarah, 5(2)
Wintie, 4, 5(4)
BARKER
Matthew, 6
William, 6, 96
BARNES
Bethiah, 6
Elizabeth, 6(2)
George, 6, 7, 50
John Weston, 6
Margaret, 6(2), 7
Mary, 6
Robert, 6, 7
Roger, 6
BARNET
William, 72
BARNS
George, 112
BARNSE
Scytie, 7
Tyse, 7
BARREMAN
Leonard, 177

BARROW
Catharine, 69
BARTELEAU
John, 7
Margaret, 7
BARTON
Joseph, 80
Sarah, 80
BARTOW
Thomas, 210, 215(2)
BASFORD
John, 144
BASS
Jeremiah, 188
BATY
Edward, 171
BAYARD
N., 11
Petrus, 81
Samuel, 12, 197
BAYEUX
Ann, 8
Henry, 7(2), 8,
27(2)
Mary, 8
Thomas, 7(3), 8,
27(5)
BAYLEY
Catharine, 27
Catherine, 28(2)
Mary, 27, 28
BEATTIE
Edward, 172
BEATTY
Ann, 8(2), 9(2)
Charity, 8, 9
Edward, 9(2), 38
Elizabeth, 8, 9
Isabel, 9
John, 8(2), 9(3),
80, 172, 184
BEBANT
Jacobus, 134
BEBOU
Jacobus, 211
John, 211

BEBOU (continued)
  Mette, 211
  Peter, 211
Bedel
  Annettie, 58
  John, 58
BEDELL
  Ann, 10
  Catharine, 10, 150,
    179
  Cathren, 107
  Cornelius, 9, 10(2)
  Hannah, 9, 10(2)
  Israel, 9, 10(2),
    167
  John, 9(2), 10(3),
    70, 129(2), 155,
    179, 204
  John Jr., 114, 150,
    168
  Joseph, 10(3), 69,
    78, 105, 155, 169,
    203
  Justis, 166
  Miriam, 10
  Silas, 10(2), 105,
    199
  Silas Jr., 200
  Stephen, 54, 70,
    112, 200
BEDINE
  Hester, 18
BEEK
  John, 10(2), 34
  Robert, 202
  Sarah, 202
BEEKMAN
  Gerardus, 35, 111,
    185
BEGALL
  Israel, 173
BELEW
  Peter, 13
BELLIN
  Isaac, 109
BELLVEALLE

John, 102
BELLVILLE
  John, 45
BELVEALLE
  John, 101
BENNET
  Jacob, 117
BERGEN
  Cornelia, 11(2)
  Elsie, 11(3)
  Grietie, 149
  Jacob, 11(5), 97,
    149
  Maria, 11
BERGER
  Cornelia, 48
  Jacob, 48
BERINS
  Samuel, 59
BERNARD
  Moyse, 45
BERRIE
  Jacomintie, 149
  Samuel, 149
BERRY
  Henry, 79, 153, 211
BEVINS
  S., 144
BIBOUT
  John, 211
BILJOU
  Ariantie, 11
  Francina, 11
  Ida, 11(2)
  Isaac, 11
  Jacob, 11(2)
  John, 11
  Peter, 11(2)
BILLAN
  Jacob, 51
BILLIEW
  James, 126(3)
  Peter, 126(3)
BILLOP
  Anne, 13(2), 14
  Christopher, 13(2),

14(3)
J., 112
Jasper Farmer, 14
John, 45
Joseph, 13(2), 189
Sarah, 13, 14
Thomas, 13, 14, 124
BILLOPP
Christopher,
135(3), 140
BILLOU
Catharine, 12
Frances, 12
Isaac, 12(2)
Jacob, 12
Maria, 12
Perrive, 12
Peter, 12(2)
BILLOW
Jacob, 104
BILLVE
Annie, 51
Jacobus, 51
BILLVEE
Jacobus, 51
Martha, 51
BILYOU
Hester, 145
Jacob, 50
BIRD
Abraham, 15
Anthony, 14, 15(3)
Catherone, 15
Elizabeth, 15
Joshua, 15
Judiah, 15
Thomas, 15
BLAKE
Margaret, 202
Thomas, 202
BLANCHER
Elizabeth, 145
Isaac, 145
John, 145
Marian, 145
Peter, 145

Susanah, 145
BLAW
Affie, 38(2)
John, 38(2)
BLOM
John, 36
Rebecca, 36
BLOOMFIELD
Moses, 55
BOBIN
Isaac, 110
BOCKELL
Hermanus, 54
BODEIN
John, 15(2), 16
BODIN
Esther, 18
John, 18(2)
BODIN
John, 18
BODINE
Ann, 16(3)
Darcus, 17
Dorcas, 16(3)
James, 16(3), 83
John, 16(3), 17, 45
Martha, 16(2)
Mary, 16
Rachel, 16, 172
Vince, 16(3)
BOGARDUS
Everardus, 81
William, 71
BOGART
Aeltie, 216
Charity, 9
Elizabeth, 16, 17
Gilbert, 17(2)
Isaac, 16, 17, 202
Jane, 17
Mary, 16
Sarah, 17(2)
Simeon, 191
Simon, 16(2), 17,
143, 192
Thunis, 216

221

BOGART (continued)
  Tunis, 17(2), 143
BOGERT
  Roelof P., 216
BONDET?
  Tabitha, 201
BORROW
  Samuel, 60
BORROWS
  John, 212
BOUDINOT
  Mary C., 74
BOWMAN
  Andreis, 82
  George, 47
  Harmah, 177
  William G., 47
BOWNE
  Obadiah, 31
  Philip, 31
BRAISTED
  Catherine, 17(2)
  Egbert, 17(2)
  John, 17(2)
  Rachel, 17(2)
  William, 63
BRASHEN
  John, 211
BRAT
  Anthony, 75
  Nelly, 75
BREASTED
  Catrina, 75
  John, 75
BREATH
  John, 207
  John Jr., 205
BREESTEDE
  Catharine, 158
  Johanes, 158(2)
BRESTED
  Catrina, 75(2)
  Egbert, 75
  John, 75(2)
  Peter, 75
BRESTEDE

Catharine, 76, 202
Johans, 76
John, 183, 202
BRETON
  Francis, 18(3)
  Hester, 18
  Susannah, 18
BRIDGES
  Elizabeth, 18(2),
    19
BRIDON
  Francis, 19
  Susanah, 18, 19
BRITING
  Nathaniel, 79
BRITON
  Samuel, 202
BRITTAIN
  Abraham, 154
  Benjamin, 71
  Frances, 20
  Francis, 20, 51
  Francke, 21(2)
  Martha, 20, 21(2),
    51(2)
  Mary, 20, 21
  Nathaniel, 19,
    20(2), 21, 45, 66,
    154
  Nathaniel Jr., 42
  Nathaniel Sr., 42
  Nicholas, 20, 21,
    51
  Rachel, 21, 51(2)
  William, 22, 51
BRITTAN
  Benjamin, 105(2),
    162
  Frances, 162, 163
  Hannah, 105(2)
  Martha, 162(2)
  Mary, 163
  Nicholas, 162, 163
BRITTEN
  Benjamin, 168, 201
  Israel, 166

James, 21
Mary, 21
Nathaniel, 95, 107
Samuel, 21
BRITTENE
Samuel, 188
BRITTIN
Benjamin, 202
William, 90
BRITTON
Abigail, 19
Abraham, 19
Alice, 19, 20
Ann, 131
Benjamin, 21, 130
Elizabeth, 19(2),
20
John, 19(3), 20(3)
Mary, 19, 20, 131
Nathaniel, 19(2),
20, 50, 118, 157
Nicholas, 19,
20(3), 65, 131
Rachel, 19, 20
Rebecca, 19, 20
Richard, 19, 117
Samuel, 19(3),
20(3)
Sarah, 19, 20
William, 19(3), 20
BROOME
Abigail, 22
Elizabeth, 22
John, 22, 23
Mary, 22
Samuel, 22(2), 23,
99
BROTTON
Nathaniel, 19
BROUN
George, 212(2)
John, 212
William, 212 ·
BROWER
Abraham, 212, 213
Lea, 212

BROWN
John, 159, 160
Mary, 169
BROWNE
George, 212(4)
John, 212
Obadiah, 174
William, 212
BUCH
Elizabeth, 118
BUDD
John, 36(2)
BUFFLERY
Jacob, 60
Margaret, 60
BURBANK
Abraham, 80(3)
Ann, 80
John, 76
BURGER
Elias, 68, 128
Frederick, 147
Jacob, 161
Minnah, 190
Susannah, 68, 128
BURNET
Ann, 23
John, 195
Samuel, 23
William, 145
BURNETT
William, 110
BURROWE
Dr., 69
BURROWS
Samuel, 106
BURY
William, 213
BUSH
Edward, 108
BUSKIRK
Abraham, 202
Ann, 202
BUTLER
Belitya, 23
Catharine, 192

BUTLER (continued)
  Christian, 192
  Daniel, 192
  Elizabeth, 24
  Frances, 24
  Henry, 2, 23(2),
    24(3)
  James, 13, 23,
    24(3), 80
  John, 24(2), 77,
    148, 192
  Mary, 24, 76, 197
  Nathaniel, 24(2)
  Nelly, 24
  Peter, 192
  Rachel, 192
  Sarah, 24
  Thomas, 24
BUTTERFIELD
  Edmund, 203
BYBAN
  John, 61
BYVANCK
  Aeltie, 24, 81
  Bellikie, 24
  Evert, 24(2), 178
  Johanes, 24(2), 81

        -C-

CAMERON
  Susannah, 190
CANER
  Jane, 203
  Richard, 203
CANNAN
  Abraham, 212
  Isack, 212
  Sarah, 212
CANNON
  Abraham, 25(4), 138
  Andrew, 25(4), 26
  Anna, 25(3)
  Catalina, 25
  David, 25(4), 53,
    138

  Hester, 25
  Isaac, 25
  Janake, 25
  John, 25(2)
  Joseph, 87, 88
  Richard, 200
CANON
  Abraham, 133
  Andre, 18
  Eleanor, 115
  Isaac, 115
CANTWELL
  Richard, 186
CARHART
  Thomas, 34
CARLTON
  Mary, 8
  Richard, 161
  Richard Rev., 8
CARMAN
  James, 20
CASHIE
  Peter, 26
  Philip, 26
CASHIRE
  Elizabeth, 26
  John, 26(2)
  Peter, 26(2)
  Philip, 26(2)
  Sophia, 26
  Susannah, 26
CASIER
  Jean, 214
CASIERS
  John, 41
CASON
  John, 102
CASPER
  Isaac, 145
CASSIER
  Jean, 41
CASSON
  John, 133
CASTELLI
  Catharine, 215
CHADEN

Henry, 50
CHADINE
  John, 18
  Judith, 18(2)
CHADYNE
  Elizabeth, 26
  Henry, 26
  John, 26(2)
  John Sr., 26(2)
  Martha, 26
  Mary, 26(2)
CHAMBERS
  John, 162, 186, 187
  William, 186
CHARLTON
  Catherine, 28
  John, 27(4), 28(8)
  Richard, 14, 27(2),
    79
CHASHEE
  Philip, 25
CHEADEAYNE
  Jean, 26
CHLINDINNY
  Eloner, 83
CHRIPS
  Ann, 168
  Martha, 168
CHRISTINSON
  Jeames, 213
  John, 213
  Magdalena, 213
CHRISTOPER
  Cornelius, 97
CHRISTOPHER
  Barent, 29(3), 126
  Catharine, 126
  Clement, 165
  Edmund, 52
  Elizabeth, 52
  Gerritt, 148
  Hance, 29(2)
  Hans, 29, 159
  Joseph, 75, 206
  Martha, 140
  Nicholas, 29

Stoeffel, 140
Susannah, 29
CHRISTOPHERS
  Barent, 68
  Christentre, 29
  Christofell, 29,
    140
  Stoefel, 139
CHRISTYSON
  Jeames, 213
CHURCHWARD
  Thomas, 201
CLAASON
  Magdalena, 61
CLANDENNY
  Moses, 203
  Walter, 203
CLARK
  Henry, 29(2)
  Jeremiah, 76
CLARKE
  George, 92, 161
  Thomas, 29
CLASON
  Rem, 23
CLAUSON
  Gustavus, 138
CLENDENING
  Mary, 118
  Moses, 40
CLENDENNE
  Jacob, 203
  Nelly, 203
  Walter, 203
CLENDENNEY
  Moses, 86
CLENDENNING
  Mary, 203
  Moses, 85, 203
CLENDENNY
  Moses, 157
CLENDNE
  Walter, 34
COCHERON
  Anna, 149
  Henry, 149

CODWISE
  John C., 213
COFFIN
  Ann, 29, 30
COLDEN
  Cadwallader, 8
  Governor, 71
COLE
  Abraham, 9, 10, 17,
    18, 27, 30(5),
    31(3), 32, 66, 89,
    90, 102, 103, 104,
    115, 153(2),
    154(2), 191, 192,
    211
  Abraham Jr., 24
  Anne, 30, 32(2)
  Benjamin, 52, 85,
    86
  Cornelius, 30,
    31(3), 32(3), 94,
    126, 131, 154, 174
  David, 30, 31(2),
    32(3), 154
  Ester, 32
  Esther, 103, 115
  Eve, 52
  Hannah, 9, 10
  Isaac, 17, 30, 31,
    32, 102, 103, 115,
    154
  Jacob, 2, 30, 31,
    32(2), 154
  John, 32, 154, 215
  Martha, 113
  Mary, 30
  Patience, 131
  Peter, 154, 215
  Rebecca, 30, 31,
    153
  Richard, 30(3), 32,
    89, 142, 143, 168,
    169
  Stephen, 30, 31,
    154
  Susanah, 30

Susannah, 30, 215
William, 32
COLES
  Abraham, 31
  Benjamin, 31
  Hester, 31
  Isaac, 31(2)
  John, 31
  Mary, 31
  Peter, 31
  Richard, 31(2)
COLON
  Abraham, 33
  Daniel, 33
  Elizabeth, 33
  George, 80
  James, 33, 38, 184
  Jonas, 33
  Mary, 32
  Mary M., 33
  Peter, 32
COMEING
  Ann, 181
COMES
  Solomon, 21, 203
CONGAR
  David, 141
CONNER
  Richard, 55(2),
    107, 131, 146,
    166, 173
  Richard Jr., 107
CONNOR
  Jeremiah, 63
  Richard, 72
COOPER
  Benjamin, 61
CORBET
  Isaac, 153
CORBETT
  Abraham, 29
  Jacob, 102
CORCHON
  John, 26
CORNBERRY
  Lord, 81

CORNBURY
  Edward, 163, 167
  Lord, 103, 142,
    149, 163
CORNE
  Simeon, 109
CORNELL
  Hannah, 199
  John, 126
CORNU
  Elizabeth, 181
  Peter, 181
CORSEN
  Ann, 33(2), 34(2),
    35(2)
  Antee, 34
  Antye, 36
  Benjamin, 36(5)
  Capt., 45
  Catharine, 35(2)
  Charity, 203
  Christian, 33(3),
    35, 36(2), 158
  Clashe, 203
  Cornelius, 5, 6,
    33(7), 34(4),
    35(6), 111, 148
  Dan'l, 209
  Daniel, 11, 33(9),
    34(3), 35(4)
CORSEN
  Daniel, 35
CORSEN
  Daniel, 36(2), 77,
    111(2), 138, 150,
    162, 171, 203
  Dowe, 36(2)
  Elizabeth, 36(2)
  Henry, 25
  Jacob, 10, 36(7),
    48, 184, 196
  Jacobus, 35(4)
  Jane, 33, 34
  Jannettie, 35(2)
  John, 36
  Katharine, 34

Katherine, 33
Maritie, 34, 35
Mary, 33(3), 34(2),
  35(3), 36, 171,
  203
Neetiea, 33
Peter, 33(2), 34,
  35(3), 111
Rebecca, 36
Richard, 33, 34(2),
  45, 203
Sarah, 36
Suster, 36(2)
CORSING
  Jacob, 158
CORSON
  Cornelius, 151
  Daniel, 182, 203
  Danl., 157
  Esther, 37
  Gurtie, 209
  John, 24, 37
  Peter, 209
CORTELYOU
  A., 80
  Aaron, 2, 3, 7,
    152, 165
  Cornelius, 38, 85,
    148
  Eleanor, 38
  Elenor, 38
  Elizabeth, 2
  Jacob, 38(4)
  Jaques Sr., 97
  Martha, 38
  Mary, 38
  Peter, 9, 38(3),
    49, 173, 184
  Sarah, 38(3)
COSBY
  William, 90, 92
COSINE
  Affie, 38
  Altie, 37, 38
  Cornelius, 37(2),
    38(2)

COSINE (continued)
  Garrit, 37
  Jacob, 37(2), 38(2)
  James, 37(3), 38(2)
  Wilhelmes, 37(2),
    38(2)
COSSON
  John, 18
COSYNE
  Garret, 38
COURSEN
  Cornelius, 188(3)
COURSON
  Daniel, 35
  Jacob, 35, 196
COWARD
  Alice, 20
  John, 20
COX
  William, 68
COZEER
  John, 103
COZIER
  Sarah, 71(2)
COZINE
  Games, 83
  Wilhelmas, 83
CRAIG
  Andrew, 215
CRANE
  William, 190
CRAVEN
  Richard H., 73(2)
CRECHERON
  John, 141
CREUSE
  Hendrick, 76
CRIMSHIER
  Althis, 189
  John D., 189
CRIPS
  Lawrence, 48
  Richard, 40, 171,
    203
CROCHERON
  Abigail, 43, 44

Abraham, 39(2),
  40(5), 42(4),
  43(4), 44(7), 109,
  184
Ann, 44
Anna, 150
Anne, 45
Anthony, 41(3)
Ariantie, 39
Catharine, 39(2),
  40
Daniel, 39(2),
  40(2), 85, 86
Elizabeth, 40, 42,
  43, 44
Henry, 43, 44, 150
Jacob, 40(3)
Janne, 44
Jean, 41
Johanah, 43
Johannah, 44
John, 40(3), 41(3),
  42(6), 43(4), 44,
  109, 150
Mary, 39, 40,
  41(2), 42(2), 43,
  44
Nicholas, 40(2),
  41(3), 44(2),
  45(2)
Sarah, 43, 44
CROESSEN
  Henry, 183
CROSUIVER
  Cornelius, 188(2)
CRUSE
  Abraham, 47(2)
  Charity, 47
  Clausia, 47(2)
  Cornelius, 47(3),
    48(2)
  Garret, 47
  Garrett, 47
  Garritt, 47
  Gerritt, 48
  Hendrick, 47(3)

229

DE HART (continued)
Samuel, 119
Samuel Jr., 100
DE MEYER
Nicholas, 161
William, 162
DE PEW
Moses, 118
DE PUE
Barent, 2
DE RAMP
Laurence, 4
DEARE
Jonathan, 213
DECKER
Barnet, 52
Charles, 51(2),
52(2), 118, 119
Chas., 52
Elenor, 51, 52
Elice, 52(2), 53
Elizabeth, 52
Eva, 52
Eve, 52
Hester, 52
Jacob, 54
James S., 52
Jemima, 52
Jenny, 53
Johanes, 52
John, 52(3)
Margaret, 53, 119
Mary, 52(2), 204
Mathew, 33, 199
Matthew, 52(8),
53(2), 76, 204
Matthew Jr., 10
Matthias, 52(6),
53(5), 204
Mercy, 52, 118
Miriam, 10
Moses, 52(4)
Peter, 52, 149, 204
Rebecca, 52
Richard, 53(3), 119
Silvanus, 52

DEDICKER
Peter, 54
DEGROOT
Robert, 48
Sarah, 106, 214
William, 214,
215(2)
DEHART
Mathias, 3
DELANCEY
James, 193
DEMAREST
David, 91
Johannes, 216
DEMOTT
Hendrick, 175
Margaret, 175
DENYS
Anne, 53
Denys, 53
Helma, 53
Isaac, 53
Jacques, 53(2)
Teunis, 53
DEPEAW
Aaron, 169
Martha, 169
DEPUE
Johanes, 89
Leah, 126
Moses, 126
DEPUY
Aaron, 55
Barent, 52
Catharine, 55
Elizabeth, 55
John, 55
Moses, 55
Nicholas, 55
Peter, 55
DES MARETS
David, 213(2)
Jaquemine, 212
John, 212(2),
213(2)
Lea, 212

231

57(2)
  Mark, 56(3)
  Mary, 55, 56, 57(6)
  Susannah, 57(5)
  Violetta, 57(5)
DUXBURY
  Elias, 42
  Ellis, 61(2), 163
DYE
  James, 19
  Sarah, 65

-E-

ECERT
  Andrew, 127
EDGAR
  David, 122
EGBERT
  Abraham, 48, 62, 63
  Ann, 62
  Anthony, 205
  Benjamin, 62(2)
  Catharine, 62(3)
  Caty, 62
  Elizabeth, 62
  James, 62(2), 63
  John, 53, 62
  Lawrence, 62
  Mary, 62(2)
  Nicholas, 62
  Peter, 62
  Susanah, 62
  Tunis, 62, 63(2),
    205
EGBERTS
  Abraham, 44, 166,
    205
  Anthony, 17, 44, 54
  Elizabeth, 76, 205
  Fransentie, 61
  Mary, 16, 44
  Tunis, 171, 172
EGBERTSE
  Abraham, 63
  Egbert, 63(2)

Harmitie, 63
Isaac, 63
Jacques, 63(2)
James, 21, 61
Janettie, 63
John, 63
Laurence, 63
Mary, 63, 115
Susannah, 63
Teunis, 63(2)
EGBERTSEN
  Abraham, 165
ELDER
  Thomas, 187(2)
ELIS
  Garrit, 176
ELLIS
  Anattie, 63
  Ariante, 63
  Bastian, 63(3),
    64(2)
  Catharine, 63(2)
  Cornelius, 63(2),
    64
  Eagge, 63(2)
  Garret, 156, 167(2)
  Gerritt, 64
  Hendrica, 63(2)
  Magdalen, 64
  Mary, 63(2), 167
  Sarah, 63, 64
ELLISS
  Hankey, 147
ELLSTONE
  William, 30
ELLSWORTH
  William, 177
EMOTT
  Mary, 74
EYTERS
  Teunis, 132

-F-

FALLEN
  Laughlen, 1

FARMER
  Jasper, 14
  Thomas, 165
FARNER
  Anne, 13
  Thomas, 13
FEY
  Francis, 180
  John, 180
FIELD
  Elizabeth, 205
  Thomas, 205
FILLYER
  William, 41
FITZ RANDOLPH
  Elizabeth, 213(2)
  Jacob, 201
  Martha, 213
  Nathaniel, 213
  Reuben, 213(2)
FITZRANDOLPH
  Nathaniel, 55
FLEMING
  Patrick, 205
FLETCHER
  Benjamin, 15, 35,
    40, 101
  Governor, 16, 41,
    71
FLOYD
  Richard, 64
  Ruth, 64
FONDRILL
  William, 213
FOORD
  Oswald, 24, 82,
    128, 196
FORBES
  Gilbert, 50
FORD
  Oswald, 26, 84(2)
FORREST
  James, 32, 140
  Margaret, 140
FOUNTAIN
  Anne, 64, 65(2)

Anthony, 64, 65(3),
  175
Cornelius, 44
Elizabeth, 65
John, 65
Martha, 65(2), 135
Sarah, 65
Vincent, 21, 64,
  65(4), 175, 196
Vincent Jr., 20,
  115
Vincent Sr., 64,
  115
FOUPET
  Johannes, 103
FOWLER
  John, 146
FOY
  Francis, 180
  John, 180(2)
  Mary, 180
FRASER
  George, 110
  William, 110, 147
FRAZEE
  George, 214(2)
  William, 214
FREELAND
  Helmus, 48
  Jacob, 175, 185
  Wilhelmus, 165
FROLICH
  Christian, 173
FROST
  Thomas, 22, 27, 28,
    92

-G-

GAMBOLD
  Hector, 79, 80
  Mr., 85
  Rev. Mr., 172
GANO
  Lewis, 43(2)
GARREAU

234

GOELET (continued)
  Philip, 187
GOLDERS
  Anna, 61
GOLDSMITH
  Sharmin, 96
GOOLD
  John, 129
GOULD
  Abraham, 70(2)
  Catharine, 113
  Catherine, 70
  John, 70(3), 113
  Mary, 88
  Peter, 70(3)
GOUVERNEUR
  Abraham, 12, 81,
    133
GOVERNEUR
  Isaac, 144
GRAHAM
  Augustine, 76
  Augustus, 197
GRANDINE
  John, 108
GRASSET
  Samuel, 214
GRASSETT
  Augustus, 26, 70
  Hester, 70
  Martha, 70
  Mary, 70
GRAZILIER
  Elias, 214
GREEN
  Margaret, 215
  Sarah Mary, 215
GRIFFITH
  Christian, 103
GRIGGS
  Teunis, 18
GROENENDYCK
  Peter, 181
GROESBECK
  Ann, 8(2)
GRONDAIN

Esther, 71
John, 70, 130, 155
Leuis, 3
Lewis, 71(3), 122,
  124, 180
Margaret, 70, 71(2)
Mary, 71
Peter, 71(2), 122
Samuel, 71(2)
GRONDEN
  John, 60
GROOM
  William, 182, 188
GROVER
  Barzilla, 49
GUERING
  John, 88
GUION
  James, 135
GUYEN
  Jacques, 71(2)
  Sarah, 71
GUYON
  Addrie, 205
  Adransha, 71
  Andrasha, 72
  Anne, 72
  Ariantie, 72
  Catharine, 92
  Elizabeth, 72
  Jacques, 71(2)
  James, 22, 71(3),
    72(4), 170
  John, 9, 72(2)
  Joseph, 9, 27, 28,
    57, 72(3), 96, 170
  Mary, 71, 72(3)
  Peter, 72
  Philip, 72(3), 205
  Sarah, 72
  Stephen, 72, 205

-H-

HADING
  Catharine, 97

236

Thomas, 97
HAGAWOUT
  Altie, 76
  Diritie, 76
  Egbert, 76
  Geritie, 76
  Harmettie, 76
  Isaac, 76
  Jacob, 76
  John, 76
  Leah, 76
  Leffert, 76
  Peter, 76(2)
  Rachel, 76
HAGEWOUT
  Catharine, 76(2)
  Dirckje, 76(2)
  Egbert, 76
  Gertruyd, 76
  Jacob, 76
  Margaret, 76
  Neeltie, 76
  Neeltje, 76
  Nicholas, 76
  Peter, 76(2)
HALL
  Edward, 106
HALLETT
  Jacob, 101
HALSTED
  Elizabeth, 189
  John Jr., 189
HAMILTON
  Alexander, 190
HAMPTON
  Abraham, 214
  Andrew, 215(2)
  Jonathan, 214
HAND
  Hannah, 205
HARDY
  Charles, 90
HARRIS
  Abraham, 73, 206
  James, 73(2)
  Margaret, 72

Martha, 73(2)
Richard, 72, 73,
  125
William, 215
William S., 215
HARRISON
  George, 158
  John, 186
  Morley, 159
  Richard, 158, 159
  William, 73, 74
HART
  Michael, 193
HASTE
  Bartholomew, 74
  Benjamin, 74
  Catharine, 74, 75
  Charles, 74
  Cornelia, 74
  Jacob, 74
  Johanes, 74
  Sophia, 74
HATFIELD
  Jacob, 44
HAUGHWOUT
  Catharine, 202
  Egbert, 75, 202
  Nelly, 75
  Peter, 75
HAUSMAN
  Peter, 52, 108(2),
    165
HAYWOOD
  James, 92
HAZEWOUT
  Peter, 76
HEASTON
  John, 77
HENDRICKS
  Susannah, 59
HERTTELL
  John, 173
HETFIELD
  Joseph, 214
HICKS
  Catrina, 177

237

HICKS (continued)
  Thomas, 177
  William, 60
HIGGINS
  Gershom, 214
HILLYARD
  Lawrence, 200
HILLYER
  Benjamin, 8, 79
  Catharine, 78(2)
  Elizabeth, 78
  Frances, 77
  Hester, 77, 78, 97
  James, 78
  John, 8, 34(2),
    40(3), 44, 77(2),
    78(3), 79, 97,
    117, 142, 208
  John Jr., 77, 97,
    146, 168
  John, Jr., 140
  Laurence, 78, 79(2)
  Mary, 78
  Nathaniel, 142
  Simon, 39
  William, 79, 142
HOCK
  Mattler, 198
HOGERWERT
  Nicholas, 206
  Peter, 206
HOGLANDT
  Dirck, 82
HOGLANT
  George, 47
HOLLAND
  Henry, 64
HOLLY
  William, 88
HOLMES
  Anne, 79(4)
  Joseph, 72, 79(4)
  Joseph Jr., 72
  Joseph Sr., 79
  Lucy, 80
  Mary, 79, 80(2)

  Obadiah, 79, 91,
    125, 133, 164
  Samuel, 21, 72(2),
    79(2), 80(2), 92,
    95, 130
  Sarah, 79
  Thomas, 80(2)
HOOGELAND
  Christophel, 187
HOOGEWATER
  Peter, 84
HOOGHLAND
  Altie, 81
  Arient, 81(2)
  Cornelia, 187
  Dirck, 81(2)
  Elizabeth, 81(2)
  George, 81(2)
  Johanes, 81(3)
  Mary, 81
  Sarah, 81(2)
HOOGLAND
  Adrian, 81(2)
  Aeltie, 82
  Amitie, 82
  Anne, 81(2)
  Beeltie, 81
  Christophel, 188
  Cornelia, 187, 188
  Daniel, 82(2)
  Dirck, 81(2), 82(2)
  Elizabeth, 81, 82
  Helena, 81
  Joris, 82(2)
  Katharine, 82(2)
  Maritie, 81, 82
  Sarah, 81, 82
  Widow, 196
  William, 149
HOOGLANDT
  Aeltie, 81
  Dirck, 82
  Elizabeth, 82
  Johanes, 81(2), 82
  Joras, 81
HOOGWERT

238

Peter, 89
HOOPER
  Daniel, 32
  Elizabeth, 145
HOPPER
  Barneck, 139(2)
  Mary, 51
  Oreck, 139(4)
HORN
  Peter V., 198
HOUGHWOUT
  Catrina, 75
  Dirckje, 75
  Egbert, 75(2)
  Maritie, 75
  Nelly, 75(2)
  Nicholas, 75
  Peter, 75
HOUSEMAN
  Aurt, 83
  John, 38
  Peter, 38, 45, 119
  Richard, 83, 188
HOUSMAN
  Abraham, 83(2), 93
  Anthony, 83
  Aurt, 83
  Benjamin, 82(2), 83
  Cathrin, 83
  Elisabeth, 83
  Isac, 83
  Jacob, 83
  James, 83
  Jemima, 83
  Johanah, 82(2), 83
  Johannah, 92
  John, 82(2), 83(2),
    93, 206
  Maregret, 83
  Martha, 82(2), 83
  Mary, 83(5)
  Peter, 5, 6, 75,
    82(3), 83, 92,
    93(2), 206
  Richard, 83, 93
  Sarah, 83

HUBBARD
  Benjamin, 67
HUDDLESTON
  William, 26
HUDDLESTONE
  Joseph, 115
  William, 115
HUDE
  Adam, 212(2)
HUGHES
  Timothy, 50
HUGHS
  William, 176
  William E., 157
HUISMAN
  Johanes, 119, 149
  Johannes, 150
  Wyntie, 150
HUNTER
  Governor, 62
  Robert, 62, 81, 163
HUTCHESON
  Benjamin, 7
HUTCHINSON
  Catharine, 106
HUYLER
  Jones, 216
  Marya, 216
HYER
  John, 212
  Rachel, 212
  Thomas, 212

-I-

INGART
  Annanetia, 84
  Antea, 84
  Charles, 84
  Christine, 84
  John, 84(4)
  Tice, 84
  Trientie, 84
  Yellis, 83(2)
INGOLDSBY
  Richard, 12, 161,

239

INGOLDSBY (continued)
170, 188
INYARD
Elizabeth, 79

-J-

JACKMAN
Tho., 214
JACKS
John, 175
JACKSON
Gilbert, 2, 57, 169
JACOBSEN
Christian, 95, 117
J., 33
JACOBSON
Ann, 84(2), 85, 172
Catharine, 84, 85
Christain, 172
Christian, 84, 116,
152
Elizabeth, 84, 85
John, 84, 173
John B., 84
JAMAINE
Nicholas, 13
JANDINE
Catharine, 85, 130
Cathrine, 86
Charles, 85(2),
86(2)
Hanah, 86
Hannah, 85
Martha, 85, 86
Mary, 85, 86(3)
Susanah, 85, 86
JANDINS
Catharine, 103
JARMYN
Anne, 86
John, 86
JEFFRIES
David, 190
JENKINS
Jane C., 197

JENNER
John, 35, 111
John Jr., 35
Mary, 111
JEQUIEN
Louis J., 37
JOB
Elizabeth, 168
JOHNSON
Abigail, 90, 91
Abraham, 86, 90, 91
Albert, 87(2),
88(2), 89
Ann, 90
Anne, 87, 89(3),
90, 91
Belichy, 90
Catharine, 88(2)
Charity, 90(2)
Cornelius, 89
Dona, 99
Dowe, 32
Dowel?, 87
Dr., 165
Elizabeth, 88, 89,
90, 163, 197
Eloner, 172
Ephraim, 32, 90(2),
91, 194
Ephrame, 163
Harmon, 89
Henry, 59, 89,
90(2), 91, 113
Jabez, 189, 190
Jacob, 19
James, 87(2), 90,
91
Johana, 189
Johannes, 112
Lambert, 19, 69
Lidia, 90
Lydia, 91, 175
Margaret, 89
Marjorie D., 139
Martha, 87, 88
Mary, 87, 88,

89(4), 90, 115
Mathias, 89
Matthew, 90(3)
Matthias, 14, 89(2)
Nathaniel, 17,
  89(3), 90(2),
  91(2), 107, 172
Phebe, 90, 91
Rachel, 87, 88(2),
  90, 113
Robert, 87, 88(3),
  90, 115
Sarah, 89(3), 91,
  107
Seiley, 197
Sophia, 175
Susanah, 89
Thomas, 143
William, 17, 58,
  89(5), 90(4),
  91(2), 175
Winants, 90, 91(2)
JOHNSTON
  John, 159
JONES
  Abraham, 54, 146
  Isaac, 206
  John, 108
JOURNEAY
  Anne, 185
  John, 135
  Nicholas, 185
JOURNEE
  Elizabeth, 91
  Malliard, 91
JOURNEY
  John, 69, 78, 113,
    124, 125
JURNE
  Elizabeth, 51
  Mary, 51

-K-

KARL
  Thomas, 206

KEARNY
  Philip, 214
KEEN
  John, 184
KEIZEAN
  Philip, 148
KELSY
  Benjamin, 138
KETTLETAS
  Catharine, 92
  Elizabeth, 92
  John, 91, 92(3)
  Stephen, 92(3)
KIERSTEAD
  James, 92, 196
  John, 206
  Samuel, 206
KIERSTED
  Samuel, 92
KIERSTEDE
  James, 95
KILSEY
  Benjamin, 92
  Daniel, 93
  Hannah, 92(2)
  Lydia, 93
KING
  Andrew, 98
  John, 190
KINGDOM
  John, 125
KINGSLY
  Thomas, 153
KINGSTON
  Thomas, 16, 40, 53
  William, 38
KINNEIS
  Arian, 186
KITCHEN
  John, 67
  Joseph, 67
KROESE
  Gerrit, 77
  Klaes, 77
KROESEN
  Hendrick, 48, 146,

LAKE
  Alice, 95
  Alleday, 95
  Ann, 152
  Daniel, 12, 33, 72,
    94(2), 95(2), 96,
    130, 135, 152,
    159, 170
  Daniel Jr., 152
  David, 95
  Elizabeth, 95(3)
  John, 95, 188
  Joseph, 22, 94, 96,
    151, 207
  Margretha, 95
  Mary, 169(2)
  Sarah, 52, 94, 95,
    206
  Thomas, 43
  William, 95(6),
    137, 169(3), 206
LAKEMAN
  Abraham, 15,
    101(2), 102, 115
  Peter, 12
LAKERMAN
  Abraham, 97
  Isaac, 87(2)
  Mary, 154
  William, 32, 154
LAKERMANS
  Abraham, 96
  Anje, 96
  Catharine, 96
  Elizabeth, 96
  Hester, 96
  Jacob, 96
  Mary, 96
LAMB
  Catharine, 85
  James, 86(2)
  Mary, 85, 86(3)
LANGDON
  Solomon, 206
LANSING
  Gerrit A., 181

LARGELLER
  Frances, 12
  Nicholas, 12(3)
LARGILLIER
  Frances, 12
  Nicholas, 12
LAROE
  Abraham, 214
  Alche, 214
LARZALERE
  Nicholas, 103
LARZELEAR
  Nicholas, 160
LARZELERE
  Benjamin, 73,
    97(4), 129, 204
  Catharine, 97
  Elizabeth, 97
  Jacob, 97(2)
  Nicholas, 97, 102,
    125(2), 126, 128
  Nicholas Jr., 102,
    125
LARZLERE
  Nicholas, 88
LASILLIER
  Nicholas, 187
LATIMER
  Solomon, 98
LATOURETTE
  Catharine, 103,
    133(2)
  David, 99(2),
    100(3), 103, 106,
    107, 126, 133(2)
  Easter, 98
  Elizabeth, 105, 107
  Henry, 99, 100(3),
    107, 179
  James, 93, 99,
    100(2), 105,
    107(3)
  Jean, 103
  John, 106, 215(2)
  Jonathan, 100(5)
  Mary, 214

LATOURETTE (continued)
  Peter, 206(2)
  Phebe, 100, 107
  Sarah, 107, 214
LATOWRETTE
  John, 112
LATURETTE
  James, 163
  Mary, 163
LAURENCE
  Jonathan, 101
  Richard, 101
  William, 100
LAWRENCE
  Ann, 100
  Catharine, 3,
    100(2)
  Edstel, 100
  Elisha, 131
  Governor, 69
  Hanah, 86
  Hannah, 85
  John, 3, 100
  Leggett, 6
  Mary, 6(2), 104,
    147
  Mary Jr., 147
  Nicholas, 100
  Richard, 34, 64(2),
    100, 104(2), 146,
    147(2)
LAZALERE
  Benjamin, 114
  Nicholas, 157
LAZELIER
  Hester, 96
  Nicholas, 96, 97
LE COMPT
  Johanes, 139
  Johannes, 139(2)
  Mary, 139(2)
LE COMTE
  Peter, 11
LE CONTE
  Frances, 102
  John, 102(5), 115,

  133, 144, 157, 177
  Margaret, 206
  Mary, 22, 102
LE COUNT
  Hester, 50
  John, 51, 88, 89,
    104, 144
  Margaretta, 87
  Marguerite, 89
  Martha, 51
  Mrs., 87
  Peter, 51
LE COUNTE
  Frances, 102
  James, 103
  John, 37, 102(2),
    103(5), 130
  Margaret, 102(2),
    103(2), 130
  Martha, 102, 103
  Mary, 102, 103
  Peter, 102, 103(3)
LE FARGE
  Adrian, 134
LEA TOURETTE
  Henry, 128
LEADBEATER
  James, 158
LEADBETTER
  James, 159
LEAKE
  Daniel, 184
  Daniel Jr., 9
  Joseph, 52
LECONTE
  John, 193(3)
LECOUNT
  Anne, 103
  Margaret, 104
  Mary, 104
  Peter, 103
LECOUNTE
  Hester, 101(2)
  John, 101(3),
    102(2)
  Peter, 101(3)

244

LOTT (continued)
  Englebart, 23
  Englebert, 108
  Johanes, 149
LOURENS
  Hans, 15
LOW
  Daniel, 18
LOWRIE
  Richard, 67
LOZIER
  Nicholas, 49
LUDLOW
  Cary, 85
LUTINE
  Abraham, 109(2)
  Ann, 109
  Hester, 109
  Mary, 109
LYNN
  David, 98(2)

-M-

McCARROL
  John, 21
McCLEAN
  Charles, 210
McDANIEL
  Joseph, 78, 135
McDONALD
  Joseph, 99
MACHILERSE
  John, 76
MACKENZIE
  Aeneas, 109, 110
  Elizabeth, 109,
    110(2)
  Eneas, 62(2), 110
MacLEAN
  Ann, 150
McLEAN
  Catharine, 111(2)
  Charles, 35(2),
    110(2), 111(2),
    177, 207

  Cornelius, 110,
    111(2), 207
MACLEAN
  Mary, 34
McLEAN
  Mary, 35, 110,
    111(3)
MACLEAN
  Solomon, 51
McLEAN
  William, 110,
    111(2)
MACMOE
  Mary, 192
McNEIL
  Anthony, 80(2)
  Mary, 80(2)
McSWAIN
  Catharine, 111
  Daniel, 111
  Elizabeth, 112
  John, 111(5), 112
  Mary, 111, 112
  Sarah, 111
  Vincent, 111(4),
    112(2)
MAKLYS
  Jan, 84
MALDREN
  James, 79
MANCE
  Abraham, 70
MANE
  Isaac, 132
MANEE
  Isaac, 113
  John, 90
MANETT
  Abraham, 112(2)
  Isaac, 112
  John, 112
  Mary, 112
  Peter, 112(4)
MANGLES
  Janette, 61
MANGLESONE

246

247

MARTINO (continued)
  Stephen, 11, 116(2)
MARTINS
  Abraham, 117(3)
  Ann, 117
  Benjamin, 117(3)
  Charity, 116, 117
  Cornelia, 117(2)
  Cornelius, 116,
    117(2)
  Elenor, 117(2)
  Elizabeth, 116, 117
  Mary, 117
  Sarah, 117(2)
  Stephen, 116(2),
    117
  Susanah, 117
MARTLING
  Barent, 20, 177
MARTLINGS
  Barent, 51
MATISEN
  Mary, 96
  Nicholas, 96
MENTOSS
  Mary, 6
MERALL
  Philip, 139
  Richard, 139
MERCEREA
  Richard, 94
MERCEREAU
  Aaron, 120
  Anne, 94
  Christian, 94
  Frances, 114
  Joshua, 36
  Martha, 114
  Stephen, 69, 201
MERCHEROW
  Daniel, 127
MERELL
  Catharine, 118
  Elizabeth, 118(2)
  Mary, 118
  Neley, 118

Nicholas, 118(2)
Philip, 118(3)
Richard, 118
Susanah, 118
MERIL
  Anne, 117
  Catharine, 117
  Charity, 117
  Charlotte, 117
  John, 117(3)
  Richard, 117
  Susannah, 117
MERILL
  Altie, 207
  John, 207
MERRALL
  John, 75
MERREL
  Richard, 117
MERRELL
  Alse, 25, 118(3)
  Ann, 117
  Gertruy, 117
  Jodia, 117(2)
  John, 25, 117(3),
    119, 124
  Mary, 119
  Richard, 118(2),
    119(2)
  Sarah, 117
  Weintia, 117
  William, 117, 119
MERRIL
  John, 118
  Leanah, 118
MERRILL
  Elice, 53
  John, 53, 76, 119
  Magdalen, 53
  Richard, 25, 33,
    53, 119, 163
  Sarah, 119
  Susanah, 119
  Thomas, 118(2),
    119(2)
  Tyon, 119

MERSELISM
Peter, 198
MERSEREAU
Abigail, 123
Abraham, 138
Allede, 138
Anne, 105
Bathsheba, 105
Catharine, 120(3)
Cornelia, 119, 188
Cornelius, 122, 148
Daniel, 61, 119,
  120(3), 121(3),
  122(3), 123(2),
  188
Daniel Sr., 122
David, 114(2),
  121(4), 122(2),
  123(7), 147
Elizabeth, 6,
  120(2), 121(3),
  122(3), 123, 207
Esther, 122
Henry, 120(5), 121
Jacob, 129, 208
Johanes, 122
John, 15, 114,
  120(3), 121(2),
  122(3), 123(4),
  138, 179(2), 192,
  205, 207, 210
Joshua, 15, 24, 36,
  122(2), 138, 147,
  206, 207(2)
Jude, 121(2), 122
Lawrance, 148
Margaret, 121(3),
  122
Martha, 114(2), 121
Mary, 36, 121, 122,
  123, 138, 148, 207
Nancy, 121
Paul, 6, 73, 114,
  121(2), 123, 136
Peter, 121(3), 122
Richard, 93, 180

Sarah, 105, 121
MESEREAU
Frances, 113
John, 132, 207
Joshua, 26
Joshua Jr., 36, 100
Martha, 207
Mary, 26
Paul, 113
Stephen, 200
MESSEREAU
Stephen, 71
MESSEROLE
John, 157
MESSIER
Abraham, 198
METZELAER
Gertie, 181
MICHAUD
Anne, 51
Paul, 103
MICHAUX
Anne, 124
Catharine, 124(2)
John, 124(2)
Paul, 14, 37, 51,
  124(3), 134, 162,
  201, 209
MICHEAU
John, 96, 97, 105,
  113, 114, 127,
  137, 140, 194
Paul, 2, 17, 49,
  88, 90, 91, 96,
  97, 100, 105, 107,
  113, 115, 127,
  137, 140, 154, 203
MICHEAUX
Paul, 37
MICHELL
Richard, 15
MIER
Marcus, 75
MILLER
M., 103
Thomas, 153

NICHOLLS
  Wm., 208
NICOLL
  Benjamin, 8(3)
  Mary M., 8
NICOLLS
  Elizabeth, 27, 28
NIELL
  Anthony, 112
NISSEPAT
  Jasper, 12
NOBLE
  Thomas, 128
NOE
  John, 2
  Peter, 2
NORRIS
  Elizabeth, 208
  Samuel, 208(2), 215

-O-

OGDEN
  Robert, 3
OLDFIELD
  Joseph, 70
  Martha, 70
OLPHERTS
  Duncan, 159
OSBORN
  Samuel, 75
OSBURN
  Catharine, 132
OUENMOUFE
  Zacharis, 189
OZANS
  Henry, 37
  Mary, 37

-P-

PALMER
  Anna, 50
  John, 29
PARELIE
  Peter, 61

PARKER
  Benjamin, 99, 147,
   148
  Easter, 99
  Elisha, 144
  Elizabeth, 147
  John, 99
  Mary, 148
PARLEAY
  Abraham, 129(2)
  Barnet, 129(2)
  Catherine, 129
  Jacob, 129
  Martha, 129(2)
  Mary, 129
PARLEE
  Abraham, 115, 129
  Bornt, 114
  Catharine, 129
  Henry, 191
  Jacob, 129
  Margaret, 129
  Peter, 114
  Rebecca, 191
PARLIEA
  Martha, 129
  Peter, 129(2)
PARLIER
  Abraham, 128(3),
   155
  Ann, 145(2)
  Barent, 128
  Catharine, 128
  Henry, 128
  Jacob, 128
  John, 88, 128
  Mary, 113, 128, 155
  Peter, 128
PARMAR
  Saxton Sr., 160
PARMER
  Elizabeth, 58
PEARCE
  Joseph, 73, 74(2)
PEARSE
  Abraham, 31

PEATMAN
  Daniel, 154
PERINE
  Ann, 130, 131(2)
  Anne, 64, 65
  Daniel, 132
  David, 31
  Dinah, 131
  Edward, 130,
    131(5), 154
  Hendrick, 80
  Henry, 24, 31(2),
    64, 67, 98,
    130(2), 131(5),
    132, 135, 153(4),
    154, 191, 194
  James, 131, 132(2)
  Jane, 17
  Joseph, 130, 131
  Margaret, 131(2)
  Mary, 131(3)
  Peter, 38, 131(3),
    132(2), 133
  Sarah, 131(2)
  Susanah, 153, 154
  William, 17, 131,
    132(2)
PERLE
  Abraham, 130
  Ann, 130
  Elizabeth, 130
  Esther, 130
  John, 130(3)
  Martha, 130
  Mary, 130
  Peter, 130
  Sarah, 130
PERLEY
  John, 87
PERLIEU
  Peter, 108
PERRINE
  Daniel, 130
  Edward, 98
PERSONET
  George, 61

PERSONETT
  George, 144
PHILLIPSE
  Frederick, 187
PIERSON
  John, 55
PIGGOT
  Robert, 197
PILLION
  James, 208
  Sarah, 208
POILLON
  Abraham, 133(2),
    136(3), 137(2),
    206, 208
  Adaontia, 134
  Adriana, 133(2)
  Adriance, 132
  Adrianna, 133
  Catharine, 132,
    133(2), 136(2)
  Elizabeth, 20,
    133(2), 134
  Frances, 134
  Heletye, 155
  Hillitie, 135,
    136(4)
  Jacques, 45, 104,
    134
  James, 20, 77, 108,
    112, 124(2),
    133(3), 134, 136,
    208
  James Jr., 137
  Jaques, 132(6),
    133(2)
  John, 22, 63, 72,
    77(2), 131,
    132(2), 133(3),
    134, 135(2),
    136(2), 137, 204,
    208
  Judeth, 134
  Judith, 133(4)
  Margaret, 131, 132,
    206

Margerett, 136
Mary, 127, 133, 134
Peter, 130, 133(3),
   134(2), 135,
   136(5), 137(2),
   155
POLHEMUS
  David, 11
POLL
  John, 23
POLYON
  Alice, 135
  James, 135(2)
  John, 135(2)
  Martha, 135
  Sarah, 135
PORTER
  John, 144
POST
  Adrian, 137
  Antye, 137
  Catharine, 137
  Francyntie, 137,
   138
  Garet Jr., 156
  Garret, 214
  Geesie, 137
  Gerritt, 137(2)
  Helena, 137
  Janettie, 137
  Johanes, 137(2),
   138
  John, 3
  Klaartje, 137
  Leah, 137
  Maritie, 137
  Peter, 137(2),
   138(2)
  Rachel, 137
  Sarah, 137
POTTER
  Katharine, 143
POUILLON
  Jacques, 12
PRAAL
  Aaron, 140, 141(2)

Abraham, 141(3)
Alida, 141
Anne, 141
Catharine, 141
Cornelius, 140
Elizabeth, 97, 141
Isaac, 141(2)
Johanes, 140,
  141(2)
Mary, 97
Peter, 97, 140(2),
  141(2)
PRALL
  Aaron Jr., 165, 183
  Abigail, 141(2)
  Abraham, 56, 138(3)
  Aeltie, 66
  Aleda, 138
  Altie, 140
  Arent, 12, 41, 138,
   139(4)
  Barneck, 139(2)
  Benjamin, 53,
   138(2)
  Catharine, 140
  Elizabeth, 141(2)
  Esther, 140
  Frances, 139(2)
  Hans, 29
  Isaac, 57, 140(2),
   142(2)
  John, 139
  Lewis, 140
  Madlenor, 139
  Margaret, 140(2)
  Maria, 12
  Martha, 139, 140
  Mary, 138, 139(2),
   140(2), 141
  Matthew, 139
  Matthews, 139(2)
  Peter, 66, 138,
   139, 140, 141, 142
  Richard D., 139
  Sarah, 139
  Wolfert, 142

PRALL (continued)
  Wolfort, 142
PRATT
  Benjamin, 169
  Sarah, 169
PRAUL
  Isaac, 71
  Isaack, 174
PREVOOST
  David Jr., 81
PRICE
  Abigail, 142
  Benjamin, 52
  Dily, 142
  Hannah, 142
  Sarah, 142
  Thomas, 142, 161
PRIME
  Mary, 168
PRIOR
  Hannah, 143
  Jacob, 143, 208
  James, 143
  John, 143
  Peter, 143
  Rachel, 208
  Samuel, 143(2)
PRITCHARD
  James, 156
PRYOR
  Andrew, 143
  Jacob, 142, 143
  Johana, 143
  Johanes, 142, 143
  Leah, 142
  Peter, 143
  Samuel, 143

-Q-

QUIN
  John, 36, 45, 177
  Sarah, 177

-R-

RACHOW
  Jacob, 175
RAISEAU
  Mary, 110
RAL
  Jan, 117, 118
RALPH
  John, 182
  Joseph, 60
RAMAH
  Susannah, 51
RANDOLPH
  Caty F., 57
RAPALYE
  Daniel, 81
RAVART
  Peter, 37
RAY
  John, 143
  Katharine, 143(2)
  Mary, 143(2)
  Winifrede, 143
READE
  Joseph, 176
RECKHOWS
  Jacob, 13
REEV
  Catharine, 189
  Matthew, 95, 189
REGRENIER
  Paulus, 144
REILLY
  Terence, 190
REMSEN
  Cornelius, 164
  Isaac, 164
RENAUD
  Catharine, 37
  Vincent, 37
RESOE
  Peter, 144
REZEAU
  Ann, 145
  Dorcas, 144(2)
  Jacob, 31, 69,
    144(3), 167, 198,

199, 208(2)
Jacob Jr., 31
James, 144(2)
Mary, 145(3)
Peter, 137, 144(6),
  145(2)
Rinier, 144, 145(2)
Susanah, 144
RICHARDS
  Aaron, 22
  Paul, 12, 15, 16
  Paulus, 7, 91,
    144(2)
  Stephen, 115
RICHMAN
  William, 51
RICKETTS
  Capt., 74
  Elizabeth, 145
  Mary, 145
  William, 73, 145
RICKHOW
  Abraham, 197
  Jacob, 143, 154,
    169, 193
RICKIT
  Jos., 135
RIDGWAY
  Joseph, 52, 145(2),
    146, 208
  Mary, 145
  Sarah, 208
  Thomas, 52, 145,
    146
RILEY
  Christopher, 20
ROBERTSON
  James, 85
ROBINSON
  John, 183
RODNEY
  William, 146
ROIZEAU
  Jacob, 117
ROLL
  John, 208

John Jr., 77
ROLPH
  Abraham, 47,
    147(4), 178
  Ann, 146, 147
  Cornelia, 147(2)
  Elizabeth, 147(2)
  Joseph, 10, 48,
    146, 165, 178
  Lawrence, 146,
    147(2), 178
  Mary, 146, 147
  Nealtie, 146
  Nealtje, 147
  Patience, 131(2)
ROMAN
  Andrise, 208
ROOK
  Amos, 137
ROOME
  Ann, 148(3)
  Laurence, 4
  Lawrence, 64, 147
ROWLAND
  Jonathan, 187
  Mary, 187
ROYALL
  Joseph, 203
ROZEAU
  Peter, 213
RUE
  John, 58
  Matthew, 161
RULYEA
  Frankey, 79
  Henry, 79
RUSSKEA
  Susannah, 18
RUTGERS
  Hendrick Jr., 4
RYCKMAN
  Albert, 148
  Caternichie, 148
  John, 148
RYERS
  Aris, 79

RYERSE
  Adrian, 148
  Auris, 148
  Avis, 65
  Esther, 148
  Fametye, 148
  Gozen, 148(2)
  Lewis, 148
RYERSON
  Lewis, 173
RYERSSE
  Gozen, 122
RYERSZ
  Aris, 148
  Catharine, 85
  Lewis, 85
RYERZ
  Lewis, 131
RYNLANDER
  Bernard, 8

-S-

SALTER
  Daniel, 5, 6, 147,
    157, 176
  Ebenezer, 20, 51
  Rebecca, 160
SANDERS
  John, 181
  Richard, 3, 93
SANTVOORT
  Cornelius, 183
SAYRE
  Daniel Jr., 20
SCHARS
  Christophel, 149
SCHLECT
  Barent, 27
SCHUYLER
  Adonijah, 74(2)
  Myndert, 181
SCOOBY
  John, 105
  Sarah, 105
SEABROOK

  Mary, 162
SEAMAN
  Bemjamin, 91
  Benjain, 73
  Benjamin, 3, 7, 8,
    10(2), 14(2), 24,
    31, 34, 40, 48,
    60, 63, 64, 67(2),
    71(2), 78, 87, 90,
    91, 93(2), 94,
    100, 105, 108(2),
    113, 114, 117,
    119, 124, 126,
    127, 129(2), 131,
    136, 138, 140,
    146, 150, 151,
    155, 160, 168,
    170, 171, 172,
    180, 190, 194(2)
  Benjamin Jr., 127,
    129
  Edmund, 202
  Elizabeth, 14,
    127(2)
  John, 129
  Mary, 208
  Richard, 85, 93,
    127, 135(3), 179
  Silvanus, 208
  Thomas, 15
SEARLE
  James, 96
SEE
  Jacob, 115
  Rachel, 115
  Sarah, 132
SEGANY
  James, 87
SEGINE
  Henry, 164
SEGUIN
  Catharine, 155
  Frederick, 150
  James, 13, 134,
    150, 155
  John, 94

257

SIMONSON (continued)
152(2), 154, 155,
216
  Margaret, 149
  Mary, 152, 203
  Marya, 216
  Ram, 151
  Rem, 209
  Simon, 53, 90,
    149(2), 150,
    151(2), 152, 215,
    216
  Suster, 36(2)
  Symon, 216
  Van Pelt, 215,
    216(2)
  Wyntie, 150
  Zena, 152
SIMSON
  Aerte, 117
  Alexander, 153
  John, 153
  Martha, 153
  Sarah, 153
SKILER
  Adr., 74
SKINER
  Samuel, 57
SKINNER
  Wright, 31
SLAGHT
  Abraham, 129
  Anna, 91
  Barent, 108, 136,
    153, 192
  Barnet, 201
  Barnt, 124
  John, 91, 154
SLEAGHT
  Barent, 153(3)
  Christina, 153
  Cornelius, 153
  Hellitie, 153
  Henry, 153(2)
  Hillitie, 153
  John, 153

SLEGHT
  Barent, 17, 155(2)
  Catharine, 155(2)
  Heletye, 155
  Hendrick, 155
  John, 155, 209
  Mary, 155
SLEIGHT
  Barnt, 154(2)
  Catharine, 193
  Elizabeth, 154(2)
  Hendrick, 193(2)
  Henry, 154(3)
  Jacob, 154
  John, 193
  Margaret, 193
  Robert, 191
SLIVE
  Randal, 21
SMITH
  Ann, 171
  Christian, 31, 95
  Deborah, 34
  Elizabeth, 155, 168
  Gilbert, 155, 156
  Hester, 31
  Jas., 211
  Nehemiah, 168
  Samuel, 155
  Samuel I., 155
  Talman, 156(2)
  William, 16, 17,
    85, 86(3)
SMYTH
  Lawrence, 211
SOPER
  Joseph, 1
SPEAR
  Abm., 203
SPEARS
  Abraham, 156(2),
    157(2)
  Anna, 156
  Closon, 157(2)
  Gitty, 157
  Hendrick, 157(2)

STILWELL (continued)
  John, 46, 98
STORER
  Thomas, 196
STOREY
  John, 2
  Rebecca, 2
STORY
  Catharine, 197
STOTTENBOROUGH
  Anthony, 2
STOUGHTENBUROUG
  Widow, 83
STOUTENBERGH
  Anthony, 105
STOUTENBOROUGH
  Anthony, 123, 163,
    164
  Elizabeth, 163
  James, 164(2)
  John, 164(3)
  Leanah, 164
  Mary, 163, 164(2)
  Stephen, 164(2)
STOUTENBURGH
  Anthony, 100, 194
  James, 194
  John, 194
  Phebe, 100
STOUTENBURROUGHS
  Anthony, 45
STRAGG
  Joseph, 210
STUART
  Alex., 163
SUNDERLAND
  John, 209
SUTTON
  Ambrose, 164
  Thomas, 18
SWAIM
  Abraham, 64, 164
  Benjamin, 209
  Catren, 166
  Elisabeth, 166
  Elizabeth, 164, 165

Hannah, 176
Isaac, 209
John, 164, 165
Lenor, 139
Lloyd B., 139
Martinus, 209
Mary, 139, 164, 166
Mathias, 166
Matthias, 166
Matthias M., 209
Mortimes, 209
Sarah, 139
Simon, 166, 184
Tice, 139
SWAME
  Barent, 165
  Benjamin, 166
  Elizabeth, 165
  Hester, 166
  Johanes, 139,
    165(2)
  John, 166(2)
  Lena, 165
  Martha, 140, 165
  Mary, 165
  Mathias, 166
  Matise, 166(2)
  Simon, 166(2)
  Ties, 165
SWAN
  Cornelia, 48
  John, 48
  Sarah, 167
  Tice, 167
SWEEM
  Anthony, 165(2)
  Cornelius, 165
  Elizabeth, 165(2)
  Hannah, 165
  Jacobus, 165
  Johanes, 165(2)
  Leah, 165
  Mary, 165
  Mathyas, 165
  Matthias, 31
  Mattys, 169

Adrian, 198
Zelitie, 198
VANAME
Peter, 176
VANBROCKLE
Mathias, 193
VANDER BILT
Gertie, 181
Ryck, 181
VANDERBEAK
Hannah, 170(2)
John, 170
Rem, 170
VANDERBECK
Rem, 183
VANDERBEEK
Elizabeth, 108
Mary, 116, 117
Rem, 65(2), 96
VANDERBILT
Aaron, 172
Adrian, 171
Anne, 170
Aris, 9, 171
Balitie, 172
Catharine, 9, 171,
187(2)
Catrin, 172
Cornelia, 171
Cornelius, 170(2),
171(3), 172(2),
210(2)
Dennis, 170(2)
Doretea, 172
Dorothy, 171(2)
Edward, 172
Elendor, 171
Elizabeth, 22
Eloner, 172
Helena, 170, 210
Hellitye, 170
Isabel, 9(2)
Jacob, 40, 170,
171(6), 172(2)
Jacobus, 170(2),
171

John, 9, 22, 99,
170, 171(3),
172(2)
John Sr., 171
Joseph, 171(2)
Mary, 171(2), 172
Neeltie, 170(2)
Neltie, 210
Oliver, 171(2),
172(2)
Phebe, 170, 205
VANDERSCHUREN
Geessie, 118
VANDERVENTER
Cornelius, 38
VANDERWYCK
Cornelius, 11
VANDEVENTER
Abraham, 173(2)
Ann, 173
Catharine, 173
Cornelius, 11, 85,
92, 173(2)
Elizabeth, 96,
173(2)
John, 11, 96, 97,
173
VANDEVOORT
John, 128
VANHORN
Ann, 175
VANPELT
Tunis, 193(3)
VAUGHAN
Edward, 74, 110
Mary, 74(2)
VECHTE
Cornelia, 158
John, 158
VEGHTE
Catharine, 187(3)
Cornelia, 187(4)
Geritie, 187(2)
Gernet, 186
Gerret, 186, 187
Gerritt, 187(3),

267

WOGLOM (continued)
Andreas, 198
Andries, 198
Ann, 198
Benjamin, 197
Catharine, 197
Cornelious, 197
Dewry, 158
Elinor, 1
Jane, 197
Janettie, 158
John, 180, 197(4),
  198
Mary, 197, 198(2)
Peter, 180(2),
  197(3), 198(3)
Sarah, 198
WOGLUM
Adrian, 198
Anna, 198(3)
Blandina, 196(2)
Christina, 196
Cornelius, 196(2)
Dowe, 196(3)
Jan, 24, 81
John, 17, 196
John Jr., 81, 82,
  196(2)
Peter, 198
Sytie, 196
Zelitie, 198
WOGLUN
John, 84
Ury, 84
WOOD
Abraham, 199, 200
Anne, 198
Daniel, 199
David, 199
Edmond, 199
Edmund, 198, 199
Elizabeth, 199, 215
Eve, 199
Hannah, 199
Isaac, 215
Isabel, 52

Jacob, 200
James, 10, 199(2),
  200(5)
John, 70, 199,
  200(4)
Joseph, 10, 167,
  199(2), 200(4)
Mary, 198, 199,
  200, 215
Peter, 199
Phebe, 199, 200
Richard, 177, 200
Sarah, 199(2)
Stephen, 87, 88(2),
  199(3), 200, 215
Stephen Sr., 199
Timothy, 199(3),
  200, 214
Winant, 214
WOODWARD
Samuel, 85
WOOGLAM
Adrian, 196, 197
Blandina, 196,
  197(2)
Christina, 197
Dowe, 196, 197(3)
John, 196(3),
  197(3)
Peter, 197
WOOLF
Christian, 124
WRIGHT
Andrew, 141, 177,
  195, 200, 201
Anthony, 30, 201(5)
Christian, 154, 210
Elizabeth, 30,
  201(2)
Hendrick, 201
Hezekiah, 30,
  154(2), 195(2),
  201(3), 209, 210
Jacob, 61
Jane, 201
John, 176(5), 201

John Jr., 176
Joshua, 126, 154,
    195
Judith, 201
Mary, 141, 200, 201
Richard Jr., 55
Tabitha, 201
Zeborah, 201
WYNANT
  Cornelius, 30
  Elizabeth, 40
  Jacob, 40
WYNANTS
  Anne, 30
  Cornelius, 30
  Mary, 30
  Wynant, 30, 36, 208

          -Y-

YATES
  Abraham, 200, 201
YEATS
  Edward, 87

          -Z-

ZELUFF
  Peter, 108
ZENGER
  Peter, 98